I BELIEVED

THE AUTHOR

THE AUTHOR

I Believed

THE AUTOBIOGRAPHY OF A
FORMER BRITISH COMMUNIST

Douglas Hyde

THE REPRINT SOCIETY LONDON

FIRST PUBLISHED 1950
THIS EDITION PUBLISHED BY THE REPRINT SOCIETY LTD.,
BY ARRANGEMENT WITH WILLIAM HEINEMANN LTD., 1952

PRINTED IN GREAT BRITAIN BY RICHARD CLAY AND COMPANY, LTD.,
BUNGAY, SUFFOLK

CONTENTS

Chapter I	THE YOUNG REVOLUTIONARY	*page*	7
II	DOUBTS AND DIFFICULTIES		14
III	EXIT THE BOY PREACHER		24
IV	COMMUNISM IN ACTION		31
V	CRYPTO-COMMUNIST		45
VI	ORGANISING FOR SPAIN		55
VII	OLD SLOGANS REVIVED		64
VIII	ON THE " DAILY WORKER "		78
IX	WORKING FOR DEFEAT		88
X	WORKING FOR VICTORY		111
XI	BACK ON THE " WORKER "		127
XII	SPIES AND CONFESSIONS		138
XIII	PARTY PEOPLE		147
XIV	THE INTERNATIONAL IS DEAD		161
XV	UNDERSTANDING THE ENEMY		167
XVI	SECOND FRONT		178
XVII	THE TWO WATER-TIGHT COMPARTMENTS		194
XVIII	CONFLICT		205
XIX	TWO IN HARNESS		214
XX	LONG LIVE THE INTERNATIONAL		221

CONTENTS (*continued*)

XXI	THE CUL-DE-SAC	*page* 233
XXII	MAKING THE BREAK	245
XXIII	OUT OF THE STRAIT-JACKET	260
XXIV	THE GOD THAT DID NOT FAIL	275

ILLUSTRATIONS

THE AUTHOR—*A Drawing by A. E. Berbank, N.R.D.*   Frontispiece

A COMMUNIST-SPONSORED MEETING ATTRACTS THE
    INTELLECTUALS
. . . AND THE PROLETARIAT   *facing* 128

THE COMMUNIST PARTY EXECUTIVE COMMITTEE
PARTY LEADERS   129

R. PALME DUTT
A STAFF MEETING IN THE *Daily Worker* OFFICE   160

HARRY POLLITT   161

*All photographs are reproduced by permission of
"Illustrated" except the Communist Party Executive
Committee, which is by permission of "Topical Press"*

I

THE YOUNG REVOLUTIONARY

BRISTOL was a city of hills. Hills, ancient buildings and ships that came right up into the heart of the city itself, bringing with them the smell of the sea and memories of pirates, slave traders, and the days of the township's greatness.

But the masts of ships I knew as a youth no longer mingle in the city centre with the overhead wires of the trams that once crossed St. Augustine's Bridge. For the big ships stop now at Avonmouth, down where the Avon joins the Bristol Channel, and the trams have gone for scrap. The old buildings, many of them, have gone too, erased by Hitler's bombers, although the City of a Thousand Spires has still more than most to boast of in the way of medieval gems. And the hills remain and are likely to until some fool uses something deadlier even than the hydrogen bomb.

One hill, at least, is said to have been volcanic in its day, but Bristol's citizens have no fears about a possible return to its youthful and dangerous indiscretions.

Much more volcanic, in its own way, when I was a youth, was a neighbouring hill, crowned with the great green open space which is the Downs.

On the Downs almost any night you could find orators representing the Conservative, Liberal, Labour and Communist Parties; "high" Anglicans, low churchmen, respectable Nonconformists who worship in chapels and the less respectable ones who carry boards proclaiming that God is not mocked and who sing revivalist hymns to the accompaniment of wheezy portable harmoniums. Any night as dusk fell and the meetings broke up you were likely to hear, mingling at one and the same time, the strains of " Land of Hope and Glory ", " England Arise ", " Abide with Me " and " Shall We Gather at the River? " And the " Internationale ". Always the " Internationale ".

On the Downs spiritual and intellectual battles were fought.

7

And not far away, behind the hawthorn bushes, other battles were fought between the young men who had accepted the spirit and morals of the period and the girls who were not quite so sure. It was the irresponsible, idiotic, ignoble first decade of the years between the wars.

Along the road which encircled the battlefield moved an endless procession. There were motor cyclists whose backs were gripped by the pink-stockinged knees of flapper pillion-riders. Youths raced each other on pedal cycles and still found time to flirt on the way. And the monkey paraders of both sexes turned out nightly in their hundreds. On their way they passed the Sea Walls, local beauty spot and target for Sunday evening strollers from the respectable suburbs on the edge of the Downs.

Look out from the Sea Walls to the west and you saw the Welsh mountains across the Bristol Channel, blue-grey on the skyline. Look south-west and you saw the Somerset sun sink in unrivalled glory into the sea, sending cold winds as messengers of night to warn the under-clad. Look straight down before you and you saw, at the bottom of the 300-ft. cliffs which dropped sheer down to the river, the recently constructed Portway which linked the docks at the mouth of the Avon with the port in the City, and at its side the still more newly constructed hard tennis-courts.

Over the Sea Walls went another procession, not of the gay but of the defeated, bankrupt small traders, hit by the gathering economic crisis, big business crooks who had been found out and the unemployed with nothing left and nothing to hold them.

They went over so frequently that suburban Bristol began to yawn and Chief Sub-Editors with news sense told their underlings: " Just one paragraph and a small head—it's only another gone over the top ".

Once four unemployed pooled all they had to hire an old car, then drove it straight through the railings and over the cliffs, and the Sea Walls hit the headlines again for a moment.

But the " comfortable " folk in the district where I lived felt secure enough in the main and their sense of comfort was heightened, if anything, by the sound of jobless Welsh miners singing, unceasingly, for pence in the street outside, the inevitable " *Cwm Rhondda* ", " Bread of Heaven, feed me till I want no more ". Then, in little groups on the Downs at night, the younger miners joined with the local communists to sing " Watch and pray, live on hay, you'll have pie in the sky when you die."

The huge, immaculately dressed negro walked across the Downs, a large suitcase in one hand, a small bamboo contraption in the other. On the fringe of " Spouters Corner " he stopped for a moment, put down his parcels and looked around, wiping the sweat from his forehead with a handkerchief which appeared quite startlingly white against the blackness of his skin.

He selected a suitable site for his purpose, then strolled jauntily across to a spot just beyond a little circle of people singing revivalist hymns around a harmonium.

Slowly and very deliberately he unfolded a small bamboo table. Then he untied the cord around the case, took from it a white cloth and carefully spread it on the table. After the cloth came a succession of small boxes which he arranged in neat little piles.

A group of young South Wales miners made their way over, curious to see what was coming next. So did people from the fringes of the various political and religious meetings dotted about on the surrounding grass.

A party of several police, including a sergeant and an inspector, appeared. The negro gave them a contemptuous look and carried on displaying his wares with all the care of a professional West End window-dresser.

When the crowd was large enough for his liking he began to address them with a broad and confident grin. " The police last week ", he said, " stopped me from selling you my corn cure because the law is that goods may not be sold on the Downs on Sunday.

" But they can't stop people from buying papers on Sunday, for they are sold on street corners everywhere. Now, I will sell you this "—and he held up a small square of pink wrapping paper —" for one shilling and threepence. I give you the corn cure, the best in the world and unobtainable elsewhere, which I wrap in the paper."

The crowd hesitated sceptically but he encouraged them with:

" Come along, don't be afraid, the police can't touch you or me."

As the first would-be purchaser stepped forward, money in hand, the police inspector stepped forward too. " Come on, pack up your traps and get," he ordered. The negro looked for a moment as though he was going to resist or argue but the inspector repeated his order, this time more sharply.

The corn-cure salesman hesitated, then ruefully began packing his little boxes, the squares of pink paper and the white cloth back into his large and battered case. By the time he had folded his bamboo table the last of the crowd had already rejoined one or other of the meetings.

Those meetings on the Bristol Downs had attracted me for years, right from the time I was a small boy. From my home on the edge of the Downs I would wander to the Sea Walls or explore the wooded slopes which run down to the banks of the Avon far below. I knew every inch and I loved every inch.

But almost always I would finish at " the meetings ", wandering from one to another, listening to cranks and others who peddled social, political and spiritual cures just as did the colourful quacks who made their living by persuading the public to buy their cures for every disease known to the flesh of man.

Among the latter was one man whose patter I knew by heart. He would hold up a little bottle of white powder which he claimed was the part that mattered of water taken from the fountains at neighbouring Bath and evaporated in his home.

" I bring to you ", he would tell his audience, " the healing waters of Bath, hitherto the exclusive prerogative of the idle rich, now brought for the first time to the ordinary man and woman, made available to one and all for precisely one shilling and sixpence per bottle."

But I knew just as well the patter of old Harry Whitchurch, septuagenarian propagandist for the Independent Labour Party, a curer of sick societies. He would take his hearers back to the days of his father, who lived in the Hungry Forties, or to his own youth; to Keir Hardie, to the Clarionites and Robert Blatchford, making them feel that there were indeed giants in the land in those early days of the socialist movement.

When he grew sufficiently excited he would throw his cloth cap into the air with a magnificent gesture and catch it again, to the delight of the crowd.   He would round off his speech with a verse from Edward Carpenter or, standing with bared and bowed head, quote his favourite verse from John Masefield: " Not the ruler for me but the ranker, the tramp of the road. . . ."

But it was not to Harry Whitchurch I went that night the negro thought he had bested the English law, but to a crowd in the middle of which was a stranger talking of the stirring days of the General Strike, which had aroused such hopes and passions in 1926, just two years before.

He reminded us that, like most such struggles, it had had its victims, its martyrs.   When men were sent to jail because of their activities during the strike, he told us, it was his organisation which had maintained their families and befriended these " class-war heroes ".

The International Class War Prisoners Aid, he claimed, had led the fight throughout the world to prevent the shameful deaths of Sacco and Vanzetti, the two emigré Italians who had been sent to the electric chair in America the previous summer after years spent in jail awaiting the end.

As he talked I remembered that day in August 1927 when the papers had said that the two pacifist anarchists were to die.   They had told of bombs which had been exploded outside the U.S. Embassies in various parts of the world.   More such incidents, they had said, were expected to coincide with their deaths.

For years, boy though I was, I had followed their cases in the daily press.   Throughout the whole of the later years of my child-hood my indignation at their treatment had steadily mounted and I had followed the course of their many appeals and retrials with increasing anger and apprehension.

From conversations with left-wingers who frequented the meet-ings on the Downs I had heard of the " bomb shop " in the old Horsefair, down in the City.   I had set off there, determined, too, to get a bomb and to register my protest at the Consulate.   I was prepared if necessary to blow myself up along with the building outside which flew the Stars and Stripes.

The sixteen-year-old from the suburbs had felt let down and

somewhat frustrated when he found that the " bombs " sold at the shabby little shop were only literary ones, in the shape of communist literature.

I still knew by heart the words Vanzetti had written after he received his death sentence:

" If it had not been for these things, I might have lived out my life talking at street corners to scorning men. I might have died, unmarked, unknown, a failure. Now we are not a failure. This is our career and our triumph. Never in our full life could we hope to do such work for tolerance, for joostice, for man's onder-standing of man as now we do by accident. Our words—our lives—our pains—nothing! The taking of our lives—lives of a good shoemaker and a poor fish-pedlar—all! That last moment belongs to us—that agony is our triumph."

I was brought sharply back to the present again when the speaker finished and got down from his portable platform. The crowd dispersed and only little knots of supporters, some of whom I already slightly knew, remained, counting the collection, check-ing the number of periodicals and pamphlets sold, speculating on the results, if any, of the meeting. I pushed through them and asked the speaker if I might join his organisation. He signed me up, took my subscription and gave me the address of the local secretary with whom I should get in touch.

I went home proud to belong to an organisation which I felt to be so obviously and so consciously fighting for the scorned and rejected. Over supper I told my parents that I was now a member of the International Class War Prisoners Aid.

" I don't like the sound of the class-war part of it," said my father. " It sounds communist to me." To which I retorted that I didn't care if it was, so long as it was doing good.

I could expect no sympathy from my parents for anything smelling of communism. Politically, this was understandable, since my father was an active member of the West Bristol Liberal Association, which my mother also supported. For social reasons, too, they would also react against it. The house we lived in at that time was modest enough, but it was at least our own. The neighbourhood was notably respectable, and throughout my childhood ran the theme that I must be " a little gentleman ", a view which had been supported in practical fashion by deep, uncomfortable, stiff white collars worn outside short jackets, and in summer, straw hats, or " boaters " as my parents preferred to call them.

The first time boaters were bought for us my brother and I rebelled. Dutifully we wore them on Sunday afternoon until we got just as far as the end of the road and so out of sight. Then, as we ran on to the Downs, we threw them spinning into the air. We spent the remainder of the afternoon using them to catch butterflies and moths. Our collection, pinned carefully in old shoe boxes, grew enormously as a consequence. The boaters when we returned were minus their brims. But in the end it was our parents who won, and new boaters were purchased and worn again the following summer.

Our home was, in short, petty-bourgeois with memories of more glorious days that had gone before and which might yet return if industry, thrift and a firmly held belief in a beneficent God could do anything towards it.

The religious faith of my parents was one which made them revolt at the idea of communism, both for its atheism and its belief in violence. Their nonconformity coloured the whole of their lives, and they sincerely attempted to practise it in their personal lives, in rearing their children and in their relations with others. And if, as we grew up, my brother, my sister and I rebelled against what we deemed to be a stifling narrowness, it never occurred to us to doubt their complete sincerity.

It was obvious that in such a home there would be little enthusiasm for the I.C.W.P.A.

But, for me, the act of joining " Icky Woppa ", as the I.C.W.P.A. was called among its members, represented a very definite step in a process which had been going on for some time. I had for weeks now been mixing with people whom I knew, or suspected, to be communists, but this was the first time I had joined one of their organisations. And it was a step of some significance, too, for I was studying theology at the time with the intention of later going to India as a missionary.

II

DOUBTS AND DIFFICULTIES

ONLY a few months before I had started my theological studies, but things had not gone at all smoothly and I was already wondering if I would ever see the inside of a clerical collar.

What in nonconformist circles is known as " the call to preach " had come to me shortly after my brother had died on the eve of his twenty-first birthday.

Until then the idea of my going into the Ministry had not occurred to anyone, least of all myself. At the age of thirteen I had, schoolboy fashion, called myself an agnostic. The Sunday School teachers who took the senior classes at the local chapel were mainly recruited from among the undergraduates at Bristol University; many of them were going to be teachers and were glad enough, therefore, of a chance of getting in a little practice.

When I expressed my first doubts about the Creation story, and, indeed, about the very existence of God, the student who taught me on Sundays suggested that I should read Darwin's *Origin of Species*. Whether he felt that this would confirm me in my doubts or strengthen me in my Christianity is still not clear to me.

The result, at any rate, was that, after studying *The Origin of Species*, followed up by *The Descent of Man*, I felt I was equipped with an adequate explanation for everything visible and invisible, proudly proclaimed myself the descendant of the ape and, in response to my Sunday School teacher's request, proceeded to write and deliver to the class a paper on the whole question. I seem to recall that I devoted a disproportionate amount of time to Darwin's argument about the quantity of flowers in a given area being conditioned by the number of fieldmice resident there. There was nothing inconsistent with modern nonconformity in the lines of enquiry on which my Sunday School teacher had launched me, but the result was that that childish scepticism was as a consequence continued into adolescence.

When, soon after my seventeenth birthday, the " Call " came, therefore, I was already a veteran agnostic of some four years' standing. The " Call " was largely emotional. Child-like I had absorbed my agnosticism without realising its full implications. Now the death of my only brother brought them home in sharp and practical terms for me for the moment at least.

To become a minister it was first necessary to be a lay preacher. That meant combining practical activities, such as learning to conduct services, with studying the elements of theology in preparation for taking my local preacher's examination.

Both had to be done in my spare time since I was already apprenticed as a dental technician, working in a small workshop where we specialised in splints for broken jaws, artificial jaws for those who had had them shot away in the war, metal tubes for cancer of the throat cases and a variety of other practical reminders of the folly and mortality of man.

Before conducting my first Methodist service, it was decided that I might make a useful start by one night taking the weekly Friday prayer meeting—one of the few which had survived from the days when such meetings were the very life-blood of evangelical devotions.

The normal routine was for someone, usually a lay preacher, to open the proceedings with a short and edifying talk, after which those present engaged in extempore prayers. I was at the time reading with considerable enthusiasm a book which set out to relate modern psychology to Christian practice, and so, in preparing my little piece for the occasion, I based my notes on ideas which flowed from what I had been reading.

At the prayer meeting I found eight or nine elderly men and women, the youngest of whom was probably at least fifteen years my father's senior. The average age must have been somewhere in the region of sixty-eight to seventy. They represented the unconquerable and uncompromising old-guard of local Methodism. Awed with the solemnity of the occasion, so terrified that I could not stop my legs from visibly shaking, I delivered my little address on psychology in the service of the soul. I sustained myself with the thought that its delivery might be bad but at least it was good, helpful stuff.

The instant I finished, and as we were still all getting down on our knees, a white-bearded octogenarian with egg-bald head and creaking joints started off with the first prayer. In a cracked but unmistakably furious voice he began: " We thank Thee, O Lord, that we don't need any psychology, nor sociology, nor zoology, nor any other ology to bring us to Thy throne of Grace but only the saving blood of Thy Son Jesus Christ, our Lord. Ah-men."

He spat out the " Ah-men " with such obvious fury that it was clear that what he really meant was, " Now put that in your pipe and smoke it."

I was left with the certain knowledge that so far as the old-guard were concerned I had failed completely.

Soon I was sent out, accompanied by a lay preacher, an elderly commercial traveller, to conduct a Sunday morning service in a little zinc-roofed country chapel. He preached the sermon and I did the rest. When it was over he told me I had done well, offered some friendly, helpful advice and said he would send a report to the Superintendent Minister on the following day.

Two days later a detective called on me at my place of work and asked if I could confirm that a letter, which he showed me, referred to myself. I did so, and he then told me it had been discovered in the pocket of an elderly man whose body had been found in a river. It was my local preacher, whom they had identified by an unaddressed letter containing the report of my service which he had intended sending to the Superintendent Minister. It seemed a grim beginning to my mission.

Although it was not long before I was preaching my first sermon and then going out week after week to country chapels, becoming known as the " boy preacher ", I soon began to have serious doubts about the theology I found in my text-books. The local Methodist minister who was coaching me told me that these doubts were perfectly normal and advised me not to worry about them.

My first studies were of Methodist origins and history, which I found both interesting and stimulating. The clarity and apostolic character of John Wesley's message appealed to me as something the usefulness of which, in its day, was undeniable. He had, I felt, come to a generation which needed his message and which responded to it. He had both fire and vision. He saw a spiritual need and set about meeting it. He was unorthodox in his methods, impatient of those who were smug and complacent. But his, it seemed to me, were not the characteristics of the twentieth-century Methodists I knew.

Those I met were mostly lacking in fire and in any sort of self-critical approach to their lives. They were resentful of change and of anyone who wanted change. In their West Bristol suburb they lived sheltered, comfortable lives, remote from the world about them.

I remembered how, when on one rare occasion we had a preacher whose sermon was remarkable for its passion and conviction, I heard a wealthy old widow say as she went out through the chapel door, " I didn't think much of *that* sermon. It had precious little comfort in it." Her phrase sank deep into my mind for it seemed to epitomise the attitude of so many. Having achieved, through thrifty living, material comfort which they enjoyed to the full all the week, they went to chapel on Sunday to get their quota of spiritual comfort too.

Theirs was an intensely personal religion which had little or nothing to say about social injustice or on a world in crisis. It was personal in the sense that it laid down a great many " dont's " which they imposed upon themselves and which they had come to regard as the deadliest of sins. For these respectable people there was no temptation to blaspheme, commit adultery, kill or steal. Such sins need passion—if you like, humanity. Admittedly, in the businesses which they ran with such success all the week, they might commit robbery by legitimate means, or even kill by slow starvation, but that was outside their ken.

And so, recognising none of the Ten Commandments as applying to themselves, they created new ones, which they had equally little difficulty in keeping. To indulge in " strong drink ", to paint the house or weed the garden on Sunday, to go to the theatre or the dance hall were elevated to the worst of sins. These were the restraints about which I had heard most as a small child at chapel and at Sunday School. To be " good " was to live without doing any of these things. To be " bad " was to do them.

But when I started the serious study of my theological text-books I could find no authority there for the things about which I had heard so much. Theology had nothing to say about them at all. They had grown, not out of the moral law, nor out of Divine revelation, but out of Wesley's early campaign in which he had taught thrift to the impoverished cotters, temperance to the intemperate miners and a need to observe the Sabbath to a generation to whom it had come to mean little or nothing.

The religion I had known was essentially " Bible " Christianity; yet neither the Bible nor the text-books gave support to the things which had come to be seen as all-important.

In practice there seemed to be little authority for anything else either. " There are two points of view on most of these things today," the Minister at the chapel told me, " and some believe one thing and some believe another." The higher criticism had robbed them of their certainties and put little in their place. I could doubt the resurrection of the dead, have doubts about the miracles, occupy almost a unitarian position on the question of the Trinity, believe that first and foremost Christ was just the ideal man, the Great Example, and the Son of God only in the sense that all are also sons of God—and still become a Methodist minister.

But if I put a shilling on a horse, was seen going into a public-house or spent my Sunday afternoon mowing the lawn or painting the garden gate, I should most certainly never get into the Minis-try. It so happened that I had no particular wish to do any of these things, but the sense of values seemed nonetheless dis-torted and, indeed, utterly unbalanced.

I expected two things of my religion: that it should be con-cerned about the world about it, with all those social abuses and manifold injustices of which I was sharply, almost excessively, aware, and, in addition, that it should feed the inner life. But in the form that I knew it, it satisfied me on neither point.

On the Downs I met young unemployed Welsh miners who told me of the poverty and unemployment in the valleys on the other side of the Bristol Channel from which they came. Their choirs going up and down the road in which I lived had become a regular part of life. But there seemed to be no message for them.

The war-wounded, too, were everywhere. Vividly I remembered the 1914–18 days. Remembered in particular the endless streams of ambulances which passed near my home day after day on their way to Southmead Hospital. We had cheered them as they passed. Sometimes the men inside waved back in return. Sometimes they had no arms to wave and would wave a foot instead. Sometimes they had neither hands nor feet.

I remembered, in a way which still made me feel physically sick, seeing one man in particular being unloaded from a train into a waiting ambulance. He had travelled in a cage to prevent anything from touching his flayed body, and the thought of his suffering had kept me awake at night.

I remembered, too, how my brother and I had found the body of a man hanging among the ivy of our favourite tree, in which we would sit for hours reading our books. He had hanged himself, it was revealed, rather than be conscripted.

Now the war-wounded were everywhere. They stood on the road-side selling matches. Blinded, they teamed up into bands; holding each other's shoulders, they toured the streets, single file, playing musical instruments. And endlessly, one after the other, they knocked at front doors waiting with their big cases to sell writing-pads, brushes, lavender, matches, pins or cotton. And there seemed to be no message for them either, nor anything to be said on the whole appalling question of war.

Why don't we do something for the unemployed? Why don't Christians do something to tackle the problem of poverty? Why do they not take up a positive stand against war and set about seriously trying to prevent another one? I asked these questions over and over again and got no answers which would satisfy me.

I went to the services of other denominations to see if it was just Methodism which was at fault. I sampled everything from the Plymouth Brethren at the one emotional extreme to the Quakers at the other. The Quakers seemed to have something, but not enough for me.

Then, oddly enough, I was started on a new line of enquiry by a man with no interest in social questions at all. He attended our chapel and took a leading part in the discussions which were a feature of a men's class I attended there on Sunday mornings.

He was a mystic. The interior life was the only one that mattered to him. He had steeped himself in the ancient religions of the East and was dabbling, too, in the new religions of the West, Christian Science, Theosophy and various small and mystical cults.

Methodism, he told me, would never satisfy me. It did not go deeply enough. The only Gospel in the New Testament which really appealed to him, he said, was that of St. John. He was happiest with the Mahâbhârata and the Vedantas, copies of which he lent me. I studied them, hoping that I might arrive at some synthesis which, whilst owing most to Christian thought, took account of the best in all other religions as well. Subconsciously, I think, I wanted if I could to escape from the preoccupation with social questions which threatened my whole religious life. I studied the works of the modern Hindu thinkers. Annie Besant's translation of the Bhagavad-Gîtâ and Sir Edwin Arnold's poem based also on the Gîtâ became my companions in long, solitary walks all over the West Country. Sometimes I would walk from early morning to late at night chewing over a single passage from the Gîtâ.

I reasoned that it could and should be reconciled with Christianity, that at some point in mysticism all religions met, and that there was nothing in Methodism to conflict with the idea that some sort of compromise could be arrived at.

Under the influence of the Eastern writers I began to exercise a discipline over myself. Sleep seemed an obvious beginning. It had always appeared very much a waste of time and I begrudged the time given to it because it interrupted my reading. Reduce the amount of sleep and my intake of the things in which I was interested could be increased enormously.

Gradually I cut it down until it was reduced to four hours each night, but I found that, in bed, I could not make it less. By lying on the floor without pillow or cover each night for several weeks, however, I reached the point where my sleep could easily be reduced to two hours nightly. In the morning I would get into bed for a minute, ruffle the clothes and bang the pillows so that my parents should not suspect what I was doing.

With sleep reduced to a minimum I could read still more books or spend hours in contemplation. A copy of Thomas à Kempis' *Imitation of Christ* lent itself particularly to contemplation and I read it over and over again.

I was talking to a Bristol University student one day about Hinduism when he told me that he knew a group of students who also were interested in the subject but who knew little about it. Would I, if he could get them together, go to talk to them? It would, he assured me, all be very informal. Under pressure I agreed and in due course went along to the hostel where they lived. He seemed rather more than usually cheerful when we met in his room. I for my part was extremely nervous. Then he took me to the hall where I was to speak. He pushed me through the door and disappeared. To my dismay I found myself facing row upon row of brown faces. The room was full of Indian students, most of them Hindus.

For a moment I panicked, then saw that even though it was intended as a joke so far as he was concerned, the Indians were all perfectly serious about the whole thing and so I decided to see it through. After my talk questions were asked, which I answered as best I could. Then someone moved a vote of thanks. He got considerable applause when he said that I had taught them a great deal about Hinduism that night. Few born Christians know and understand the fundamentals of the Christian religion, he said. So, too, very few born Hindus know anything more than the external practice of theirs.

Among the many books about India I read were, inevitably, some which touched upon the growing Nationalist movement then almost daily in the news. I was attracted by it and learned with joy that there were Christian missionaries who were sympathetic to it and who were admirers not only of the leaders of cultural nationalism, such as Rabindranath Tagore, but also of political leaders like Gandhi too.

In the public library one night I came across the journal of the Commonwealth of India League, which supported the Nationalist movement. Mrs. Besant, whose work I already knew through her translation of the Bhagavad-Gîtâ, was one of its leaders, writing regularly for the journal. I read each new issue as it appeared. Then one evening I found inside it a leaflet announcing a conference which was to be held in a Labour Hall in the city to discuss the League's aim of Dominion status for India.

I was admitted as an observer, so making my first direct contact with the organised left-wing political movement. A number of coloured students were present and I was soon making friends with a friendly young Indian.

At that conference I saw my first communists in action. To the intense annoyance of many of those present, they demanded immediate independence for India with the withdrawal of all British troops, despite the fact that the purpose of the conference was to demand Dominion status. They irritated me by their persistent refusal to stick to the aims of the conference, by their denunciation of Gandhi as a bourgeois reactionary and their abuse of the organisers of the conference as traitors to socialism. They irritated me, too, by what seemed the unreasonableness of their demands. Their very unreasonableness helped to influence my decision to join the League, which seemed mild by comparison. It was my first political affiliation.

The League's secretary proved to be a girl theosophist with a knowledge and love of the religions of the East which were shared by a number of the other active members whom I soon met. I had, I felt, something to share with them right from the start.

They were enthusiastic when I told them I might later go as a missionary to India. Missionaries, they said, had in the past been largely a reactionary force. It would be useful therefore to have someone who was on the right side on both political and religious questions. Most of the League's leading people were members of the Labour Party. The chairman was a member of the Independent Labour Party as well, which at that time was permissible under the Labour Party's rules.

Mixing with others, however, I discovered that, although officially and publicly supporting the aims of the organisation, they privately professed a belief in the views which had been put forward by the self-proclaimed communists at the conference. And they went to some trouble to prove to me just why these views were not really as unreasonable as they sounded.

Within a few weeks of joining I was made treasurer and so became a member of the Committee. Among my reading was now included a growing proportion of political matter, including anti-imperialist pamphlets giving facts about labour conditions on the Indian tea plantations and in the cotton mills. As I read of the appalling wages, the abominable conditions, the practice of doping tiny children so that their mothers could work unhampered in the mill, the flow of profit and interest from India to Britain which was said to be bleeding her white, I became rebellious and angry about Indian conditions just as I had been about those in Britain. My work for the liberation of India from the imperialist yoke took on the character of a crusade, which seemed to me to be a practical form of Christianity. And so, after all, my study of Indian mysticism brought me back to pretty much where I had begun, back to the fight against injustice and misery.

There were, I argued, two ways of dealing with a movement such as the Indian National Movement. One was to denounce it as revolutionary and to fight against it. The other was to get into it and Christianise it, which was what some Christian missionaries were attempting.

I favoured the second line of action and so was able to tell myself that in my activities on behalf of India's freedom I was doing a practical job related to my future work there.

Soon I was appearing as a secondary speaker on the India League's platform on the Downs. And soon, too, my sermons were noticeably coloured by my new ideas. On doctrinal questions I felt unsure of myself. I had little on which to grip. I had no difficulty in learning theology as one might acquire any other branch of knowledge, but it failed almost completely to link up with my own religious life or to bring any fresh light to bear upon it.

But when I examined the contemporary scene in the light of the Sermon on the Mount, as I interpreted it, applying it to poverty at home and exploitation abroad, I felt more sure of myself and could preach with conviction.

By the time I joined I.C.W.P.A. Christ stood for me eternally, whip in hand in the Temple, turning out the money changers in a magnificent mood of fiery indignation.

III

EXIT THE BOY PREACHER

INSIDE the International Class War Prisoners Aid I found that a majority of the members were at the same time " in the Party ", which meant, of course, the Communist Party. Amongst them were some whom I had already met in the Commonwealth of India League too. They made a point of belonging to a vast range of such organisations that stretched from those which, like I.C.W.P.A., were predominantly communist, containing only a minority of non-communists, to those which, like the India League, were genuinely non-communist in origin but which communists could join. The communists, I soon learned, always had a great advantage over those with whom they associated because they knew exactly where they were going and how they were going to get there. And their drive, energy and enthusiasm ensured that they quickly became the spearhead of any organisation in which they worked.

The Communist Party members of that period fell roughly into two main groups, the unemployed and the students. The vast majority were unemployed. Already mass unemployment was becoming a large-scale problem although it was to become vastly larger as the years went on. To become known as a " Red " on the average job meant that, at the first opportunity, you would be dismissed. And there were plenty more ready to take your place. To be the spokesman in a dispute, to be seen with communist literature or to get the reputation with the management for talking communism among your workmates was to court victimisation. The consequence was that most of the Party's members had lost their jobs in this way and were paying the penalty for it. The vast majority had been " victimised ". Some over and over again.

One, who took a particular interest in me, had been sacked six or seven times for his communism until at last none would employ him. He lived alone with his widowed mother, with no prospect of being able to afford to marry. His unemployment benefit had long ago come to an end. He was receiving public assistance which then, far more than today, carried with it the stigma of the workhouse.

He had been in the Navy during the 1914–18 war but became bitter whenever the war was mentioned. " It was an imperialist war, a bosses' war, and we were fools to fight it," he would say. " We had arms in our hands then and we should have used them. If ever war comes again we shall turn the imperialist war into a civil war."

In his hatred of war he was one hundred per cent sincere. In his communism he was utterly sincere as well. He had sacrificed everything for it, yet never dreamed of going back on his principles in order to end his poverty, as he undoubtedly might have done, for he was an intelligent man who could have " got on " had he been prepared to drop his communism.

And he never dreamed of sparing himself in the cause despite the fact that he was a chronically sick man. His very sickness was part of the price he paid for his communism. Neglect, combined with under-nourishment, had worn him down. He was a pauper. The waiting list at the Infirmary was long and, in his position, he had no sort of priority, no influence and no hope of getting in for treatment for a very long time. And so a simple ailment went from bad to worse making him for ever tired: tired standing at meetings, tired queueing at the Public Assistance Committee, tired walking miles from one end of the city to the other in the course of his communist activities, tired standing idle at street corners because there was no comfort and practically no furniture at home.

I warmed to him whenever I saw him climbing the steep hill at the end of the long walk from a city slum to the Downs, panting under the weight of the Party's heavy portable platform. From somewhere he had obtained an ancient " pork-pie " hat and an equally ancient navy-blue suit. The jacket was double-breasted, the trousers wide and very long. The entire outfit at the beginning of its life had obviously belonged to a dandy and somehow he still succeeded in conveying the impression of the dandy, despite the stains on the battered hat and the shine on the faded suit.

There was nothing of the violent agitator about either his appearance or his manner. He was quiet-voiced, by nature retiring and always understanding.

I told him how I was coming to feel, more and more, that the communists were justified in wanting to destroy the capitalist system, that I thought that the revolution might even be seen as a great crusade, that perhaps if Christ had been alive He, too, might have been a communist. But, I said, the atheism of the Marxist was a stumbling-block to me.

Characteristically he did not attack my Christianity. "I had some difficulties myself, Chief, at one time," he said, "but I grew out of them and you will too."

He told me of a book I should buy. It was D. F. Buxton's *The Challenge of Bolshevism*, which had been published only a few months before. The author was a Quaker, who had gone to Russia and on her return had written this little book which was sympathetic to Bolshevism. She had dedicated it " To the nameless host, who under the Tsars perished as martyrs to their ideals of justice and freedom " and had sub-titled it " A new social ideal."

I have it before me as I write. I thought when I took it from my shelves that I should find some marked passage which had particularly struck me at the time, for its influence upon me at that precise stage in my spiritual and political development was incalculable. But I find that hardly a page is unmarked and, reading marginal notes entered at the time in my adolescent hand, I can easily recall the impression it made upon me. It did for my generation of communists what the Dean of Canterbury by his books and lectures does today. It lulled my doubts about the Marxists' militant atheism. It provided a bridge by means of which the man with some religious belief could cross with a clear conscience into the camp of unbelief.

The author's case was that the communists had found the Christian answer to an utterly un-Christian, bourgeois system of society. " Let the atheists of Russia speak the *language* of blasphemy: is it more than the echo of the blasphemy which has so long been embodied in the social order we uphold? "

In communism this sincere Quaker found honesty of purpose, intellectual integrity, a higher morality and a system which would prepare the way for a Christianity purified and reborn. And, of course, the communists used the book for all they were worth.

It was exactly what I needed at the time. It resolved a crisis for me, clarified my position and accelerated my progress towards communism. It was the link between my Christian past and my atheist future. I was able now to read with an " open mind " Engels' *Anti-Duhring*, the *A.B.C. of Communism*, the works of Lenin and others which formerly I would have rejected because of their atheism.

Its influence, and that of the host of ideas which now became permissible to me, were reflected in the sermons I preached. As a future missionary, I was asked to go one evening to conduct the annual Foreign Missions service in a little country chapel. It was a pleasant evening and some of the people from my own chapel went out to swell the congregation. But instead of preaching on India, China or Africa I concentrated my attention on what was wrong with Britain in general, and Bristol in particular.

The outline of my sermon was as follows: Bristol is full of Oriental students who are judging Christianity by its practice around them. But the Western capitalism they find here is un-Christian, based on the profit motive; it breeds war and they find Christians and the Church supporting war; it kills men, women and children by other means as well and they see Christians by their silence condoning their murder. Their influence, when they return to their own countries, will be greater by far than that of any missionaries. The best thing we can do to aid the work of the foreign missions is to give ourselves to the task of destroying capitalism and establishing a state of society based on service instead of greed.

I doubt whether many of the villagers present understood it. They certainly did not see its political implications. They clearly thought it odd that at their annual Missions service they had heard nothing about the heathen of other lands.

But the Bristolians who had gone out there were very much alive to where my sermon would lead and expressed sorrow, consternation or anger according to their varying temperaments.

There was, not unnaturally, an immediate cooling off in the enthusiasm of those who had been pushing me for work in the missions. Interest in the progress of my theological studies noticeably decreased. The demand for my services as a lay preacher slumped.

But when the requests to preach did come I made a point of denouncing the smugness of the chapel-going public, campaigned against capitalism and imperialism and identified Christianity with communism.

I still hoped to find some Christian body into which my ideas would fit and went on searching unceasingly. But God, for me, had to be in a workman's jacket, not in boiled shirt and tails.

On the Downs one Saturday night I noticed a young man, a newcomer there, holding forth to an audience of exactly one, another young man of about his own age. Both wore brightly-patterned shirts, with little bow ties. When the first finished speaking they reversed their roles and the second took over.

I went across to see who and what they were. From their accents it was clear that they were Americans and before long the speaker revealed that they were members of the Church of Latter Day Saints. One came from Salt Lake City, the other from Paris, Idaho.

Having by now had some experience of speaking on the Downs I stayed to listen out of sympathy for their so obvious lack of success. Until the meeting closed I remained their only hearer.

They repeated the performance the following week and again there was no other member of the public but me to hear them. Then, after several such occasions, they started talking to me, and, in due course, lent me the Book of Mormon. I found nothing in their teaching or in the books and pamphlets they began to press upon me which appealed at all. But because I felt sorry for them I usually strolled across from the other meetings to spend a little time with them.

I learned that they had worked double time for two years " back home " in order to be able to live as missionaries at their own expense for another two years in Bristol. Then they would go home—and do the same again. For several months I remained their only hearer and they became noticeably and increasingly depressed at the lack of any response whatsoever to their efforts.

Then, one evening, just as it was getting dark and the crowds around the meetings were breaking up, a very flushed and some-what inebriated elderly woman who happened to be passing heard the speaker make a reference to the Book of Mormon.

She stopped for a moment on her unsteady way and then heard the word " Mormon " again. She looked in wonder, first at the man on the platform, then at his companion standing at its foot. Then she turned to me, sole member of their audience, and asked incredulously, " Are those two blokes Mormons? " I told her they were. Her reactions were surprising and, indeed, alarming. Holding her umbrella before her, as though it were a bayonet, she made for the speaker.

" I know what you've come for, you dirty blackguards," she shrieked in a high state of excitement. " You've come to pinch our daughters to take them back to Salt Lake City."

Her shouts quickly attracted the people who were leaving the neighbouring meetings. The unfortunate Latter Day Saint tried to continue his oft-repeated and hitherto neglected message, but without success.

Soon several hundred people were crowding around, many of them taking up the woman's charges. They asked him, with a great show of enthusiasm, for further details of the domestic arrangements of Brigham Young, with particular reference to his forty wives, accompanying their enquiries with a steady barrage of advice to " get back to Salt Lake City ".

The vigilant if drunken lady was obviously filled with pride at what she had achieved. She prodded first one Mormon and then the other with her umbrella to the applause of the gathering. Finally, failing to make himself heard above the din, the speaker got down, defeated, from the platform, whilst the crowd pro-claimed that he was yellow. His companion took his place but met with little more success. Above the din I could barely hear him shouting something to the effect that his father had been a virtuous man, his mother had been a virtuous woman and he himself had been born as virtuously as any Bristolian in the crowd. It began to look as if some of the crowd were going to rush the platform. I found the defeated speaker at my side. " We are going to be chased right out of town at this rate," he said in an agitated whisper. Then rather forlornly: " Some of

them seem to know you. Do you think you could get them in
hand?" I said I would try.

From the platform I told them that I, like them, was a Bristolian, that I was not a Mormon but that I had known the two
young Americans for some time and believed that they were
utterly sincere in what they had come to preach. I added that I
was quite certain, on the basis of my knowledge of them, that
they had not come over for the purpose of shipping back the
girls of Bristol to Salt Lake City.

As I talked I saw the woman who had started all the fuss
quietly disappear, with a view, presumably, to looking for some
other form of fun. And before long the crowd decided that there
would be no more excitement and quietly went too. Things returned to normal with the three of us once more comprising the
entire meeting.

Rather emotionally the man from Salt Lake City and the man
from Paris, Idaho, thanked me for what I had done and, embarrassed by the intensity of their gratitude, I got away as soon as
I could.

I was, in fact, so embarrassed that I avoided them for some
weeks. But one night after I had spoken at an India League
meeting, I tried to hurry past them on my way home. One stood
on the small portable platform preaching his usual sermon. The
other stood before him, his only listener. But the instant they
saw me they declared the meeting closed and called me over.

They had, they told me, got a " proposition " to make. It was
this : They had come to Bristol with the idea of making converts.
But not only had they not made any, they had never, except on
that one disastrous occasion, had an audience of more than one.
The indifference of Bristol had hurt them, but the realisation that
when the moment of opportunity had come they had failed to
use it hurt still more.

They had, they reasoned, failed the folks back home who had
collected for the purpose of a Mormon Church which seemed
destined never to have a congregation. The trouble was, they
felt, that they were Americans coming from known Mormon
strongholds, which immediately aroused suspicion in the minds
of any potential converts. But now, supposing that I, a Bristolian

already known to many people, became the pastor of that church, what a better chance there would be of striking their roots in the city.

If I would take on the pastorate they and others in the States would work to maintain me, which would be more sense than working double time for two years in America in order to talk to each other for the next two years in Bristol.

They were disappointed, although, I cannot help feeling, perhaps not exactly surprised, when I declined. I was, in any case, by now giving most of my time and a great deal of my thought to political matters. I was writing for the *Bristol Labour Weekly*, and active in a variety of organisations.

Had my theological studies gone according to plan I ought by now to have taken my local preacher's examination and been on the next stage towards becoming a missionary. I had been examined orally, very early on, by the local minister responsible for supervising my work, who said that already I had reached a point where the examination would present no difficulties to me. But as my reputation for preaching " Red " and unorthodox sermons grew, all talk of the examination receded into the background. And in time it was quietly dropped.

It seems natural enough to me now that those responsible should have behaved as they did. They wanted to see just where I was going to finish up. But it seemed then only to confirm my belief that modern Christians were on the side of privilege, and that you could believe anything provided only that you did not question the desirability of the social system within which so many of them prospered.

IV

COMMUNISM IN ACTION

I STILL have on my bookshelves Lenin's *Preparing for Revolt*, published in 1929. On the fly-leaf is drawn a Cross on which hangs a hammer and sickle. Written in an immature hand

beneath it is: "For God and the Workers' Commonwealth".
On the title-page is written the slogan: "Workers will turn war
into civil war".

And, reflecting the way in which the semi-Marxist intellectuals
who profess opposition to the Communist Party can assist in the
making of a communist, there is written on the opposite page,
copied at, I should say, a somewhat later date, a quotation from
Professor Laski's *Democracy in Crisis*. It reads: "Circumstances
calculated to create a revolutionary situation in this country.

1. If we drift into war;
2. If there is a serious attack upon the workers' standard of
life, which culminates in a series of great strikes with, it may be,
an unwise use of the troops or police;
3. If there is a passion for economy so drastic that the social
services are gravely undermined;
4. A grave increase in the number of unemployed resulting
in widespread demonstrations suppressed by troops with con-
sequent loss of life."

Those words may be interpreted as a warning to the "ruling
class" or a call to action by the "ruled". They were most
certainly the latter to me.

Professor Laski, no doubt, was analysing the processes at work
in capitalist society in ice-cold fashion as became a Professor of
the London School of Economics. But the young communist
was able to surcharge the Professor's scientific analysis with
revolutionary warmth.

For those situations, enumerated by him as likely to lead to
civil war in Britain, are ones which every communist would recognise as being exactly in line with all that the Marxist theorists
have said and written. The communist, not unnaturally, longs
and works for communism, which he recognises can only come
via such situations, disastrous in appearance to everyone else, but
to him, even though he will not say so in public, necessary and
desirable. He has a vested interest in disaster. Economic crisis,
social upheaval, defeat in war or a victory which leaves a nation
bled white even though victorious—these are the pre-conditions
of communism. It would be less than human and, indeed, idiotic
for the communist not, in his heart of hearts, to long for them.

It would be still more idiotic for the world leaders of communism not to work for the creation of precisely such situations. Beneath the propaganda and the smoke-screen of concern for social justice, this is always the real aim and purpose of the Communist Party line, nationally and internationally.

Yet it was indignation at the consequences of economic crisis, a revulsion against social injustice and hatred of war which had brought me, as they have brought so many, to communism.

The contradiction is more apparent than real. Examine, for example, my hatred of war, which in itself would have been sufficient to keep me working night and day as the world drifted crazily over the years nearer and nearer to war. The Communist Party skilfully exploits that hatred which so many feel, in order to make recruits to its ranks and also in order to keep its members' anger for ever white-hot.

The first Communist Party public meeting I attended as a member was called to warn against the immediate danger of war —and that was in 1928. The speaker, on the basis of his Marxist diagnosis of the situation, made war with either France or the U.S.A. appear to be likely at any moment. There is always enough combustible material lying about the world for the communists to be able to paint such pictures and they do not appear too grotesquely improbable to their followers.

When I had worked for a few months as a Party member inside the No More War Movement, whose members vowed to take no part in war, neither international nor civil, I was myself arguing along the approved Marxist lines: The immediate question is not one of civil war but of the danger of imperialist war, and pacifists and communists can find common ground in opposing it if only because neither will be left if imperialist war comes. As for the civil war: if we get communism there will be no more wars and so that is completely in accord with the aims of the No More War Movement.

The amount of bloodshed and suffering required to carry through a successful communist revolution would, I reasoned, be so small by comparison with that resulting from any world war that it would lead in practice to a reduction of the world's sum of suffering, not an addition to it.

B

In theory, were it not for the ethics of the thing, one could, I suppose, justify such reasoning if there were conclusive proof that communism did, indeed, mean the end of war for all time. But the idiotic part of it was, and is, that there is no such proof. Experience, in fact, now points in exactly the opposite direction. But it would be foolish to ignore the fact that I, and thousands like me all over the world, worked and fought for communism and for civil war believing just that; believing with colossal conviction that modern war was so appalling that anything which would end it for all time was justified, whatever its methods.

And, I reasoned, if war came—and it was laid down with all the weight of a self-evident dogma that come it must so long as capitalism continued—then it would not have been in vain if out of the blood and the mud and the tears came a new and saner communist world from which the causes of war had been removed. " Workers will turn war into civil war " was not, therefore, to me just a cry for violence but for the ending of all war.

That may all sound very idealistic; its reasoning may, to the superior, sound slipshod or paradoxical. But the backcloth to my childhood and that of my generation was a war which we had been told was to end war—and millions died believing it. Yet already, in the late 1920s, it was widely held that much if not all of the slaughter of that war had been senseless and unjustifiable, viewed from any angle. And it was clear, too, that it had been based on a falsehood, for already there was talk and fear of the next war.

A strong resentment against social injustice was another of the things which drove me into the Party. The injustice likely to be done by communists to " the exploiters " troubled me at first. But the communist answer was clear and seemed fairly logical. The masses have never known social justice, which has been only for the few. Under communist rule there will admittedly, during the transitional dictatorship of the proletariat, be injustices so far as the individual former rulers are concerned. But, because of their past, this will in fact be no more than a grim, rough justice. They will be paying for the injustices perpetrated by their class over the centuries. And, in balance, how much better that injustice should now be confined to the tiny minority. For the vast majority, the erstwhile exploited, there will be justice for the first time. It became almost a matter of arithmetic. And for good measure there was the appeal of retribution as well.

It had everything to it. And, extraordinary as it may seem, I, and millions like me, may at first have questioned its ethics, but we hardly stopped to question the main hypothesis, i.e., that there would be justice for the many " when the revolution comes ", or to question whether the Party which would make itself responsible for the imposition of that justice was in any way competent or likely to make this possible or even probable.

Economic depression, with its attendant suffering which had appalled me so much, had played its part in driving me into the ranks of the communists. Yet was it so strange that before long I, like my comrades, was believing that economic crisis might, in fact, be the means by which communism would come? For it was laid down as a dogma that so long as capitalism continued the world would be subjected to ever-recurring, ever-more-frequent and ever-deepening crises, which could be ended only by the triumph of communism throughout the world. And we were, even then, sliding into just such a depression.

The queues at the Labour Exchanges were growing longer, malnutrition was becoming more widespread. If out of the misery, squalor, insecurity and disease which were the accompaniment of crisis we could get civil war and communism, then these things would not have been in vain. Let the crisis deepen and let the ruling classes tremble. Already the riots were beginning in the unemployed centres, the masses were coming into conflict with the capitalist State's repressive machinery, and who knew but what sooner or later, when anger and misery had increased still further, local riots might not blossom into full-scale revolution?

And then? The end of capitalism and the end of all crises, all unemployment.

After all, there was evidence which appeared to support this argument for the communist and left-wing Press was daily proclaiming the liquidation of unemployment in the Soviet Union. And if the opposition Press said that Russian unemployment was concealed by the millions in forced labour camps, why, that, we knew, was just bourgeois propaganda and, as such, suspect.   Was it really to be wondered at if a generation which had grown up in the din and strife of modern propaganda rejected all that which came from official and " respectable " sources and accepted only what fitted in with what it wanted to believe?   There was a certain " kick " to be had out of rejecting all that came from the most respectable quarters and accepting all that came from those who were most abused and distrusted.

My Christianity did not die easily.   The individual who, retaining some remnants of religious belief, nonetheless joins the Communist Party will in almost every case tell himself that, even though the Party and the individuals who make up its membership are militantly atheistic, there is no reason why he should be so too.   Party members will put up a show of agreeing, so confirming what he wishes to believe.

He may even tell himself, and believe, that the big job is to Christianise the movement.   Communism, he will reason, has in any case come to stay, and so Christians must do one of three things.   Either they may pretend to ignore it, in which case it will triumph despite them; they may oppose it, in which case they will be banging their heads against a wall, or they may get into it and Christianise it.   And so he will tell himself and others: " I am choosing the third course, which is the only sensible, Christian one."

It is a course of action which has glamour and excitement to recommend it—for what more exciting than pursuing a reforming mission among those who see themselves as the greatest reforming missionaries of all time?

It is attractive, it is exciting and it is fatal to his Christianity, for he will, almost inevitably, quickly reach the point where his Christianity more and more loses its strength whilst atheistic communism takes a firmer and firmer hold.   For how long he will continue publicly to call himself a Christian and still have some religious influences—or prejudices and superstitions, as his new associates will call them—still at work within him will depend upon the individual.   But the process will be much the same in any case.

That is what happened to me.   For a time I set about the

attempt to evangelise my new friends. I tried to persuade them and they in turn tried to persuade me. But they were bound to win, for I had, after all, given away half my case already. I had to convert them entirely, whereas I was already converted to the idea of communism and they had only to prove that Christianity was a barrier to its achievement. That took time but the outcome was a foregone conclusion.

Marx and Engels appeared to be able to account in scientific language for most things in heaven and earth, and the post-Reformation world has all but lost the ability to provide the philosophic answers anyway. Yet I had, after all, had what had seemed a very real personal religious experience at the time when I first determined to become a missionary. It was not easy to explain that away. How to account for it if there were no God? Modern jargon and pseudo-science helped.

" That ", I was told, " was really just a sublimation of your sex instincts. It is significant that it came during your adolescence and so soon after puberty. It did not have its origins in any omnipotent God but in your own glands. Take a look at your own chapel and see what proportion of the congregation is made up of sex-repressed spinsters." Such evidence was there in plenty, I knew. I knew well enough, too, the intensity of the sex instinct and guessed that if it were " sublimated " it would surely add up to something pretty considerable.

Complete and ribald debunking has been proved to be peculiarly attractive to our cynical age. Biographers of the between-the-war years discovered this and exploited it to the full. And what greater debunking than to accept that it was not the Holiest in the Heights but the lowliest in the depths of one's own sex mechanism which explained one's greatest spiritual experiences?

It would be wrong, of course, to say that this facile argument was alone or even mainly responsible for the destruction of my religious belief. The Marxist interpretation of history provided the intellectual argument, the sublimation-of-the-sex-instinct theory gave it emotional support. Drifting out of all Christian activity and becoming utterly absorbed in communist thought and practice, mixing the whole of my spare time with atheists, I came gradually to both feel and believe that I could get on perfectly well without a God. The whole of the emotion, thought and activity which had formerly gone to my religion were now canalised into new channels. Zeal, enthusiasm, idealism, study, sacrifice, ceaseless activity, all were now needed for the new cause as much and more than they had ever been demanded of me by my nonconformity.

There was, of course, a period when the frontiers were blurred; when, although subscribing intellectually to my dialectical materialism, and habitually blaspheming in a peculiarly rich and ribald way as became a militant atheist, I would nonetheless, in moments of stress, just barely stop myself from offering up a prayer for the success maybe of some communist exploit in which I was engaged, or on some purely personal matter. That was the transitional period which preceded the fifteen or more years in which no doubt about the correctness of my Marxist atheism, or any twinge of conscience about my denial of God, disturbed me at all.

I discovered that William Morris, whose works as an artist, poet and craftsman I knew and loved, had also been a Marxist, and that his communism had grown out of his revolt against the sham and the shoddy of the new machine age and his desire for a return to the popular culture and gaiety of the pre-capitalist period.

I found myself in agreement with everything he had written, and the realisation of just how much the proletariat had lost and what they must recapture excited me and provided just that touch of warmth, colour and humanity which the Marxist text-books manifestly lacked. Morris made my communism a colourful crusade, appealing to the spiritual as well as the purely intellectual. Best of all, he made the pattern of the future Communist State, as I wanted it to be, more clear in my own mind. After a fantastically busy day I would spend hours reading Morris and developing his ideas.

The communist theoreticians have been careful to avoid describing, except in the most general terms, what life under communism would be like. They have said that it would be a " classless society "; there would be an end of exploitation and none would live on rent, profit or interest. But that is not a way of life—it is little more than a collection of slogans.

But now the pattern of my communist Britain became clear. In a society in which the means of production were owned by the people the machine would truly become man's slave and not his master.

Man's leisure would increase until at last he had more leisure hours by far than those required to assist the machine to do the humdrum but necessary jobs for the community.

From this would come the desire and opportunity to use that leisure well; every man and woman would become an artist-craftsman and, as æsthetic standards rose, none would be content with anything which was mass-produced if it could possibly be made by his own effort.

There would be a great blossoming of the arts, with the common people themselves producing things to compare with the glories left to us by the medieval craftsmen. Communism in practice would in fact lead to a great outpouring of the human soul.

The fact that communism is little more than a word, a name to which almost any meaning can be given, a mould into which each individual communist may pour his own content, is of tremendous assistance to the cause, and it was this that I did. It meant that it became in a very real way my own personal ideal.

I had early learned to love the magnificent old churches of Bristol, to revel in the artistry revealed in every stone. That interest in the medieval never waned, and it coloured my communism throughout.

The personal life of some of the communists I met troubled me at first, but there I was confronted with a paradox, for the best communists seemed to live the worst lives. In practice the shock effect did not last long and was eased by the fact that I was in process of ridding myself of most of the restraints which had been the be-all-and-end-all of the nonconformity I had known.

I was shocked when the speaker I had listened to with such admiration, and who had spoken with such feeling and conviction, paired off nonchalantly and as of right with the equally sincere, attractive girl comrade I had marched and demonstrated with—taking her off from under my nose to bed and doing so quite openly and unashamedly. It was shocking maybe, but also disturbing; it left one restless and a little resentful with oneself for not having got there first.

It was disturbing to know that the girl who put the case for the new communist world before the unconverted with such skill and such violence would, if you wished, nonetheless finish up in your arms at the end of the evening, leaving nothing left to be done, and that hardly a " by your leave " was needed to accomplish this.

Such behaviour seemed curiously inconsistent to me at first, but it had its attractions and, as always, a Marxist theory to justify and support it. That Marxist theory and practice has been not least among the attractions of communism in our day. It has lured on those who did not want to be restrained and provided a haven for those with guilty consciences.

In such matters there was, as with everything else, only one rule to observe: it must not interfere with one's communism.

The very first communist leader I met gave me my initial shock of this sort. I suppose that it was my nonconformist background which made me expect that any man with a mission would, in his personal life, be something of an ascetic, who denied himself the pleasures of the flesh.

But here was a man, an unemployed South Wales miner, who could sway great crowds with the burning intensity of his concern for the down-trodden and his anger at the injustices which they suffered; who was equally sincere and impassioned about these things in private conversation and who gave practically his whole effort to the cause.

Yet, on the rare occasions when he could afford it, he would drink to excess on the grand scale and, since it was free, would " love " whenever he had the opportunity on an even grander scale. He took it for granted that every girl comrade was his for the asking.

I came to see in time that there was no need to doubt the sincerity of his Marxist beliefs because of such elements in his personal life, that they sprang, indeed, quite naturally from the Marxist views he held.

He later proved his sincerity in quite spectacular fashion. One of his drinking and philandering bouts had seriously interfered with his work as a communist. Not for the first time he was missing when he should have been addressing a meeting. The Party's District Committee " carpeted " him and told him that if he continued to let his personal life interfere with his Party responsibilities he would be expelled.

" I'll show them," he said.

That week-end he went out carrying a chair and addressing open-air meetings in every mining village he came to. Ill-nourished and exhausted by years of Party activity and by his hectic personal life, he nonetheless in a single week-end addressed forty meetings. Then, as he finished the fortieth, his heart gave out and he dropped dead. He was sincere, he was brilliant, but his life had been distorted by the views he held.

Increasingly the Party based its activities upon the organisation of the unemployed. I was made treasurer of the local branch of International Labour Defence, which was now doing the work formerly done by the International Class War Prisoners Aid (the name had been changed in order to give it a broader appeal).

Our job was to provide defence for those who found themselves in court, to organise demonstrations of protest or support, to look after the dependants and to raise the necessary cash for it all.

Bristol became a battle-centre. The communist-led-and-created National Unemployed Workers' Movement would organise a demonstration for more relief, for winter coal or special allowances. The unemployed, after listening to flaming speeches from the communist leaders in the Horsefair (Bristol's popular meeting place), would start to march and quickly come into conflict with the police, who would use their batons, to which the unemployed would reply with a shower of the wooden blocks which seemed always conveniently to be stacked for road repairs in the city's main streets. Arrests would result and a number of " class-war victims " would appear before the magistrates.

That meant an International Labour Defence demonstration to boost their morale before they appeared in court, a meeting to raise the cash for their defence, a protest outside the Bridewell whilst their cases were being heard, and another when they had been sentenced.

When they went to jail there would be more I.L.D. demonstrations to raise funds for their wretched families. And so, in the process, more riots would occur, more arrests be made and the whole grim business be repeated again. So it went on, week after week.

The unemployed man with little or no sympathy for communism might listen on the fringes of the crowd for want of something better to do. There would be a fight with the police and, maybe, he would be batoned or trampled upon by the " mounties' " horses and would disappear into hospital. When he came out he was a hero; he was lionised and before long he was drawn into the movement of revolt.

Or perhaps he was arrested, and the only ones who appeared to care were the communist I.L.D., who saw that he was represented in court. If he went to jail we looked after his family, and he, when he came out, would join our ranks.

Those of us who were receiving Party instruction knew the meaning and purpose of it all, how it was intended that class anger should be built up and up by such means until the lean men of the unemployed queues dreamed of revolution and not simply of reform.

But it would be wrong to conclude from this that our approach as individuals to the unemployed, as we worked to turn riots into revolution, was completely cynical, that we felt no concern for their present plight.

As I watched and helped to lead each demonstration of unemployed, my feelings were a compound of both anger and pity. As I saw them trampled under the horses' hooves during baton charges, or tugging with bare hands at paving-stones in their search for ammunition to be used against the police, hope and pride would mingle with my anger. Each man who disappeared between warders from the court-room into the cells added to my own hatred of the capitalist system and of the capitalist class, and strengthened my revolutionary determination.

The constant activity carried one along. There was action, there was colour and there was a grim comradeship which gripped one more and more. We sang of the revolution, dreamed of it, fought for it, studied for it, worked for it and, often enough, suffered for it too.

As the economic crisis deepened, the poverty, and the vast scale of that poverty, appalled me. We sold our National Unemployed Workers' Movement pamphlets, which explained the rights of the unemployed or exhorted them to " action ", at a halfpenny each—and still there were plenty who could not afford them. When the *Daily Worker* began to appear, the unemployed queued at the " bomb shop " in the Horsefair in order to be able to read it free of charge. And the Bristol demonstrations, riots and prosecutions featured more and more in its columns. We knew that, as Marxists, we were doing a good job. This was the real test and we were standing up to it. The strength and influence of the Communist Party cannot be gauged in times of normalcy, when democracy is working smoothly. They cannot be judged by success or failure in the ballot box. The real test is in time of crisis. The crisis had come and we were proving our ability to lead as trained Marxists should.

There later came the day when the Party decided that there should be united action by both employed and unemployed, for there were increasing signs of the one being played off against the other. An evening demonstration of solidarity at a time to suit both was arranged. There followed what has come to be known in communist working-class history as " the Bristol Ambush "—and in it I was seriously batoned for the first time.

The route which our march was to take through the city streets was discussed with the police and for once we found them accommodating. On the night itself the police who accompanied us were unusually helpful, too, giving us permission to follow almost any route we pleased.

It had been our hope that we might go down Castle Street, now bombed but in those days a popular rendezvous. To our surprise permission was given for us to do so. But as soon as our long crocodile of " employed and unemployed " was well inside Castle Street the street lights failed, leaving us in darkness.

Within a few seconds fights had broken out between demonstrators and police. I do not now pretend to know who or what was responsible for touching off the battle.   Certainly at that time I and all my comrades were convinced that it was the police.

No sooner had the fighting begun than, as though by pre-arrangement, mounted police charged through the darkness from both ends of the street and others came from side streets.

But as they did so, thousands of people streamed out from nearby cinemas, for the electricity had failed there too, and found themselves in the middle of a terrific police charge.   The consequence was that many were injured before they even knew what it was all about.

As foot police attacked on either side of our procession, a girl I was with rushed into a shop doorway for safety.   But she found no safety there, for hidden in the arcade was a policeman with truncheon drawn, before which she went down screaming and fighting.   I struck out at the constable as he beat her on the head; within a few seconds I had joined her in a heap on the ground.

The night's incidents led to a considerable outcry for a public enquiry in the local press, for among those injured were some quite important people.   But the brief demand for a Watch Committee investigation fizzled out when three of the communist leaders were arrested, sent to the Assizes on serious charges of incitement to violence and finally sent to jail.

Incitement there had certainly been, but not, I felt, in the crude and public form alleged by the police.

Incidents like that of the " ambush " effectively killed any lingering doubts I might have had about the need for violence in the achievement of the ending of capitalism and the establishment of communism.   And the silence and indifference of the " comfortable " chapel-goers, to what seemed to me an appalling outrage, killed any lingering regrets I had for my lost Christianity.

In its place was a bitter hatred which became a dynamic force in my life.   " What we need is a jolly good healthy hate," I would say with terrific conviction, and I would seek to awaken and spread that class hatred which was beginning to flourish as one of the fruits of the great depression and on which we placed our hopes.

The Party decided that we should also try to win the support of the " workers in uniform "—the men in the armed forces whom we expected to be used against us sooner or later if we did not win them first.

A seditious paper, the *Soldiers' Voice*, was brought out from time to time, and Party headquarters expected us to get the bundles which were smuggled down from London into the hands of the men for whom they were intended. Sometimes members would hurriedly distribute them during a military parade or tattoo and then try to lose themselves in the crowd. A number who were caught served long prison sentences as a consequence. They were our martyrs and their example served only to strengthen our faith and our willingness to sacrifice.

In Bristol we were blessed with the presence of a large barracks, and a group with whom I was connected was one night given the responsibility of dropping parcels of the *Soldiers' Voice* over the wall in the hope that they would fall into the hands of the soldiers inside. Since the risks were high, volunteers were called for, who then drew lots. I volunteered but drew a blank. The unlucky one that night was caught in the act and disappeared inside the neighbouring jail for eighteen months. And again my resolution was strengthened along with my hatred.

V

CRYPTO-COMMUNIST

WHEN I had " learned my communism on the streets " of Bristol, my work in dentistry took me to North Wales, away from the excitement of almost daily battles to an area where, at that time, no communists were to be found. I was, indeed, the only communist between Chester and Holyhead. At once, as any good communist should, I began to seek recruits, but there appeared to be little prospect of making any by means of direct or open communist propaganda and activity.

But there was an Independent Labour Party, composed almost

entirely of men who had been active in the pioneering days of
Keir Hardie, or who prided themselves on having worked with
Philip Snowden and Ramsay MacDonald.   The I.L.P. was still at
that time affiliated to the Labour Party and I joined it as a means
of taking my communism inside the enemy camp.

Soon, as the only young and active member of the branch, I
was made its secretary, and its policies quickly swung to the Left.
Before many months had passed I had been given responsibility
for organising the Party throughout North Wales—which provided me with an excellent opportunity for prospecting for the
Communist Party at the expense of the I.L.P.; contacting the
Left-wingers in the coalfield, in the stone- and slate-quarrying
areas and elsewhere, turning them into *Daily Worker* readers and
getting them to accept the " Party line ".   But always I came
up against a brick wall when I tried to get them inside the Party
itself.

To maintain my own morale I continued to keep in touch with
Bristol for some time, motor-cycling down occasionally and
taking part in demonstrations there.   But more often I went
across to Lancashire, drawing inspiration from the communism
of the cities, assisting the communist candidate in Liverpool's
Scotland Division in the 1931 General Election and dashing across
to Birkenhead when unemployed threw up their barricades
after fierce street battles with the police.

I needed such tonic from time to time, for after nearly two
years in North Wales I still had not one fully organised branch
of the Communist Party to my credit, although I had built up
a considerable following among busmen and railway workers,
had made a number of sympathetic contacts among miners,
quarrymen and others, and had converts scattered here and there.

But invariably when I tried to get people actually into the Party
I came up against the deeply-entrenched nonconformity of the
North Wales workers.   I searched for ways of " breaking
through ", believing that its hold was mainly an emotional one
and calculating that if I could once get recruitment to the Party
started it would quickly grow.

Then, in line with Lenin's words, " morality is subordinate to
the class struggle ", I thought of a way of getting them on their

own ground. I was, in theory at least, still a lay preacher. I would exercise my right to preach, so paving the way for Party recruitment and at the same time obtaining an audience for the message which I burned to get across.

I had to meet and defeat considerable hostility on the part of the established lay preachers and ministers of the area, who put forward every possible reason for keeping me out of the pulpit, but in the end I won and started preaching again.

From the first I gave my sermons a " social slant " which I built up more and more as time went on.

The Communist Party's main activity at the time was the organising of a hunger march to London from all parts of the country. I longed to join the marchers, to identify myself with their savage pilgrimage, to be with them if riots or worse developed, and in any case to help them by building up support on their behalf. I decided to burn my boats and to preach directly about the march and the marchers' demands.

On the first Sunday after my decision my text was: " I was an hungered and ye gave Me no meat ". I told my prosperous-looking congregation about the misery of the unemployed, the suffering of the children, the human consequences of a capitalist world in crisis and the need for an alternative.

As I looked down on row upon row of well-fed, smug faces, I felt that the ragged, desperate men marching on the capital might have belonged to a land a thousand miles away. I felt angry and contemptuous, and made no attempt to conceal my feelings. On the spur of the moment I recited to them some verses of Joe Corry, the rebel poet, which compared the unemployed agitator with " one named Christ two thousand years ago ", and which had some harsh things to say about the bankers, parsons and police who were His enemies.

As I recited the poem the faces before me became less blank. But at its end a number of people got up and went out. I announced the last hymn. By the time it was finished the chapel was almost empty.

In the vestry afterwards a pillar of the church, in morning coat and with a large flower in his button-hole, told me my sermon had not been appreciated.

" I don't believe in mixing politics with religion," he said.
Then he added: " And I personally didn't like your reference to
bankers."

I discovered later that he was himself a banker.

During the week the Superintendent Minister asked me to go
to his house for a chat. A protest deputation had gone straight
from the church, he said, and had demanded that I be prevented
from again appearing in a Methodist pulpit.

I refused either to stand down or to keep off controversial
subjects. He appealed to my " better nature ", but my only conscience was my Marxist one, product of a blending of real human
sympathy at the suffering of the " victims of capitalism " with the
cold logic of Marxism and the belief that out of the present crisis,
if we used it aright, might come the Revolution and the Workers'
State.

On the following Sunday morning, with the hunger marchers
now in London, I took as my text, " Give us this day our daily
bread ". Before I had finished a tall old man with a beard that
seemed to advance fiercely before him like a medieval pike
came down the aisle and shook his fist at me over the pulpit.
" You should be in jail," he told me before stamping angrily out.

On the radio that afternoon I heard how the unemployed in
their tens of thousands had battled with the police in Hyde Park,
tearing up the railings to use as spears.

In the evening I preached on " I came not to bring peace but
a sword ". I told my sober, respectable audience that things had
reached a pass where the violent overthrow of capitalism should
be seen by Christians as a crusade, that any Christian worth his
salt should be prepared to fight alongside the Communist Party
for and in the Revolution.

In the half-lit chapel I watched them streaming out as I
preached—the hypocritical who wanted to be told that those
whom the gods love grow wealthy and who instead had been told
to become revolutionaries; the pious, too, who had come for
" comfort " and had been given communism.

When I closed the service one old woman alone remained. I
went down to her. " I am a member of the Society of Friends.
I want to thank you for your brave words," she said. She told

me that it was not for her to apologise for her fellow Christians but that she wanted me to know that although she had disagreed with everything I had said she still believed in my right to say it. " We are both Christians," she added simply.

I shocked her when I answered: " Quite frankly I'm not, I'm a communist."

I did not preach again.

It did not seem at the time as though I had achieved much for the Party by my brief return to the pulpit, but there was, some time later, a curious sequel to it. I had been either shunned or attacked by most of those with whom I had come in touch during that period and had been denounced from the pulpit in some of the chapels in the mining areas.

Then, one day, I met a local preacher who was also the leader of a young men's class. He told me that in his view I had been badly treated, that had I been handled more charitably I might still have been an active Christian.

I disagreed, pointing out that I was already a communist when the local Christians had turned on me. He said that he wanted to prove that there were still some who tried to practise charity, and asked me to give two talks to his class, one on " Why I am an atheist ", the other on " Why I am a communist ".

I told him that I thought that, from the point of view of his class, it was the greatest possible folly. " Your young nonconformists don't know where they stand," I said. " I, as a Marxist, do."

" Come along and you'll see," he said. " We'll turn you into a Christian yet."

Half-way through my first talk one young fellow got up in a magnificent rage. " It's daft getting him along," he said, " he's got all the answers and we haven't. We come here to be made better Christians, not atheists." He threw a book he was holding on the floor with a bang and slammed the door as he went out. He had my sympathy and, indeed, my admiration.

But the class leader called on me during the week, apologised and told me that he had talked the offending member into coming next Sunday after all.

He came, and the proceedings began with a handsome apology

from him.   I replied that I had left the previous week feeling that
he was the one sane man among them but that I now had my
doubts about it.

They listened quietly and charitably to my case for atheistic
communism and for dialectical materialism, seeing it as a demonstration of tolerance and charity.   I heard no more from any of
them for two or three months.   Then one day as I left my place
of work I found the member who had protested waiting for me.
He told me that since my second talk he had thought about what
I had said and had ordered the *Daily Worker* and some communist literature.   " I realise now ", he told me, " that none of the
people there really know what they stand for, but you do."   He
was my first communist supporter in that area.

When a hunger march was organised the following year, I
joined it in London, backed by a number of branches of the
National Unemployed Workers' Movement and Friends of the
Soviet Union (both " Party " organisations) which I had created.

Going from the isolation of North Wales to London was a
colossally stimulating experience.   Up there the fight was a lonely
one, my enthusiasm maintained only through knowledge of what
was happening in the class war elsewhere, and by persistent study
of the Marxist " classics ".

But marching from Bermondsey Town Hall to Hyde Park with
the hunger marchers after a spate of rousing speeches at a " Congress of Action ", I was carried along on a great wave of excitement and certainty of victory.

To those who watched the ragged marchers from the windows
of Grosvenor House we were, I suppose, just a rather ridiculous
if slightly terrifying sight as we plodded by in anything but
military formation.

But to me and my comrades this was the proletarian army, forerunner of the great Red Army which Britain would one day boast.
They were the men who had, as Marx had prophesied, in this
crisis of capitalism, nothing to lose but their chains, the meanest
and lowliest under the present system who would be the rulers in
the system of tomorrow.

When we swung into a long straight road I looked back down
the line of marchers stretching as far as the eye could see.   Their

challenging, threatening banners, sailing along above their heads, brought tears of hope and excitement to my eyes. The memory of that spectacle and of the vast crowds which greeted us at the Marble Arch provided a tonic and a stimulus which kept me going at fever pitch for months in the totally different life of North Wales.

I was running a smallholding in my spare time, breeding poultry, goats and dogs; living high up in the hills. My next-door neighbour on the one side was a farmer living three-quarters of a mile away.

On the other side lived the local squire, with whom I had a close friendship, for we were bound together by common interest in the soil. Politically, we were poles apart, but as he leaned over my five-barred gate of an evening, exchanging opinions on the harvest prospects, on the best breed of table poultry, or the points of the gun dogs we both bred, we had everything in common.

That friendship saved me in more than one awkward situation. The squire's great pride was his walled rose garden, and within it a tree which was, in his gardener's language, known as the " black " rose, bearing the darkest of dark red blooms, over which hung tiny shades to protect them from the bleaching of the sun.

When I returned to my holding one autumn evening I found that the billy goat, who sported a more-than-usually large beard and so had been named Karl Marx, was missing and I had a presentiment that he was up to mischief. Passing the squire's walled rose garden I heard a suspicious sound; I scrambled up the wall and peeped over the top. There, in the middle, stood Karl with an uprooted rose tree in his mouth. Sticking out from one side were the roots. From the other limply hung a mass of dark red roses. Then he took the final, fatal bite through the middle of the stock and the little protective shades tinkled sadly in the soft evening air as they fell to the ground.

I spent some time bracing myself before I went to break the dreadful news to the squire. But perhaps there is a point in human suffering at which the senses become numbed and nothing registers.

" My God, that's too ghastly even to think about," he said when I told him. Then, marching indoors, he added : " We both need something to put us on our feet after this. Come and have the biggest Scotch you've ever had."

The same degree of tolerance, however, was not shown to Trotsky, my small black-and-white cat, so named because from the start it was a little devil, spitting and clawing at everyone who came near.

Trotsky learned to poach, for which there were plenty of opportunities, for on some land adjoining my own little coops were neatly set out row upon row, in which were hens rearing broods of baby pheasants fed on chopped hard-boiled eggs and, even in those days, costing 10s. each to rear.

I was standing in my doorway one Sunday afternoon when the squire and gamekeeper stopped at the cottage gate.

" We're trying to trace a poacher," said the squire. " We're losing a lot of pheasant chicks."

" He may have two legs or he might have four," added the keeper significantly.

" If we catch him we shall shoot him," said the squire.

I heard a scuffle and, I fancied, a squawk from inside the house. Taking a sidelong glance inside I saw Trotsky playing with a half-fledged pheasant chick which came running towards me. I kicked it back through the door with the side of my foot.

" Excuse me a moment," I said, " I'll close the doors. Lot of wind today, blowing things about."

Squire and keeper looked suspiciously at the trees, where no leaf moved, and at the sky, which reflected the calmness of the day.

" They say that good ratters are good poachers," observed the keeper, coming round to the point. " And the farm bailiff tells me that your cat is the best ratter he ever came across."

From within the house came the last dying squawk of the unfortunate pheasant chick. Ignoring the gamekeeper, I turned to the squire. " My cat is too busy keeping your farm buildings free of rats to have any time left for poaching," I observed. They went away, but I feared for Trotsky's future.

Daily she came home with a pheasant chick and nothing I could do would stop her. One day she disappeared and I saw no sign of her for weeks.

Then, one evening I was passing the place where the keeper had his little hut. On its side was a board on which he hung his trophies. Nailed there were the usual crows, blackbirds, a hawk, some rats and a stoat, all hanging by their tails. And in the middle of them all, also nailed by the tail, was the unfortunate and now rapidly decomposing Trotsky, who had died, as became a good Marxist, engaged in the job of expropriating the expropriators.

Neither the squire nor I ever mentioned the fate of Trotsky, but one evening, as we stood together watching the sun setting across the hills and over the sea, a cock pheasant called from the spinney.

" All that poaching nonsense stopped some time ago," he said. " Stopped quite suddenly too. Something must have happened to the poacher."

" I'm sure it must," I said.

I was with the old squire only a few minutes before his death. I had been with him to his kitchen garden to see a new variety of lettuce. He left me to join his family, but on his way fell to the ground on the drive with an attack of high blood pressure and within a few minutes was dead.

As a Marxist I should have rejoiced at his death, for he represented everything most hated by communists. His social background was, in communist eyes, feudal, and therefore detestable; his politics were " reactionary "; when his farm staff staged a miniature strike on a trivial issue he sold up the model farm which had been the apple of his eye rather than give in. Yet I grieved at his passing. Only the tiny few among the Marxists can be one hundred per cent rational the whole of the time in the practice of their faith.

When I was asked to be a pall-bearer at the funeral the recollection of his considerable girth filled me with apprehension lest I should not be up to taking my full share of carrying the heavy coffin. But I need not have worried. The coffin, covered with branches from the trees he loved, was taken down the drive on an old farm cart, and then at the gates the pall-bearers took over, our job being to carry it right down the road to the church.

My fellow bearers, I found, were all a good deal taller than myself, and I thanked whatever Marxist gods there were when I discovered that all I needed to do was to keep in step with the rest and walk at the appropriate funereal pace, for the coffin conveniently missed my shoulder by a couple of inches. I could almost imagine the stout old man inside chuckling at the joke.

Those years in the early '30s which I spent on the smallholding were busy ones. I was functioning as a local correspondent for a number of national papers and writing for periodicals, in addition to looking after my livestock and continuing to hold a job in dentistry. Added to this were my constant efforts to build up communist organisations and maintain them. Yet I still made time for a considerable amount of Marxist reading even though most of it was done after midnight.

My parents had moved into a little Somerset village, dominated by a magnificent Gothic church. A place which had once been a medieval inn became their home, with low ceilings, great beams which you could touch when you sat up in bed in the morning, and walls so thick that they could house deep cupboards in their bosoms.

I got down there as often as possible and loved every minute spent there, studying each ancient inn and building in the village, cutting mistletoe from the trees in the orchard at Christmas and re-creating the spirit of the great feasts of the past; accompanying the carol singers who went, lanterns in hand, to the oak-panelled halls of the great houses of the neighbourhood, or spending New Year's eve in the high belfry to see the ringers take the muffs off the bells at midnight.

Every hamlet for miles around contained a magnificent Gothic church, every lane concealed an ancient inn or fascinating cottage. It was easy there to recapture what life must have been in those centuries when men built and worked for a faith in which they truly believed.

Those days, I thought regretfully, were dead and the faith in which they had believed was dead, too. But the treasures those men of the past left were nothing compared with those which the men of tomorrow, with their new faith, their new proletarian culture, would create.

Somewhere I discovered a curious communist poem which I illuminated in Gothic lettering. Its text was blasphemous, and I embodied in the initial letter a portrayal of the crucified Christ. It read: " Good-bye, Christ. You did all right in your day, I reckon. Make way for a new guy now with no religion at all. . . . Marx, Communist, Lenin, Peasant, Stalin, Worker, Me—I said ME."

Illuminated and medievalised, and with its worker-mystique, it summed up my faith.

On my bookshelves *Piers Plowman* and Chaucer took their places quite naturally at the side of Morris's *Dream of John Ball*, Marx's *Das Kapital* and Lenin's *The Proletarian Revolution.*

VI

ORGANISING FOR SPAIN

THE fundamental change which was made in the policies and particularly the methods of communists the world over when Hitler came to power in Germany helped my work in North Wales enormously, for the scope of our activities was suddenly broadened and new possibilities loomed up at once.

The effect of the Nazis' victory upon the world communist movement is still not fully understood even to this day, yet it is vital to an understanding of the communists' methods.

The Communist International, and Party members throughout the world, by 1930 believed that a Soviet Germany was " in the bag ", that the " crisis of capitalism " was something which the German ruling class simply could not survive. The *Daily Worker* of August 1, 1931, for example, published a picture of uniformed members of the German Workers' Defence Force which was captioned " Red Front Fighters . . . ready to defend Soviet Germany against Imperialist War ". No communist believed that the Nazis could triumph. We took it for granted that the great German State would fall like a rotten plum straight into the lap of the Party.

The shock to the world communist leaders caused by Hitler's virtual destruction of the mighty German Communist Party was terrific. If this could happen, then anything was possible. And so, in approved Marxist fashion, the Comintern did a complete switch. " The communists disdain to conceal their views and aims," said Karl Marx and Friedrich Engels in the Communist Manifesto, and that, so far, had been the attitude of the Communist Parties everywhere.

Communism had been our aim and we had said so. It could only be achieved by bloody revolution, civil war and Red terror —and we made no bones about it. The capitalist world was rotten, we hated its traditions, we rejected its conventions, its morality, and we did not hesitate to proclaim and to practise these things. As communists, we publicly defied all " bourgeois " conventions and gloried in being " outrageous ".

Communism was militantly atheistic and we said so, publicly blaspheming at our meetings, caricaturing God in our Press. We had our League of Militant Atheists and gloried in its title and its intentions. We proclaimed the bankruptcy of marriage, the futility of the family, the freedom of unrestricted sexual intercourse. And we practised these things too.

If we worked to assist the return of a Labour Government we did so only that the social democrats, or " social fascists " as we more often called them, might reveal their bankruptcy and so that the disillusioned workers would then turn to us. And we told the world that this alone was our reason. There was at least a certain grim, contemptuous honesty about our attitude.

But the new situation created by the Nazis' successes ended all that. It resulted in the tactic of the Popular Front, the decision to enlist the aid of the middle class, the intellectuals, the " social fascists "—anyone who could be brought in to fight fascism, the victory of which would mean the end of all our hopes. It was a temporary retreat, but justifiable in the light of Marxist thinking.

The new tactic was to soft-pedal in public whilst sticking to everything as before in private.

Books published before that date, which stated our position
with frankness, such as *The A.B.C. of Communism*, published by
the Communist Party of Great Britain, were withdrawn and
destroyed. (Thoroughness was carried to a point in the Soviet
Union where the two authors of that work were, in fact, liquidated.) The leaders were already equipped with copies of such
books, which was what mattered. In the Party's bookshops they
tore up or burned former " classics " by the thousand.

It was all very thorough but very phoney, for we went back
on none of the fundamentals; we simply put some into cold
storage and found new methods of dishing up the rest.

That is still the tactic today, and in the intervening years the
technique has been developed to a point where the communists'
public propaganda never at any time bears any relation whatsoever to their real aims as expounded in their text-books and
as taught in the privacy of their members' study classes.

Communism has, in fact, become a gigantic hoax, a deliberate
and total deception of the public.

I accepted the new tactic with enthusiasm and began to cultivate
those whom I had fought or ridiculed in the past. And, such is
the essential charity of the average man, it worked. Despite
everything they welcomed the chance of working with me as a
friend.

When the Left Book Club began early in 1936 it provided me
with just the weapon I wanted. To all those who had so often
told me that they were of the Left rather than the Right I said,
" Join the Left Book Club and prove it." To the liberal-minded
who argued that they liked to read both sides I said : " Here's your
chance." To those who claimed to take an intelligent interest in
the contemporary scene I said : " You can't do so without reading
the Left as well as the Right."

Soon I had dozens of people whom I had regarded as political
foes reading a Left book each month and then discussing it with
me.

By the time the Spanish civil war began in July of that year,
I had the movement already well established, organising a wide
variety of well-intentioned people.

The events in Spain were a challenge and a showdown. Here

was the war and fascism against which we had warned, already beginning in one corner of Europe. Who knew where it might end if all those who stood for peace and democracy failed to unite?

All over Britain and right across Europe, recruits to the Party came thick and fast—the sensitive intellectuals, the troubled and disillusioned pacifists, and solid working-class, trade union types who had distrusted us in the past but now believed that, if what they stood for had some day to be defended, arms in hand, it would be the communists who would lead and fight as no one else.

When a Welsh section of Spanish Medical Aid was formed I at once organised a public meeting to raise cash for a Welsh ambulance. I asked all my Left Book Club members to prove their sincerity by giving it their active support. The platform at the first meeting was solidly lined with clerical collars and it had been announced from pulpits all over the district. The cause was presented as a great humanitarian issue on which all men of goodwill could unite. But we communists knew that an ambulance could be as useful to the Spanish Government as a gun and that each meeting, each collection, was shot and shell for communism.

Our first ambulance left within a few weeks for Spain. With it went the Welsh national secretary as driver and I took his place. In the months that followed I worked as I had never worked before.

Organising two or three meetings daily kept me fully occupied. Speaking at every one of them meant that I slept little and hardly ever stopped working. I showed the propagandist film, *Defence of Madrid*, at each meeting. After hiring a cinematograph machine and the film time after time, I bought both outright and took them everywhere with me. At one period I saw that film twice daily for four months and made as many speeches and appeals. I learned a lot about the geography of the district, but, more important, I learned a great deal about the willingness of men and women to sacrifice for causes in which they have been brought to believe. Often the sacrifices were so huge as almost to appal me.

At a meeting in a village near Bethesda, for example, I had an audience entirely composed of working folk, to whom I made my speech, showed the film and then made an appeal during the course of which I " Dutch-auctioned " a Spanish militia man's hat and a militia girl's scarf.

Two men made the final bids for the first. When I knocked it down to the purchaser he passed up an unopened pay packet. The same happened when I followed with the militia girl's scarf. Both went to slate quarrymen earning pitifully little.

Similar sacrifices were later made at our meetings by miners, agricultural workers, railwaymen and other low-paid workers. With such sacrifices being made all over the country there seemed little reason to doubt the rightness of our cause.

At great London meetings men and women were throwing on the platforms their wedding rings, pitiful little heirlooms or everything they had in their wallets at the time. Our political opponents, who charged us with faking these things, most foolishly under-estimated the depth of feeling we had succeeded in creating. But the widespread, often quite unreasoning and almost instinctive hostility to everything to do with Franco Spain, which still survives to this day, is a tribute to our achievement.

Often at my meetings I would get volunteers for the International Brigade and I would pass them on to the appropriate quarters. More often than not they were lads with no political background at all. Some never came back, and I and others working in the cause felt that we owed it to them to work even harder. We worked all the harder for our ambulances, too, when we learned of the machine-gun parts and other arms which were being smuggled out in so many of them.

In the early days of the Spanish struggle the Party sent many of its own members to fight. One of my own converts to the Party came back after years in jail, minus an arm.

The communists went to Spain for quite different reasons from those of the non-communists. We saw it as a chance of learning the art of insurrection in practice so that it might one day be applied at home; to get experience of the barricades, to learn to use the modern weapons of death and destruction for the cause of communism.

Every Communist Party in the world sent numbers of its members there to gain such experience. The leaders went out one after the other for a few months' experience. Very few lost their lives or received serious wounds. The type of jobs they took there were not calculated to make this likely, and every Party member felt that this was rightly so, since the leaders should not lightheartedly be thrown away.

But the rank and file in the early days died in great numbers and set an example in heroism. Too many died, in fact, for the Party's liking. It was not intended that Party members should be slaughtered wholesale. Dead men could make no contribution to the fight for Soviet Britain.

So I and others doing similar work were dissuaded from sending out any more Party members. The new recruits must be non-communists whose deaths would assist the immediate aims of the Party without jeopardising the coming struggle for power at home.

When cannon fodder, above all else, was needed, one Party organiser's job was to go around the Thames Embankment in London at night looking for able-bodied down-and-outs. He got them drunk and then shipped them over the Channel.

They sobered up in Paris, were dined and primed, then made drunk again. Paralytic they went over the Pyrenees and, when next they were sober, they were already members of the British Battalion of the International Brigade.

Communists have little regard for those whom they contemptuously term the lumpen-proletariat, and if a few down-and-outs could be made to serve the cause in this way, then by their lives, or at any rate their deaths, they had served the cause after all.

One of the high spots of my own emotional experience as a communist came one May Day during the Spanish civil war. I was marching with the traditional London demonstration and many contingents had joined us along the route. Going down Oxford Street I looked back down the ranks. I was at the end of my own contingent. I expected, as I turned, to see the usual red flag or trade union banner heading the next. Instead, I saw a black one with white lettering which read: " For every man marching behind this banner one member of the Bethnal Green Communist Party has died fighting fascism in Spain."

Behind it came row on row of men, with heads proudly carried, the living who represented the dead in that bitter May Day rally. I carried my own head more proudly, too, and looked with greater pride than ever before at the hammer and sickle badge I wore in my button-hole.

From Bethnal Green those lads had gone out from slum homes to give their lives for the defeat of what they believed to be the decadent and the corrupt and for a brave new world.

They, who had never known life as it should be lived, gave their lives for what was the best they knew. They died with hatred in their hearts and the slogans of the Revolution on their lips, and they died gloriously. There lies the strength of communism. It is in its ability to take hatred, desire for retribution by those who have been ill-used, youthful idealism and the desire for a cleaner world, and then to harness all these powerful horses to its chariot.

But there was a very different side to the story. At the top of the anti-Franco movement was every sort of jealousy and intrigue, and a lot of straight, sordid racketeering. Members of other parties who were taking the same risks in the International Brigade in Spain, inspired by nothing but anti-fascist or liberal-democratic motives, were appalled when they became aware of the communists' determined efforts to direct operations and manage affairs at all levels in what, after all, had been named the Major Attlee Battalion.

From Wales we were sending up to London the money for one ambulance after another, but squabbles between those responsible for their purchase and those who were waiting for them on the other side led to such an accumulation of scandal, and threats and counter-threats of libel actions, that I had to go hurrying up to try to sort things out.

Wherever I went I took pamphlets on Spain with me, selling them or leaving them in buses, trams and trains. And, like other communists, I would sometimes hurry into the porch of a Catholic church and make for the Catholic Truth Society's literature rack, where pamphlets were exhibited for sale. I would take out any which appeared to be anti-communist and put others on Spain in their place. I did not bother even to spare a glance for the churches themselves.

One Saturday, just as it was growing dark, I hurried into a church, pamphlets at the ready. Three little girls wearing convent school hats came out. To pass off what I was about, I asked them what they had been doing.

" We've been to Confession," said one.

" What on earth have little girls like you got to confess? " I asked incredulously.

" Little girls sometimes forget to say their prayers," replied the bright one of the three as they made for home.

I was appalled. Appalled to a point of fascination. I had not had a religious thought in my head for years. I had consciously made my life as blasphemous as I could.

Having put my pamphlets into the rack, I was turning to leave when I saw that lights were shining inside the church. Out of curiosity I peeped inside.

Through the gloom I could see a figure of Christ standing with garment opened at the chest on which was painted a vivid red heart—a Sacred Heart statue which meant less than nothing to me.

Other figures in gaudy colours, and equally lacking in taste, stood here and there. Red, blue and gold paint—lashings of gold —appeared to have been splashed about almost indiscriminately on the masonry, woodwork and stone walls. It jarred almost to a point of physical hurt. In the body of the church here and there people knelt and I watched lest they should make for the door and find the communist pamphlets in the rack, whilst I had my pockets stuffed with the Catholic ones I had removed.

One man rose and went into what I took to be a confessional box, as the woman who had just left it went to kneel in silent prayer.

It was all utterly alien to me. It represented superstition at its lowest depth. Yet suddenly for one brief moment the craziest and most outrageous of impulses took possession of me. I, too, wanted to go and confess. To say to the priest inside: " Look here, you who live in a world of your own, you are wasting your time. The children whose confessions you have heard have not come within a million miles of sinning. That man and woman still go to church. They live respectable lives. They believe in God. Here's a real job for you. I'm up to my eyes in sin. I sin more in one day than they'll sin in their whole lives. Confess me."

The impulse was so mad, so preposterous, yet so strong and urgent that it all but swept me inside. Instead I stuffed a few more Red pamphlets into the rack, went out into the night— and blasphemed all the harder to get myself back to sanity again.

A point was reached where I had shown my film throughout the whole area, a meeting had been held in every possible town, village or hamlet and collections had been made over and over again. It was clear that a new type of appeal was required if the political work I was attempting was to be carried forward. Direct appeals for cash with which to buy machine-guns and for volunteers for the front were bound to be confined to very select and limited audiences. What was now needed was a new humanitarian appeal.

The arrival of the Basque child refugees in Britain provided me with just what I needed. I at once launched a local appeal for a Welsh Basque Children's Home. A committee, the broadest and most " Popular Front-ish " yet, was formed and a large empty school taken, which in due course housed a number of the loveliest of little Spanish children.

I fell in love with them at once. I parted with a good deal of my own furniture for their home and I was delighted that the party line was such that it had become a politically useful thing to undertake such work. But they were, nonetheless, just an excuse for yet one more campaign " against war and fascism ", an excuse for making new sympathisers and, one hoped, new Party members too.

VII

OLD SLOGANS REVIVED

EARLY in 1938 I made for the London area. The life on the small-holding had been good and, since I had always had other irons in the fire and so did not depend upon it, was successful even at a time when smallholders and poultry farmers were going bank-rupt all over the country. But I had had to give up the holding because it was too much of a tie at a time when I spent so much time travelling about.

The political work in North Wales had been useful. But it was clear, as the war-clouds gathered, that history was going to be made in the next few years. And it would be made much more in the cities than in " backward " rural areas. I wanted to be near the hub when things began to happen.

But for a time, even in the South of England, I again found myself in a " backward " area, this time in a district of Surrey of military rather than industrial importance and hardly likely, in peace time at least, to be a revolutionary storm-centre. But because of the presence of large numbers of barracks and training areas, it was of vital importance in the event of war.

My first political task was to get a Communist Party branch established. But how? There was practically no industrial working-class, no factories on which it could be based. It was a situation where the frontal attack was almost bound to fail. So I tried the familiar communist infiltration methods instead, using the local Labour Party for the purpose.

I was in luck, for at my very first meeting after making a con-tribution to the discussion I soon had a group of keen young members around me, arguing about what I had said. I noted the most hopeful and sat with them at the next meeting. We left together, had a meal, and by that time I knew those on whom I would work first. I selected the keenest and most intelligent.

My luck continued, for the next meeting was the Annual General Meeting. I was made an executive member and dele-gate to the Divisional (or Constituency) Party. And, on my proposition, most of those whom I hoped to get into the Communist Party went on to the Executive too. From then on they looked to me for leadership.

Two or three weeks later I got the first of them into the Party, telling him to keep quiet about his membership and to continue to work in the Labour Party. Then another, another and another. Each thought that he or she was the only one.

When the Constituency Party's Annual General Meeting came round we decided in advance whom to support and whom to fight. The result was a triumph for the Left. We had formed a " ginger group " which by now was well sprinkled with Communist Party members. The group captured a majority of the positions in both the local and Divisional Party and was soon doing most of the work of the Labour Party throughout the entire district. And we got a foothold, through the local Trades Council, in the trade union movement too. It was not long before I had got every likely man or woman at executive level into the Communist Party.

Then, one night, I got them together. I did not tell them the purpose of the gathering but left them to assume that it was just an extended " ginger group " meeting. When all had arrived I revealed that everyone present was already a Communist Party member and suddenly they realised what had happened and just what strength the Party already had in the local Labour movement. Then we got down to business.

The Party leader who was nationally responsible for infiltration within the Labour Party came to meet the new Party group. He wore a more-than-usually dirty mac., an ill-fitting suit and an ancient hat. It was a surprisingly simple yet effective disguise, for by day he was a super-sleek lawyer and in that role was also known as a Party member. But at night, simply by dressing in completely contrasting clothes, he could go to well-known Labour Party members' houses without arousing suspicion.

From then on we functioned as a Communist Party group, continuing to keep our membership secret and working inside the Labour Party and Trades Council. Not unnaturally the constituency quickly got the reputation with Labour headquarters for being Left.

We decided that it would be good to have a local Labour Party

C

paper, which would in fact reflect Communist Party policy.   The necessary resolutions were steam-rollered through the Divisional Committee authorising the starting of the paper and making me its editor.   Before long the paper was circulating over a wide area, using *Daily Worker* cartoons, discreetly publicising Communist Party national activities and never under any circumstances deviating from the Communist Party line.   It was, of course, published as a Labour Party organ.

This state of affairs continued until after the Munich crisis, when Communist Party headquarters decided that most of its " under-cover " members in the Labour Party should come out into the open as a political demonstration against the Labour leadership.   Almost the whole of our group resigned from the Labour Party, getting maximum publicity for their action.   They gave their " reasons " at length to the local press and announced that they were applying to join the Communist Party (of which they had, of course, in fact been members for many months).   In due course a second statement was issued saying that their applications had now been accepted and announcing the formation of a local Communist Party branch.   The result was that the Labour Party in that Division was all but wrecked, losing all its most active and leading members at one move, and a brand " new " Communist Party branch appeared on the scene.

I was officially complimented by Party headquarters for my performance.   It was a typical, although particularly successful, piece of communist infiltration, and I have described it in some detail for that reason.

By the time the episode was over I was editing a local paper in West London but conducted operations from a distance, which I continued to do until after the commencement of the war.

The period following Munich was one of intense political activity.   For years the Party had worked throughout the West for a policy, based on Russian needs, which aimed at the encirclement of Nazi Germany by the " peace-loving nations ".   Chamberlain's deal with Hitler put it all in peril.

But although our campaign for peace continued throughout the early months of 1939 and it was said to be defeatist to suggest that war was now inevitable, each of us believed, on the basis of

the Party's earlier analyses, that the worst had happened at
Munich and that war would come despite all our efforts.

But we also believed with increasing conviction that it might
well take the form of a Nazi attack on the U.S.S.R., with Britain
backing Germany. The thought that that was possible was to us
so appalling as hardly to bear thinking about. In such an event
it would be the job of communists to work for the defeat of their
own Government and the success of the U.S.S.R.

That was, and remains, binding upon every communist.

But, although such a situation might bring with it the possibility of the Revolution in Britain, the threat of a combined attack
on the U.S.S.R. was something to make every communist ready
to do anything, and " at any price ", for what each one of us saw
to be the " workers' fatherland ". And that is precisely how
the communist sees the Soviet Union. It is how I had seen it
for years.

Quite briefly and simply this is how I reasoned and how
hundreds of thousands of others, trained in Marxism, in all parts
of the world still reason:

Communism is necessary and desirable above all else. The
fight for communism stretches across the world, which is divided
horizontally by the two opposing classes and not vertically by
different races and nations. In fighting for a communist Britain
I am fighting for a better Britain and for the destruction of all
that is rotten and decadent. In that fight I have the assistance
of all who are operating on the same world front against capitalism. My desire to make my country communist therefore makes
me an internationalist.

But at one point in that world front there is a whole nation
on my side, a great State, the U.S.S.R.,where a strong-point has
been established, around which all future battles will tend to turn
and without which any other, local victories must fail. At all
costs, therefore, Russia, bastion of communism, must be defended. The defeat of the U.S.S.R. would mean the end of any
chance of world communism for generations.

Therefore, in order to get my communist Britain I must at
all costs work to assist the continued survival of the Socialist
Sixth of the world. Who attacks Russia attacks my hope of a

communist Britain.   In helping Russia " with all the means at his
disposal and at any price ", therefore, the British communist is
working for a better Britain, the French communist for a better
France, and the Icelandic communist for a better Iceland.   He
is, in his own eyes and that of his Party, the super-patriot.   The
need is for Russia at all costs to survive, and anything, anything
at all, which contributes to this is permissible.

The Soviet-German Pact therefore in August 1939 did not
trouble the trained Marxist at all. The Soviet leaders had a
responsibility to the working-class of the world to defend the
U.S.S.R. and could, if necessary, for this reason make an alliance
with the devil himself. The rawer rank-and-filer may have his
doubts and difficulties at such moments but not the well-instructed
Marxist.

Many of the intellectuals who had joined us in our popular
front campaigns, admittedly, quickly left in disgust, but this was
what we had expected them to do.   Their attitude was summed
up in a letter I received from a well-known poet who, after being
drawn to the Party because of its anti-fascist propaganda, wrote:
" A plague on both your uncles, Uncle Joe and Uncle Adolf "—
then disappeared into an ivory tower from which he has never
since emerged.

The difficulty with which the communist propagandists were
confronted posed itself simply in terms of the question: " Now
how do we get *that* across to the uninitiated? " and the leaders
proceeded to think of the best propaganda line under the circumstances.

The harassed rank-and-filer, having to face his workmates'
questions and, maybe, jeers in the factory, at times when such
somersaults are turned, grabs only too gratefully at whatever
" line " the leaders hand out in their directives and in most cases
trusts to their superior knowledge of dialectics to ensure that it
is doctrinally permissible.

According to all Marxist reasoning it seemed likely that our
own Government would strike at the Russians rather than at
Germany in their own " class interest ".   When Britain, in fact,
declared war on Germany it seemed to the Party's leaders as
though, despite everything, Chamberlain had been forced by his

own political ineptitude to do something which was in conflict with the best interests of the capitalist class, and which must contribute to the world fight against fascism and, therefore, indirectly aid communism.

The communist leaders in Britain and right across the West for this reason supported the war in its earliest days and declared it to be an anti-fascist struggle which should have the support of every worker.

The rank and file, however, although maintaining an outward appearance of unity, on this occasion tended to be privately divided. Those who had fought in Spain or had been in direct conflict with fascism in Britain tended to welcome the chance of " having a go at the Nazis " under any banner, even that of Chamberlain.

Others distrusted Chamberlain to a point where they could not believe that any war fought under his leadership could be of any use to the workers and that he would still, if he could, do a deal with Hitler and switch the fight to the East.

I found myself in the second group and so, for the first time in years, doubting the correctness of the Party's policy. I felt miserable and demoralised, finding excuses for dropping almost all my political activity. For the first time in my life I began to spend almost every evening in a road-house where I made the consumption of a drink of beer, a plate of green cheese and a few olives last as long as possible.

My mood was not helped by the rather tricky question of Russia marching into Poland on September 17. I was sharing a flat with a leading communist shop steward, one of the Party's most active factory members.

I learned the news from the Sunday papers, took them home and showed him the headlines: " Russia Invades Poland ". On the face of things, for any communist, the news was devastating. His reactions were typically violent.

" B— Uncle Joe, b— Molotov, b— the whole bloody lot of them," he cursed. Then he rallied himself. " But communism is still right," he said, trying to comfort himself. " But how the hell am I to explain this in the factory tomorrow? "

He missed work the next day, and by the time he returned to

the factory on the Tuesday the *Daily Worker* had got its line straight, and he proceeded, as communist shop stewards all over Britain were doing, to explain Russia's great new peace move to a specially-convened lunch-time meeting in the factory.

Then the Party line switched to opposition to the war.

The Party's Central Committee had met one day at the King Street headquarters to draw up a stirring manifesto to the British people calling upon them to sacrifice all in the great anti-fascist struggle. After hours of discussion the text was finalised. Then, unexpectedly, in walked the British representative to the Communist International whom everyone had thought was still in Moscow.

He took one look at the manifesto and told the leaders they would have to scrap it. It was, he said, an imperialist war. The Comintern had said so, and that meant opposing it in the classical Marxist way.

Out of the confusion which followed this bomb-shell came a demand that he should produce proof. He did, in the shape of a crumpled and much-thumbed postcard, on which the position was stated tersely but unambiguously and signed " Georgi Dimitroff, General Secretary of the Communist International ". There was no further room left for doubt as to its authenticity.

Pollitt, the General Secretary, and J. R. Campbell, a Political Bureau member, both refused to accept the new line, although they publicly recanted some time later. But the remainder of the Central Committee sat down again and with the assistance of the Comintern delegate proceeded to re-draft their manifesto on which so many hours had been spent, but this time declaring it to be an imperialist war in which the workers could have no interest.

Once again the old, beloved slogan began to be repeated at Party meetings: " Workers will turn war into civil war ", and in Dimitroff's new formulation: " The working-class will end the war after its own fashion ". This, then, after all, was to be one of those crises out of which our Soviet Britain might come. I think it would be true to say that every Marxist thrilled at the thought, even though it meant that we had first to face a world war with all that that meant in terms of human suffering. The new turn brought to a sudden end my brief period of demoralisation, there was now no question of spending evenings in pubs. This was the hour of opportunity.

The invasion of Poland had prepared us for what happened in Finland when the Red Army began its assault. But, although it was plain to Marxists that Russia was taking steps to forestall any attempt at intervention from the West, it was a little disconcerting for the Party propagandists and ordinary members who had always claimed that Russia was the one dependable friend of the small and weak. In our demonstrations we had sung the Soviet Airmen's song: " We drop them leaflets whilst we bomb their bosses ", but when the raids began on Helsinki we saw just how optimistic and unreal those words had been.

We emphasised more and more the danger of the phoney war against Germany becoming a real one against Russia, and so sought to turn attention from the disturbing events in Finland to the alleged treachery of the leaders at home. But, such is the nature of communism, I would say that the anti-Soviet campaign which resulted from the attack on Finland strengthened most of the Communist Party members in their communism. For many members it was their first real test, with public opinion becoming increasingly hostile. We prepared ourselves for persecution and we got it.

Sellers of the *Daily Worker*, women as well as men, were spat upon and assaulted on the streets; canvassing, they had doors slammed in their faces, even chamber-pots emptied on their heads from upstairs windows. Often, out selling papers or pamphlets, we would have housewives shouting vituperations at us until we disappeared from their street. It was a testing time, and most Party members rose to it and gloried in their martyrdom. There were, of course, the weak ones, and the Party was glad enough to be purged of them.

In the branch in which I was working at the time was one member who was a dustman. He had been victimised over and over again, first in South Wales and then later in the London area. When the war began, he got his first work for a year, emptying garbage-cans.

So when the persecution started he was able to report to the branch committee that an under-cover Party member who was also a Labour councillor had—fearing a police raid—dumped all his books along with the household refuse into the dustbin. The dustman's Marxist library grew as a consequence, but the Labour councillor was quietly taken off the Party's books. The dustman continued to keep us informed of the behaviour of the weaker brethren who destroyed their libraries, and among whom on one occasion was found to be a member of the branch committee itself.

For most it was a period of hope—with the dream of a possible early victory constantly before us.

The Party had publicly stated that it was an imperialist war. Every well-instructed Marxist knew what that meant. Regardless of what might be our public propaganda line, we knew the Marxist–Leninist theory of how the workers should behave when imperialist war came.

Moreover, the Party took steps at every level of its organisation to ensure that this was understood, so that no member should be taken in by our own public propaganda. Georgi Dimitroff's "Workers will end the war after their own fashion" was seen as an unambiguous call to every Marxist to prepare for revolutionary action. Our London headquarters initiated one series of study classes after another on the Leninist teaching on the art of turning war into civil war.

Lenin's *War and the Workers* was republished, used as a textbook and all but learned by heart. Volume V of the *Selected Works of Lenin*, in which the most important of his writings on the subject are pulled together, became the most popular Marxist reading. Seven out of every ten of the pages in my own copy are underlined and heavily thumbed. Most popular passage in it, pregnant with meaning and with hope and inspiration, was the one which reads:

"Take the modern army. It is one of the good examples of organisation. This organisation is good only because it is *flexible* and is able at the same time to give to millions of people *a single will*. Today these millions are living in their homes in various parts of the country; tomorrow a call for mobilisation is issued, and they gather at the appointed centres. Today they lie in the trenches, sometimes for months at a stretch; tomorrow they are led to the attack in another formation. Today they perform miracles hiding from bullets and shrapnel; tomorrow they perform miracles in open combat. Today their forward detachments place mines under the ground; tomorrow they move forward scores of miles, according to the advice of flyers above ground. When in the pursuit of one aim, animated by one will, millions change the forms of their intercourse and their actions, change the place and the method of their activities, change their tools and weapons in accordance with changing conditions and the requirement of the struggle—this is organisation.

" The same holds true for the working-class struggle against the bourgeoisie. Today there is no revolutionary situation, the conditions that cause ferment among the masses or heighten their activities do not exist; today you are given a ballot paper—take it. Learn how to organise in order to be able to use it as a weapon against your enemies and not as a means of getting soft parliamentary jobs for men who cling to their seats in fear of having to go to prison. Tomorrow, you are deprived of the ballot paper, you are given a rifle and a splendid quick-firing gun constructed according to the last word of engineering technique—take the weapon of death and destruction, do not listen to the sentimental whiners who are afraid of war. Much has been left in the world that *must* be destroyed by fire and iron in order that the emancipation of the working-class may be achieved. And if anger and desperation grow among the masses, if a revolutionary situation arises, prepare to create new organisations and *utilise* these useful weapons of death and destruction *against your* government and *your* bourgeoisie."

Waking and sleeping we dreamed and planned of how to make the most of this war situation, how to build up anger, how to exploit desperation when it grew among the masses, how to make absolutely certain that we should be ready organisationally and doctrinally for the revolutionary situation when it arose. How to ensure, too, that those Party members lucky enough to be in the armed forces should be able to lead their fellow " workers in uniform " in the utilisation of " these useful weapons of death and destruction " against our own Government and our own bourgeoisie.

In Volume V, too, was all we needed to tell us about how to accomplish this. Lenin had written: " A revolutionary class in a reactionary war cannot but desire the defeat of its own government." It was our job to make the working-class revolutionary and at the same time so to instruct our own members that they would need only to be told that this was a " reactionary war " to know what to do.

Lenin had written: " Revolution in wartime is civil war: and the *transformation* of war between governments into civil war is, on the one hand, facilitated by military reverses (' defeats ') of governments; on the other hand, it is *impossible* really to strive for such a transformation without thereby facilitating defeat."

Understanding that, and having the experience of Russia in 1917 to underline it, it was not surprising that Dunkirk, when it came, troubled us not at all and served only to make what we regarded as being the almost inevitable defeat of Britain appear as a magnificent opportunity.

" The transformation of the imperialist war into civil war ", wrote Lenin again, " cannot be ' made ', any more than it is possible to ' make ' a revolution—it *grows*. . . . Such a growth is *impossible* without a series of military reverses and defeats of those governments which receive blows from *their own* oppressed classes."

Taking this to heart we administered all the blows we could, through the tactic of the People's Convention, through trying to create war-weariness, through industrial disputes, through the spread of disaffection among members of the armed forces and through exploiting every possible grievance, political, social, economic or industrial, upon which we could seize.

The study of the history of the Bolshevik success in Russia, the writings of Engels and of Lenin on the art of insurrection, were now no longer merely of purely academic interest or just a question of acquiring knowledge which might possibly some day be useful, as hitherto it had been for me and for so many others. Now it related directly to the events of the moment.

And the colossal joke of it was that all this vital reading-matter, this political dynamite, did not require to be sent out by underground means. It could be, and was, published openly and purchased legally in bookshops all over the country.

Whilst the Party had perforce publicly to pretend that it had no intention of sabotaging the war effort or of turning the war into civil war, our members could at the same time be discussing in their classes every conceivable detail of how best to achieve the defeat of one's own government in war.

There was no need for the Party's leaders to take foolish risks by issuing insurrectionary orders. It was all made so simple for us.

All that was required was that the Party members themselves should be trained to understand the inner meaning of the works of Marxist writers, to understand Leninist thought, to know the jargon. That was the purpose of the Party's classes —and still is.

It was necessary, too, for them to know what to do should the war be " switched " against the Soviet Union. The instructions laid down by the Communist International on what to do in the event of war with Russia were abundantly clear:

" At the present historical juncture," said a resolution passed at the Seventh World Congress, " when one-sixth part of the globe, the Soviet Union, defends socialism and peace for all humanity, the most vital interests of the workers and toilers of all countries demand that in pursuing the policy of the working-class, in waging the struggle for peace, the struggle against imperialist war before and after the outbreak of hostilities, the defence of the Soviet Union must be considered paramount.

" If the commencement of a counter-revolutionary war forces the Soviet Union to set the workers' and peasants' Red Army in motion for the defence of socialism the Communists will call upon all toilers *to work, with all their means at their disposal and at any price, for the victory of the Red Army over the armies of the imperialists.*"

No need, therefore, for any doubts about what was required of the Party members in the event of war with the Workers' Fatherland. The thing was to be ready. That was the keynote of all our party classes. It was the underlying theme of all our instruction.

I had been a Party tutor for some years, and the classes I took during that period were regarded as being among the most successful, so much so that at the London District Congress of 1940 my tutorial work was held up by the Party's national education organiser as being the best and most successful of any.

Classes which I tutored and which had been planned for a dozen or fifteen people brought instead some sixty or seventy regularly week by week. My week-end schools were crowded. But the classes were valued by the Party for their content as well as for the crowds they drew.

Here, then, is an outline of what I was teaching, based on the notes of one of my most successful series, which led to special praise from Party headquarters and which indicates the line of the Party at the time and its real aims.

The first class was entitled, " The Bolsheviks and the last war ". It began with an historical outline of the position of the Bolsheviks at the beginning of the 1914 war; their anti-war stand and their early recognition, under Lenin's guidance, of the need to defeat their own Government.

" The war ", read my notes, " placed the slogan of the social revolution on the order of the day."

That lesson finished with the quotation from Lenin: " We cannot tell whether the revolutionary situation will develop during or after the war, but only work in this direction deserves the name of socialism." To which I added, " The Bolsheviks saw the urgency and responsibilities of the situation. So must we."

The second lesson dealt with the national and colonial question and set out to show how the Bolsheviks used the national aspirations of the subject peoples of the Tsarist Empire on behalf of the Proletarian Revolution. I went on to survey the national movements in the British Empire and to analyse how far they might be used to assist in bringing about the collapse of capitalism at home and the weakening of capitalism throughout the world.

The third lesson was entitled: " England, whose England? "

The aim of this lesson was to show that although men, women

and children were being called on at that moment to die for Britain, it was not their Britain in any case. I examined the distribution of wealth and gave a long explanation of the Marxist definition of the State as an instrument of coercion on behalf of the ruling class. From this the lesson was drawn that the first thing a revolutionary working-class must do is to seize that instrument and use it for the coercion of the erstwhile rulers.

In the last lesson in the series I dealt with the way in which we should prepare for the Proletarian Revolution.

My conclusion was: " We can lead the masses to victory. The historic prerequisites are present. The masses are responding to our slogans. The future is ours—but not inevitably—and only you and me and common struggle can bring our time to birth."

These notes reveal the underlying purpose of all our activities during the " imperialist " phase of the war. They reveal how our minds were working. They make nonsense of the oft-repeated public assertion by British Communist Party leaders that they do not seek violence and that when they talk of revolution they mean only " drastic change ".

My lectures differed from those of many of our Marxist tutors only in this (and it was this that made them popular): always I tried to combine the purely " scientific " Marxist reasoning with an emotional appeal. I wanted both to instruct and to inspire. For me the Revolution was a crusade, even though its theory had to be studied and it must be the result of cold reasoning rather than warm idealism. I was not, at the time that those lectures were given all over London and the Home Counties, an obscure, or wild and irresponsible member of the Party. Before they had finished I was a member of the Party's London Secretariat, one of the half-dozen responsible for leading the work throughout the capital. I was directly responsible for guiding the Party in West Middlesex, which we regarded as the " reddest " and most important war-factory concentration in the London area, taking in huge aircraft works and munitions factories. And I was hailed as the " star " tutor of the period. These classes, therefore, may safely be regarded as one hundred per cent " on the Party line " and free of any " Left-wing deviations ".

VIII

ON THE "DAILY WORKER"

In December 1939 I was told by the Party that I should wind up the weekly paper of which I was editor and prepare myself to work on the communist daily instead.

On January 1, 1940, during the period of growing anti-communist feeling and when the Party was already operating on the fringes of illegality, I went to work as a member of the staff of the *Daily Worker*.

Many of the staff had been called into the Forces, others were expected to go shortly and the paper was wrestling with an acute personnel shortage. Because I had had experience of advertising and newspaper circulation-building as well as journalism I went prepared to do whatever might prove to be the most urgent job. When the Party called me to go and work on its paper I dropped what I was doing and went, as any other loyal member would have done. It meant a drop in income, and so in my standard of life, but it did not even occur to me that that might be a reason for not going. A large proportion of the paper's editorial staff, particularly at that time, had made similar or bigger sacrifices.

I felt that no greater honour could have been done me as a communist and as a journalist than to have been asked to work there at such a moment. Thousands of people in all parts of Britain had sacrificed for years to keep the paper going. Every communist looked to it for daily guidance and leadership. There were hundreds of workers in industry all over the country who regularly got up hours earlier than was necessary, adding to the length of their working day, in order to sell it or to get it from the local railway station to the factory, depot, mine or shipyard.

The *Daily Worker* for me embodied all my hopes, all that was best in the movement to which I belonged. When I entered its building on my first day as London circulation manager I felt that I was treading on sacred ground.

Before the first morning was out I was aware of strong personal cross-currents in my own office and sharp antagonisms between the various departmental heads. Before the first week was out I was equally aware of the great network of amorous entanglements which existed throughout the building. Living and working under conditions of considerable strain, with the popular tide flowing against them and recognising no moral restraints of any sort in their personal lives, it was not unnatural that what was, apparently, normally a very loose, amoral atmosphere had become one which was supercharged with sex. It was, in fact, neurotic.

I had thought myself by that time to be fairly hard-boiled, but I nonetheless experienced a certain shock at what I found on the paper, just as I had done when first I joined the Party. But the shock was only a very brief one, for, after all, what I found there was but the practical application of the theories I had for long upheld and practised to some extent as well.

I talked to members of the staff who were going the pace as much as anyone, and they agreed that they had had similar feelings to my own, in their early days on the paper. But they had soon got over them, and then did the same as the rest. And that was what happened in my case too. Gradually, you got things in perspective and came to see that, although that neurotic atmosphere jarred at first, it was not the part that counted.

Out of the activities of this curiously ill-assorted, mixed group of people each day came the paper that led the fight for communism, serving as agitator, educator and organiser of the militant working-class—which Lenin had said should be the character of every communist paper.

One thing about a young girl secretary which struck you first might be her dogmatic assertion, frequently reiterated, that contraceptives went out with the horse-drawn tram and that the only sensible thing for a girl to do was to have a regular quarterly abortion as she did.

In time you also came to realise that this made her no less a good communist; that this same young girl spent most of her evenings and all her week-ends canvassing with Party literature, getting more abuse than sales; that she burned the midnight oil night after night, studying the most turgid Marxian classics, mastering the most difficult points of Marx's philosophy and economic theories. If, in addition, she still found time for " sleeping around " then it was not for you to be shocked. She deserved it, anyway. Before long you were accepting the whole position as being perfectly normal.

Only when such activities injured the cause did they matter. Thus when one of the paper's financial organisers was known always to sleep with leading local comrades wherever she went, nothing was said against it. It was only when she let it affect her work that she was told that she must not let her personal life interfere with her political responsibilities. The Party could, of course, intervene at any point it liked. And, remember, this was an organisation in which discipline was strict and which claimed the right to order the whole of one's life if need be.

The first job on the *Daily Worker* brought me in touch with some of the best and most active of the Party's rank and file. It was my job to know them and to stimulate them, by means of pep talks, duplicated bulletins, competitions, conferences, public meetings and so on, to ever greater activity on behalf of the paper.

If ever I felt depressed about the atmosphere on the paper, I had only to look at what some of its readers were doing for the cause to dismiss the scandals with a shrug of the shoulders and then to work all the harder. For these people seemed to me to be the salt of the earth.

There was the aircraft worker who went to the station at five o'clock each morning all the year round, collected a huge parcel of hundreds of papers, took them home and then, with the aid of his wife, did them up into bundles of various sizes for the different departments throughout the works.

After a hurried breakfast, he would cycle off to the factory with the bundles tied to every part of his bicycle, meet a chain of workers from the various workshops at different points around the factory, each of whom would smuggle in his supply (there was an embargo on such sales in most war factories at the time) for sale inside. He never missed a day.

And there was Jimmie. Jimmie was doing a similar job at the big war factory at which he worked near his home in Essex. Then he was called up. Going to join his unit he fell under an on-coming train and lost a leg. He was nineteen years of age.

When he came out of hospital, still very ill and with an artificial limb which did not fit, he learned that he would get no Army pension, no compensation. He had not only fallen beneath a train, he had somehow managed to fall between being technically a Civilian and officially a Service man.

He went back to his former place of work, this time as a watchman. But he proceeded to re-establish all his former contacts and to build up all the old *Daily Worker* sales.

Early each morning he set off on his crutches to collect an enormously heavy bundle of papers and then got them around to his network of sellers.

Then came the air raids on London and trains became less regular. Sometimes his beloved parcel of *Daily Workers* failed to arrive and he would phone me, desperately pleading with me to get another parcel despatched and so ensure that his readers should not be let down. But, with bombs dropping nightly on the line between London and his local station, the number of occasions on which no parcel arrived became more frequent. He could stand it no longer.

He bought an old bicycle with a fixed wheel, had one pedal removed so that his artificial limb could hang free, and cycled at night through the blitz to the *Daily Worker* building. His course lay right down the Thames waterfront, which was a regular target for the Nazi bombers. In the black-out and at the height of the blitz, through the whole of dockland, right through the East End, he came. When he arrived on the first night his face was grey.

As he came through the door the night sky to the east from where he had come glowed red with dockland fires, and thud after thud of falling bombs sounded dully from the same direction. Anti-aircraft flak sprinkled skies and streets.

On either side of his body he had a great rucksack strapped, and another on the back of his cycle. We filled all three with his precious papers and he set off—east, the way he had come, cycling back through the night with his one leg and his huge burden. The workers in his factory did not again miss their

Daily Worker until the day the paper was banned and Jimmie's job was for the time suspended.

They did not miss it even though on more than one occasion he had to push his bike the whole of the way back, taking all night to do it, over networks of firemen's hoses, over broken glass and debris and making great detours where roads were closed, arriving just as the men were turning up for work.

There was, too, the little East End Jewish clothing worker who decided that the blitz was a heaven-sent—or Hitler-sent—opportunity for selling more *Daily Workers* than ever before.

" The workers are in the shelters," he said, " and our place is with them." So when the sirens sounded and most other people were making for safety he set out to collect the papers as they came off the press, then went from shelter to shelter selling them. He was not on official business, so there was no tin hat for him.

At a period when bombers were nightly coming over in wave on wave to his part of the East End he doubled his order.

" There have never been such chances," he told me one night, as in the middle of a raid I saw him loaded up. But going from shelter to shelter that night he became just one small part of an " incident ". And a widow and seven small children were left in one Jewish corner of Bethnal Green.

And there were many who felt their first sympathy for communism stirred when they saw the *Daily Worker* sellers standing outside the Tube stations in London's West End, selling the paper as usual no matter how hot the blitz. And when it became known that not a trace had been found of the familiar figure outside Tottenham Court Road Tube after the high-explosive bomb had fallen exactly on the spot where he had so often stood, that sympathy was likely to crystallise into something more positive.

I said then, and I believe even more strongly today that it was true, that you will never understand communism unless and until you understand such communists as these.

When the phoney war period ended with Hitler sweeping through France and the Low Countries, British Communist Party members found themselves watching the battle, as it were, from the outside. It was not our war. It was a war between rival imperialisms with several millions of workers in uniform as the unwilling pawns. Our war was coming later.

Even Dunkirk was seen in this detached light. To us, after all, it was by no means a catastrophe. It was a military defeat and as communists we had a vested interest in defeat. Out of military defeat in 1917 came the October Revolution in Russia—the Workers' and Soldiers' Councils in Germany in 1918 and the Soviets of Hungary. We had more to gain by defeat than by victory. We were busy fighting our own war and it was a very real one—with the vast majority of people almost hysterical in their hatred of us.

At the time of Dunkirk I went one lunch-time to address an open-air meeting in a market near the *Daily Worker* office. Whilst I was making my speech, the crowd rushed me and before I knew what was happening the portable platform had been kicked to splinters from under me.

I undertook to address open-air meetings in Ealing each Saturday night and our usual practice was to erect our platform half an hour before the meeting was to begin, attach a poster to it announcing the time it was to start, erect a red flag for good measure and then go away for a drink.

One Saturday night during the period when the allied armies were being routed on the Continent, we left our platform on the Green as usual and went for our customary drink, over which we discussed our plan of action should the audience get rough.

Going back we saw that there was already a crowd around our platform, on which was a man of about my own build addressing the crowd. Like mine, his hair was dark and rather long. Like me he was wearing a sports jacket and flannel trousers.

Then, across the Green from the opposite direction marched a determined little army of police, who made straight for the platform. Within two minutes the speaker had disappeared into a Black Maria.

Mixing with the crowd we learned that he was a fascist who had captured our platform in our absence. And further enquiries revealed quite clearly that the police had made the arrest thinking it was me they were taking away.

We discreetly made off, collecting the platform, from which the red flag had been torn down, after dark. The fascist was, in due course, detained " for the duration " under Regulation 18B. I was, however, to meet him again.

Two or three weeks later I was speaking one Saturday night in the neighbouring borough of Southall. I had for a long time been a thorn in the flesh of the local police, who had often ordered me out of factory premises where I was agitating for strikes or had had to deal with demonstrations I had organised which had got troublesome.

I heard before I went out that night that they were going to arrest me and that they believed that they could use Regulation 18B, which had so far only been used to detain fascists, to get me out of the way for a very long time.

The first speaker had not spoken for long when she was ordered to get down by a police inspector who stood surrounded by constables, with others dotted about the crowd.

As soon as I took over, the crowd began to heckle, and a slightly hysterical woman (whom I had reason to suppose was there as an *agent provocateur*) asked a leading question about whether " our boys are dying for democracy ". I told her they were not, they were dying for profits. The crowd roared its anger, the police threw me off the platform on to my face in the road. I went down shouting: " And this is your war for democracy." With my arms firmly twisted behind my back I was taken through the crowded main street to the local police station with a derisive, angry mob following behind.

The atmosphere of that period is reflected in the fact that when I protested that the police were using unnecessary violence in twisting my arms behind my back one of them replied that they were taking no chances, I might be armed.

At the station I was put in the cells without being charged and I repeatedly demanded throughout the night that a charge should be made. I was told that no charge was likely as they expected to detain me under Regulation 18B and were in touch with the Home Office on the matter.

The Home Office must have told them, however, that it was not intended to use the regulation against communists unless it was absolutely necessary, and so, finally, at dawn I was charged with using insulting words likely to cause a breach of the peace and was released on bail. Two days later, as I waited for my case to come up in the Court, the fascist who had been mistaken for me some weeks earlier was brought up from the cells for a few brief minutes; the Court decided that he should continue to be held pending Home Office instructions. As he went off between two warders he gave me a look which had in it neither peace nor charity.

My earlier experience with the International Class War Prisoners Aid and International Labour Defence, when I had so often assisted with the defence of others, stood me in good stead. I conducted my own defence and enjoyed myself cross-examining at length the various police witnesses, including the inspector who had arrested me, and attempting to play one off against another.

Once, in the excitement of cross-examining the inspector, I referred to him as " the prisoner ". The kindly, octogenarian chairman of the Magistrates' Bench leaned forward and explained : " He's not the prisoner, he is the witness. *You* are the prisoner."

" I am today," was my reply, " but one day *he* will be the prisoner."

And I believed it. It is that certainty of ultimate victory, bringing with it both the realisation of dreams and the possibility of retribution, which accounts for a good deal of the aggressive self-confidence of the communist. " You can hate me, persecute me, do what you like with me," he says through his clenched teeth. " One day we shall have our Revolution and our Soviet Britain and God help you when that day comes."

I exercised my right not to go into the witness-box and so avoided taking the oath and being cross-examined. In the best communist traditions I made an address to the Bench which was really a political speech, intended for the press and public rather than for the magistrates.

I got off with a fine or the alternative of a month's imprisonment. The bottom of the police case had really fallen out when the Home Office decreed that I should be charged. Within a few hours, a fund for my fine and expenses had been generously over-subscribed which gave us something in hand for any further cases that might arise.   One of the national dailies reporting the case headlined its story with a quotation from the inspector's evidence: " The crowd cheered me when I arrested him."

Some documents had been taken from me before I was put in the cells, which I now demanded back.   I was told to collect them from the Special Branch (political police) at Scotland Yard, who, I was told, were anxious to meet me.   Suspecting a plot, I refused to go and after some weeks threatened to sue for their return.

A week or so later I received a phone call at the *Daily Worker*. An apologetic voice explained that this was a Special Branch detective speaking from Scotland Yard.   He was sorry, he said, to have to phone me at my work but had had difficulty in contacting me, as I seemed never to be at home.   " It is not our policy to phone people at their place of employment, for fear it harms them in any way," he continued.

I assured him that, my place of employment being what it was, a phone call from the Special Branch was more likely to result in promotion than demotion for me.

I insisted that my documents should be returned to me at the police station in which they were first removed.   We arranged to meet there that night.   I went, still prepared for some further attempt to detain me " for the duration ".   But the documents were passed to me in the friendliest of atmospheres.

The detective asked me when I was due for military call-up. I told him I was to take my medical examination two days later. He said he supposed that I would be a conscientious objector, but I assured him that I was anxious to get into the Forces.

" The communists go where the masses are," I told him.   " And if I can get among the workers with arms in their hands I shall certainly do so."

When I went for the exam., however, they put up a show of discovering that I had almost every disease known to the flesh of man, put me in the lowest category and told me they hoped never to have to bother with me again.

But the way in which it was said made me suspect that my alleged poor state of health was not entirely unconnected with my conversation with the detective inspector two nights earlier.

A surprising number of members of the *Daily Worker* staff did, however, get into the Forces, and the ease with which many well-known communists slipped through the M.I.5 net and were only caught up with, if ever, months or even years later reassured us as to the limited scope of the department's knowledge of the communist personnel and communist activities.

For some months I was tailed by a curious assortment of police agents, including a persistent little man who tried to connect up with me each evening on my way home from the office. I knew who and what he was, and he knew I knew, and so it became something of a game trying to shake him off whilst he tried to keep up with my various subterfuges.

But my never-ending activities against the war effort were no game. They were the focal point of years of work and study.

It was a period of strain, but one also of sustained excitement when idealism, willingness to sacrifice, love of battle and adventure blended into a satisfying sense of purpose and fulfilment.

It was in that period that I met Carol, a " bourgeois " communist, who had joined the Party during the Spanish civil war and who was devoting the whole of her life, too, to the cause. Early each morning she left her comfortable home to sell the *Daily Worker* at a trolley-bus depot some miles away. Then, after a day in a stockbroker's office she would go distributing leaflets, canvassing or taking classes in Marxism as the Party instructed.

I met her first when she was the chairman at a May Day demonstration at which I was the principal speaker. Within a few months we had set up a partnership which has remained a source of strength to us both throughout the years, and had established a relationship which is as harmonious and helpful to us today, as Catholics, as when we were first thrown together in the fight for communism.

We came together, it seemed, almost casually; two communists, sharing their Marxism and their hope of a victorious revolution. My views on the home and family had for years been the Marxist ones, that marriage in a "bourgeois" society was a worthless sham, "legalised prostitution" as we called it. For years I had believed that in showing my contempt for it as an institution I was demonstrating my emancipation, that men and women, both by nature polygamous, should be free to make or break associations as and when they pleased. In common with other communists I had insisted that recognition of these "rights" was the only basis for a happy relationship.

Yet by the time I met Carol I had proved that happiness did not lie in the practice of those ideas. Others might flit from one to another without regret. I never loved that way without breaking a home. I had reached the point where, more than I realised at the time, I was deeply longing for the stability and complete surrender of what I had for years so contemptuously regarded as "conventional, bourgeois homes".

IX

WORKING FOR DEFEAT

As members of the *Daily Worker* editorial staff were called up one by one I was increasingly used for the editorial work for which I had really been engaged. We were putting everything we had into our fight against the war. All our campaigns were keyed to weakening the morale of the men in the Forces and the people on the home front too. And for this any sort of ammunition was good enough.

I discovered, for example, a pacifist doctor who was concerned at the increase in the number of elderly patients who complained of trouble with their feet and legs. This he attributed to their sitting for long hours during the air raids in their Anderson shelters (which people were, somewhat doubtfully, just beginning to use). As a pacifist he was quite ready to blame it all on the war.

I interviewed him, he explained his views at length, I wrote them up, and next day we published the story, giving it some prominence. The doctor was given a show he could never have expected had we been working to boost morale instead of seeking to undermine it.

We expected that at any moment the paper might be banned and made our preparations accordingly. Those responsible for its distribution were brought from all parts of Britain to a hush-hush meeting in Hampstead. There William Rust, the editor, explained that the paper had only been kept going as the result of a high degree of Marxist understanding and skilfully applied Leninist tactics, in combining legal with illegal activity, and that the continued appearance of the paper under such conditions had won the admiration of communists throughout the world. It was necessary, however, to be ready for any eventuality, and so arrangements were being made to get the paper distributed all over the country, even though every legal facility should be denied us.

A lawyer was given the job of explaining to each department just what should be done in the event of a police raid; which documents should be quickly burned when the warning came and how we should conduct ourselves.

The doorkeeper was put in charge of an elaborate system of buzzers which could be simultaneously sounded in every room if the police arrived, and of a police-proof door which was opened only by a switch operated from within.

Raids on Party members' homes were occurring almost daily, and we anticipated a police raid on the paper and the Party's headquarters as a prelude to a ban on the *Daily Worker* with, possibly, the Party being made illegal at the same time.

And so, in the Party too, we made our preparations for illegality. A duplicate Party organisation was created from top to bottom, with a shadow leadership at every level.

We had for some time been strengthening what was known as the Cadres Department, and it was this which was charged with the responsibility of building up the underground organisation.

In the headquarters of every Communist Party in the world a Cadres Department had been set up following a speech by Stalin to the graduates from the Red Army academies in May 1935.

In it he said: " Without people who have mastered technique, technique is dead. In the charge of people who have mastered technique, technique can and should perform miracles. . . . That is why emphasis must now be laid on people, on cadres, on workers who have mastered technique . . . cadres decide everything."

Stalin was referring in particular to Russia's internal situation, but his words were seen also to have an application to the work of communists everywhere. What was now required was a team of people, cadres, specially trained for providing the framework for the communist battalions in their fight for communism. In communist jargon to be a *cadre* meant to be someone trained and ready to do anything, anywhere, for communism.

The task of the Party was and is to produce " men of a special mould ", as Stalin called them in his speech at Lenin's funeral. They must, like Stalin, be " men of steel ", hard, inflexible, rapier-edged. To be a " steel-hardened cadre " became the aim of every good Party member.

The job of the Cadres Department was to facilitate the development of such people, to make sure that the Party's human material was used to the best possible advantage, and to see that the essential framework of the revolutionary " army " was sound. This, in time, led to Cadres Departments acquiring a responsibility for the doctrinal purity of the Party's propaganda and, in particular, for ensuring the theoretical soundness and Marxist " purity " of all members. They had, therefore, a direct interest in and responsibility for all purges; in capitalist countries one aspect of their work was to become a sort of N.K.V.D. within the Party organisation itself. The Cadres Department became almost a separate party within the Party, with over-riding authority when it came to keeping the Party free of deviations and deviationists.

A Cadres Department was created at every level of the Party, national, district, area, branch and group, and, because of its nature, those put on to cadres work were usually among the soundest of theoreticians, " safe " beyond doubt. And, whenever possible, they were those who were least known to the public as communists.

Such an organisation, therefore, provided a ready-made basis for the underground movement when it was needed. It was itself already more than half-underground, it was in touch with all the " under-cover " members in the Forces, in Government plants and departments, in the Civil Service, and within other organisations. And it knew all those rank-and-filers who had the best records for theoretical understanding and personal devotion to the cause.

From among these the underground organisation was built up. People whose jobs had prevented them from being publicly associated with the Party but who had, perhaps, done tutorial work for years would quietly disappear from the life of the Party.

Any member who enquired what had happened to them would be told: " He is doing more important work, comrade. It is part of your duty to forget he ever had anything to do with the Party." The Party membership had always consisted of " open " and " closed " members. Now a large section consisted of ones who were never seen or heard.

The public activities of some of the suburban branches in particular were heavily hit by this process, for the proportion of " closed " members was always high among the professional and middle-class elements in the Party.

At one meeting in a London suburb at which I spoke, someone complained that there should be more local Party members present, whereupon an indiscreet young man protested: " What can you expect when the Cadres Department takes all our best people? Our trouble is that so many of our members have been sent underground that there is practically none left above surface."

The effect of this public revelation upon the older and more responsible members present was rather what one might expect if an elderly local preacher playfully let off a fire-cracker at a Methodist prayer-meeting.

It became the policy of the leaders to avoid anything which would mark the Party members off from the working-class. There is an hysterical streak which runs through the Party's life and which results in violent swings of the pendulum, and an absence of moderation even when " moderation " is the current tactical line. This occasion was no exception to the rule.

Ted Bramley, London District leader, blossomed out for the first time in a cloth cap, to " set an example to the other comrades ". Phil Piratin (later M.P. for Mile End, Stepney) followed suit. When I first saw him with a large costermonger-type grey cap on the side of his head I thought that I had never seen anyone look so conspicuously disguised—until Johnnie Mahon, the District Cadres leader, took to wearing an even louder one at an even more acute angle.

Johnnie, a vegetarian and teetotaller, was now told that it was a serious political weakness that he never went to pubs and the little working-class cafés where the masses were to be found. Dutifully Johnnie followed the Party line, going with the rest of us into public-houses. But while the rest took beer, bread, cheese and pickles, proletarian fashion, Johnnie would produce from his pocket a well-scrubbed carrot or two for his first course, an apple or pear for dessert, and wash them down with a glass of milk poured from a medicine bottle carried in his overcoat pocket.

Lenin had repeatedly urged the need to " combine legality with illegality " in Communist Party work and the Party tackled the job with enthusiasm. During the process it gained an experience upon which it will always be able to draw in the future. Many of the mistakes of that period would be avoided should a similar situation ever again arise.

Our more public activities were mainly around the running of anti-war candidates in by-elections, campaigning for deep bomb-proof shelters and in running a campaign in support of the People's Convention. The shelter campaign had everything to it from our point of view, since it had the appearance of being a crusade for greater safety for the common people, whilst at the same time it spread alarm about the provisions already made by the authorities. Moreover, it gave us an opportunity to use many of our crypto-communists on public activity. It was led by our scientist-members, among whom was Dr. Nunn May, later imprisoned for passing on atomic secrets to the U.S.S.R.

The campaign for the People's Convention was, I suppose, the most effective and, from the Government's point of view, potentially dangerous thing we had done. As a communist tactic it was perfect. It united a reasonably wide and varied number of people and organisations on limited, short-term political and economic demands which deliberately did not include direct opposition to the war. Yet had those demands been won, they would have crippled the war effort—as they were intended to do. And the campaign for those demands was unhelpful in the extreme and was calculated to weaken public morale.

Into the campaign were drawn people and organisations far removed from Marxism; pacifists whom we had for years fought and derided became our allies; non-communist musicians, literary people, university professors and other well-known figures were prevailed upon to add their names to the hard core of Left-wing trade union leaders whom we had managed to entangle. The deep longing for peace which everyone instinctively felt was carefully worked on for revolutionary-defeatist ends.

Months of ideological training of our members had prepared them for being able to participate in this large-sized piece of subterfuge without themselves being taken in by their own Party's public propaganda.

By the time the Convention took place the blitz on London was at its height and, despite the stiffening of public morale which came with the great hardships caused by bombing, we thought we detected a certain war-weariness on which we could work. And where it did not exist we set about trying to create it.

The obvious way to sow distrust of the war itself among the class-conscious workers was to suggest that it was a rich man's war, and that the workers, the majority of the people, had no real interest in it.

This was the political keynote of the People's Convention, attended by two thousand delegates from all parts of Britain. It was the note underlying the preamble to the main resolution; but the programme embodied in that resolution simply ignored the war altogether, with the exception of one point on air-raid shelters, and was framed almost as though no war was being fought.

Even though the genuineness of some of the delegates' creden-
tials was doubtful in the extreme, and allowing also for considerable duplication in the compilation of the numbers they were
supposed to represent, the fact remained that the Convention
demonstrated that there were still large numbers of trade unionists
who were more concerned about continuing the class-war than
about the war with Hitler and for national survival.

The Convention had a considerable power for mischief, and it
was clear that the Government, which was preparing for industrial
conscription, would have to take some defensive action against
it. We did not have to wait long, for some ten days later the
Daily Worker was banned.

I had gone to visit one of the best of our *Daily Worker* sellers
in a West London aircraft factory. When I got back to our flat
in Maida Vale, I was told by the man in the flat below, a Communist Party member who was an organiser in the Amalgamated Engineering Union, that the B.B.C. had reported that
the *Daily Worker* building had been raided and the paper banned
under Defence Regulation 2D. Both he and all the Party
members with whom he had already been in contact were convinced that the Party would shortly be declared illegal. It seemed
likely that we should soon be putting our carefully prepared
underground organisation into action.

I contacted the *Daily Worker* the next day, using discretion, in
case it was the Party's intention to switch me off public work.
Police were in and around the building, keeping an eye on what
was going on. The machines had been sealed, and those members
of the staff who were to be seen about the place were rather point-
lessly destroying documents which had already been carefully
gone through by Special Branch detectives.

Most of the editorial staff had been switched to " other duties ".
One had panicked at the first sight of the police and had taken
the first train home to the provinces. But the vast majority
were keyed up with excitement and ready for anything that might
come.

Our carefully prepared plans for burning anything incriminat-
ing in the event of such a raid had largely failed, due to the fact
that only a few days before a land-mine had been dropped nearby,

blasting out our windows, bringing down ceilings and, worst of all, setting off the anti-fire sprinkler valves, which flooded all our offices and filled our desk drawers and filing cabinets with water. When the police arrived everything was so damp that nothing would burn.

The business manager, Henry Parsons, asked me to go out with him for a chat. " I'm like a magnet so far as detectives are concerned at the moment," he complained, " so we had better shake them off."

On his suggestion we employed a simple device which was completely effective.

" Come on out for a drink," he said, as we passed the Special Branch police who were standing at the door. Down the road we looked back and saw that a couple of plain-clothes men had taken the hint and were following us.

Anyone who had the most elementary knowledge of the social habits of the staff at that time would expect us to make for the nearest public-house—but we skirted it, and dropped unnoticed into a nearby Express Dairy instead. Henry drank the first soda and milk he had tasted for a very long time.

I was instructed to contact the editor, who had a job for me, as soon as this could safely be done. Meanwhile I must not again go to the *Worker* building but could lend a hand on another job for a day or two.

I was sent after black-out to an address in Finsbury where a little cyclostyled illegal paper was being produced in the back-room of a private house. It was small both in size and circulation, but was intended as a political demonstration, rather than as a serious underground effort. It contained the *Daily Worker's* usual signed features, with the idea of strengthening the morale of our readers and Party members, who would feel that the staff were carrying on despite the ban.

Communist Party branches had been advised that parcels of the paper would be brought to them at night and, using the courier system we had had at the ready, they had suggested the places at which the bundles should be delivered.

After helping to produce the paper, I set off in the dark at nearly eleven o'clock with a great parcel of several thousands which constituted the entire quota for Stepney—London's river-side " Red belt ". I had been told that I should be met by one of the local leaders at a spot among some bomb ruins. An air-raid alert had already sounded and bombs were dropping not far away.

At Old Street I staggered on to a trolley-bus with my great parcel of illegal papers, the wrappings of which were already coming undone. I heaved a sigh of relief when I saw that the bus was empty. But at the next stop it filled up to capacity—and entirely with uniformed police coming off duty from a nearby police station.

I sat hugging the bundle of illegal papers and expecting to be arrested at any moment. I was glad when the time came for me to get off the bus into the relative safety of the blitz.

After staggering through a bewildering network of back-streets I came to the spot where I was to be met by the local contact. But there was no one there. I waited for what seemed hours, whilst " alerts " and " all clears " followed each other in quick succession. Once someone headed for the spot where I waited, walking purposefully as though they meant business. They did. It was a prostitute. I replied irritably to her impor-tuning that I had neither the time nor the money.

At last I decided that to wait longer was purposeless, and I set off in a state of great indignation for the secretary's house. If he was afraid to come out, then I would take the papers to him, indiscreet though it might be. I knocked at his door time after time, and at last a bedroom window went up. " I've brought the papers," I told him, " and I've waited for you for hours."

" I'm sorry, comrade," he said casually; " none of my people turned up for instructions so I just don't need them." Just that and no more.

His head disappeared, the window went quietly down—and I staggered back miles through the blitz to my flat, weighed down by the torn but unopened parcel. I found that Carol had been sent out on similar work and had successfully delivered supplies to Shepherd's Bush and Hammersmith.

The " inquest " which follows any breakdown in Party organisa-tion and discipline was held next day, and by that night Stepney was doing everything possible to redeem its reputation. But at the crucial moment, when illegality had for the first time come to the Party and when worse was expected, the Stepney branch, reputedly our biggest and most successful, had failed completely.

In most places the Party organisation, however, rose to the occasion, and for several nights factory workers and intellectuals, young fellows and girls and even working-class housewives, traipsed the streets of London and elsewhere, defying bombs and police to get the paper out.

Then the Political Bureau decided that enough had been done to demonstrate our defiance and contempt for Labour Home Secretary Herbert Morrison and his ban. It looked as though for the moment, at any rate, the Party would not be banned after all, and it was decided, therefore, to combine legality with illegality, and not to go entirely underground before it was absolutely necessary.

I was given one of the most important jobs on the illegal side of the Party's activities, being put in charge of the national underground Press organisation.

I was told to drop all other Party activities for the time being, to shun " open " members and to make it seem that I had " ratted ". I was provided with a car and driver, partly for convenience and partly to give the appearance of having taken some well-paid commercial job. Finally, as a further " cover ", Carol was instructed to give up the office job she was doing in order to assist me and to accompany me when it was particularly necessary to make my activities appear as innocent as possible.

I took over an already existent but very inadequate organisation and was told to build it up as quickly as possible. The idea was to have printing-presses and print-workers ready in all parts of the country, in case the Party should be made illegal and all public propaganda be brought to an end, or, alternatively, ready in the event of the situation " sharpening " to a point where it was felt necessary to produce a paper which could say illegally what could not be said legally.

My first and largest unit was a big warehouse which had been

D

rented in Acton, a busy war-factory area. Into it we managed to
get two or three linotype machines, a large flat-bed press, one or
two smaller ones, a considerable variety of types and a mass of
printing paraphernalia of one sort and another.

The bulk of the machinery arrived on a great six-wheeled lorry,
and an obliging policeman held up the traffic for some five
minutes whilst the driver backed the huge vehicle with difficulty
down into the warehouse yard.

I was supplied by the Party with two full-time workers, a
linotype operator and a machinist to man the unit, who put
up the sound and appearance of working there each day. We
described ourselves as " general dealers ", opened a bank account
as such, put up a pretence of dealing in machine-parts and
deliberately left some of the printing-plant components un-
assembled to maintain that illusion.

Meanwhile the linotype operator practised both hand-setting
and operating the flat-bed machine, the machine operator taught
himself to work the linotype as a standby and Carol learned to
operate the linotype as well.

In the cellar of an East End saw-makers, among cobwebs and
steel-filings, I had another press. Lying about the place was a
mass of old saws of every sort; piles of the long, narrow saws
used in industry lay in tangled heaps, and in the middle of it all
we put a printing-machine, linked with the belting which drove
the machines in the works above.

The ceiling left a minimum of head-room, the light came
through a grating, and conditions were as bad as they could be.
But the great advantage was that the saw-cutting machinery
upstairs screamed all day long as steel cut steel, electric belting
whined endlessly and in the general din the sound of a printing-
press at work producing illegal papers would, we hoped, pass
unnoticed.

We made this unit ready to start up at any time. As it was to
be the first we should use if and when required, we several times
produced " dummy " papers in trial runs there.

The owner of the works was not even a Party member. He
was a fellow-traveller, active in the Labour Party but consciously " Left-wing " and militant.

In two shoe repairers' premises in Surrey I had other machines also more or less at the ready. In both cases they were in back-rooms behind the general workroom and excited no interest at all when we moved them in. Then I got another and larger machine into yet another shoe repairer's, this time in a North London suburb.

In half a dozen different places in and around London, including Twickenham, Carshalton, Slough and Wimbledon, I fixed up large stocks of type and everything required for type-setting.

One such unit was in the basement of a large house in a select Kensington square. The titled family who lived there would have been interested to know that the footman and his housekeeper-wife were both Party members and that in the basement flat with which they were provided was a type-setting unit on which every Sunday two print-workers, employed in a Government print works, laboured preparing things in readiness for publishing an illegal revolutionary paper.

I stored large stocks of newsprint of the various sizes required for the different types of machines in shops, houses and even in allotment sheds in half a dozen different counties.

I got together a team of print-workers, Party members who were prepared to risk their jobs and liberty for the cause. In order to protect both them and the organisation as a whole against spies and police, they worked in twos at each stage of production, knowing only those with whom they were to work, plus myself and the car driver who would take their completed work on to those working on the next part of the process.

Then I proceeded to build up units in several provincial towns; the largest were in Manchester and Glasgow.

I went to Manchester, did the preliminary work with a clothing worker as my contact, arranged for a ton of equipment to be sent there from London, then travelled all night to Glasgow.

I arrived on the morning following one of Clydeside's worst air raids, the Germans having made Greenock their target for the night.

But my journey was for nothing. My contact there was a

Party functionary. We varied our tactics from place to place and in Glasgow we planned to have an employee in the Party's District office at the head of the unit, on the assumption that the police would not be likely to think of such people being used for the work.

The city was preoccupied with licking its wounds after the events of the night and discussing the much worse ones sustained by nearby Greenock when I slipped into the Party office as it opened at nine. But my contact was not there and failed to put in an appearance.

The District Party leaders were clearly embarrassed by my presence. Because of the character of the job I was doing I was always likely to be tailed by the police and Party offices were getting their full share of police attention at that time in any case. But I had spent the night awake, having gone from one blitz to another, and was not prepared to accept their view that it was no use waiting for my man. In the end I got his address and set out for his home in Clydebank. It proved to be a council house where he was a lodger.

His broad-Scots landlady told me, in a minimum of words, that immediately the bombs had stopped falling early that morning he had packed his belongings into a haversack and left, saying that he was going mountaineering and did not know when he would be back. It was her opinion that he had been afraid of the bombs and had taken to the hills.

One thing seemed certain, and that was that he had panicked, whether at the bombs or the job in which I was to instruct him was never clear. But he bolted at the crucial moment, and I returned in a grand rage to the District office, rather gratified at being able to tell them what I thought of their choice of contacts, after the " cagey " way they had treated me. The District organiser undertook to find a more suitable person and I got the next train back to London.

The man who bolted was subsequently expelled from the Party and a seasoned factory worker chosen for the job.

When next I travelled to Glasgow I found everything ready for me to clinch the acquisition of some shop premises with an agent. Print-workers had been selected for the work and I was sufficiently impressed with what had been done to arrange to get the plant in right away, along with some presses bought in Glasgow itself.

The banning of the *Daily Worker* had been the signal for others to go under cover too. Occasionally I would meet them, but under no circumstances were we supposed to recognise each other.

The booking-halls of Underground stations, with their constant flow of people, were, I found, ideal for meeting my contacts for brief meetings. A crowded place was more private, I felt, than a lonely spot.

Johnnie Mahon, who as District Cadres leader was also now under cover, apparently had the same idea, and on more than one occasion I went to some busy inner-London Tube station to meet someone engaged in preparing the type or transporting machines for my press and found that Johnnie was already there briefing one of his contacts too.

Soon Johnnie went still further underground and I saw nothing of him until, one day, I went to order some paper from a duplicating agency from which I was obtaining supplies. In the back room where the mimeographing was done I found Johnnie, busy putting the last touches to a curious little journal he was now editing for a crank health organisation.

He had, it seemed, become a member, and this, he explained, involved a strict routine of personal hygiene. Members were vegetarians but in addition they took a cold-water bath each morning, then dressed, putting their clothes straight on to their wet bodies. " Your body heat dries you off and you feel absolutely radiant," he explained. He gravely explained to me that he had " secured a legal organ of which we may be glad if all other channels of expression are closed to us."

Once I had the national organisation geared up for work it was no longer necessary to put in all my time on the job.

I had, for the time being, dropped all public activity, but could now come half out into the open again.

When first the *Daily Worker* was banned it became the Party's most urgent need to restore by some means the day-to-day guidance and directives which the *Daily Worker* had given to communist shop stewards, trade unionists and other important Party members.

Then someone had a bright idea. A news agency was started in Red Lion Court, in the heart of London's Fleet Street newspaper industry.

Industrial and General Information, as it was called, had three jobs to do—or rather, one job and three means by which it was done.

First, it functioned *as a news agency*. That is to say it obtained industrial and general news which it supplied, at a fee, to the national daily papers. By this means it aimed to get *Daily Worker*-type news into the capitalist Press.

Second, it issued a cyclostyled bulletin each day which was distributed to the Press as part of its " normal " service. But these bulletins were also mailed daily to Communist Party offices, shop stewards, communist trade union officials and leading Party workers. Thus they were given their daily directives. Some of those items in it which meant least to the journalists of Fleet Street meant most to the Party members on our mailing list.

The third purpose served by I.G.I. was to keep together, as an organisation, throughout the period of the ban, the *Daily Worker's* system of " Worker Correspondents "—the volunteers who supply the " inside " news from factories and Labour organisations all over the country.

It had been made illegal to republish the *Daily Worker* or any other journal carrying on its work, but the fact that those who received the bulletin daily also supplied the news gave us an alibi for providing them with it.

It was into I.G.I. that I was shifted when I had got the underground press sufficiently at the ready. The staff were all former *Daily Worker* employees and so I.G.I. served yet another purpose in keeping some, at least, of the old *Daily Worker* team together.

The agency's editor had just received his call-up papers when I was moved in to take his place.

No job could have started under more difficult conditions. I had been " underground ", and so out of touch for some time; the blitz was at its height, with the Fleet Street area getting its full share of the bombs.

But added to this was the fact that only a few days before my arrival the office had been raided by detectives on the instructions of the Public Prosecutor, and all its files, correspondence and documents had been removed.

The Public Prosecutor was at that very moment trying to decide whether we were, in fact, a continuation of the *Daily Worker* in another form. We were, of course, precisely that, but shortly after my arrival the detectives arrived again—this time to bring back our files.

I was alone with a girl secretary when the police, headed by Special Branch Inspector Whitehead, who had conducted the earlier raid on the *Daily Worker*, arrived in taxis. Although they brought the news that there was to be no prosecution, the appearance and atmosphere were those of a raid. The offices were again searched and then our documents were restored to us, I signed the receipt and as I did so my colleague Walter Holmes walked in from lunch.

" I'm sorry you didn't come before," said the inspector. " I should have liked to get your signature too."

" No doubt you'll have other opportunities," said Holmes grimly.

But there was to be no law case, we were to be allowed to continue our work and our documents were all returned. So, as the police constables staggered in with their arms full of our precious material, we gibed at them and insisted that everything be put back in exactly the spot from which it had been taken.

But they had, of course, got the names and addresses of all our contacts and a good deal more besides.

There was a sequel to the raid, of which I only heard some time later. In my post one morning came a letter from one of our Worker Correspondents, a shipyard worker, in Scotland.

He wrote saying that he expected that we had wondered why we had not heard from him for some time (in fact we had not noticed). This had been due, he wrote, to the fact that, on the day before our raid, he had posted to us full details of submarine construction and shipping movements around his part of the Scottish coast, including some material on submerged vessels which were then holding up shipping. But the letter must, he

said, have been in the unopened post which the police had taken
away from the office the next day. A few days later he had been
arrested at his work, charged *in camera* with passing on military
information and had found himself in jail before the day was
out.

" I am, however, out again," he wrote, " and have pleasure in
appending all the information which the police got last time plus
a lot of more up-to-date stuff besides." We took no chances and
destroyed it as quickly as we could. It was not likely to be of
use to the Soviet Embassy and was much too dangerous for us
to have about the place.

In view of the Marxist training we had given our Party members,
it was inevitable that " hot " material of that sort should constantly arrive at the office. And it was most certainly arriving
in even greater quantities at Party headquarters throughout the
whole of that period. For our members were at war. Not with
Germany but with our own Government. All their thoughts
were of its defeat and of the hope of revolution.

Constant discussion of the need to help the Soviet Union under
all circumstances and to undermine our own Government led
inevitably to such indiscretions but also to the receipt of much
valuable information. It resulted in Party members sending in
reports from aircraft experimental departments, naval yards,
ordnance works, so that we should know what the " enemy " was
doing and in the hope that the information might be of help to
the U.S.S.R.

For every Party member, from the top leaders down, believed
the whole of the time that at any minute the war might be
" switched " against Russia and that we were already more than
half at war with her in any case.

By day I worked at my job of editing our Fleet Street agency,
getting into the Press stories of disputes and strikes, the activities
of the People's Convention, the campaign for the raising of the
ban on the *Daily Worker* and, from time to time, news of Communist Party activities. And, of course, getting the daily bulletin
out to our key people.

By night, I tutored classes, directed the activities of factory
group leaders and shop stewards in the West Middlesex area and

continued to supervise the print-workers' preparations on our under-cover press. This meant, also, maintaining contact with William Rust, the *Daily Worker* editor, who had the final responsibility to the Political Bureau, of which he was a member. The Bureau itself, consisting of the top half-dozen leaders who make and guide the Party's day-to-day activities, was now almost completely underground.

Rust sent for me urgently one night to go to his house. The Political Bureau, he told me, had decided that we must commence production of the illegal paper in the near future. It would not be for general consumption but would be aimed directly at the men in the Forces.

There were by now large numbers of Party members who had succeeded in getting into the Services; new members were being made and in each of the three Services they were working on existing discontents as a means of spreading disaffection. Those agitations could be spread if we aided them from outside, and that was to be the purpose of the proposed publication.

I told him of the state of my organisation and expressed the view that the Party had made a mistake in insisting upon some of my key people continuing their public Party activities. This, I maintained, meant that they were almost certainly known to the police and that, so far as I could see, they would be quickly held responsible for producing the illegal paper.

Rust's reactions were typically free of any concern for them as individuals. It was more or less inevitable, he said, that after the first few copies had appeared we should lose at least one of our presses and also our first team of print-workers. They could not be protected and it was simply part of being a communist in time of war. There would be worse to come before the revolution was won.

There were in any case, he went on, other teams to call upon. But there was only one editor. He was therefore going to disappear as soon as we went into production and would operate from the large country house of one of our wealthy secret members. A courier service would be used to maintain contact between us.

Meanwhile, I was to continue to work publicly on I.G.I. as

though nothing were happening, in the hope that this would deceive the police into thinking that that was the extent of my activities.

I doubted whether the police would in fact be deceived, and estimated that it would not be long before my deputy was functioning in my place while I pondered the hopes of revolution in the relative quietness of a prison cell.

I agreed entirely with the need for the editor, as a member of the Political Bureau, to be " protected " and so to go into hiding whilst others took the risks, and I am sure that that would have been the attitude of the vast majority of members. But I was nonetheless privately shocked at his failure to express any concern for the fate of the faithful rank-and-filers, most of them married —some to non-communists—who were going to be offered up with hardly a thought. In theory he was one hundred per cent right. In practice I should have felt better about it had he given in his briefing some indication of concern for them, even though nothing could be done to protect them. But this I regarded as being simply a personal weakness on his part. There were other leaders who succeeded in being both " human " and good Marxists at one and the same time, although those with the greatest influence inevitably tend to be those for whom human considerations count least.

There was to be no great rush about the job of producing the illegal paper. Discontents were to be allowed to " stew " for a little longer, whilst the comrades in the Forces strengthened their positions.

Bill Rust quietly prepared for his retreat to the house in the woods. I got my people at the ready, with trial " runs " on the machines.

I wrote the contents for a dummy paper, which was set in type in the Kensington basement, whilst the titled owner enjoyed a normal quiet Sunday upstairs. It was then taken by car to the saw works, where two machine operators printed it on paper which had been brought in another car from North London.

The papers were then parcelled up at yet another point by a third team as though they were to be despatched by courier to contacts in different parts of the country.

Then the entire issue was destroyed, with the exception of one copy for the Political Bureau, and the type was dispersed again. The whole try-out went according to schedule and was declared a complete success.

The Party at the same time set about getting its Forces contacts' organisation on to its toes for whatever might be demanded of it.

This organisation had been built up steadily as yet another party within the Party. The " cadres " secretary in each branch had to find some tried and trusted member who was not too well known and could put up an appearance of complete " respectability ", since their work was completely underground. Those chosen were usually women of middle-class origin.

After suitable training and instruction their task was to keep in touch with every communist from their locality who went into the Forces, to know where they were, when they were due to come on leave and to pass on directives to them each time they came home.

When the Forces men and women returned to their units it was the contact's job to see that they took back with them by word of mouth all the necessary directives for other Party members in their units.

Now the contacts began quietly to tell those who came home on leave to be ready to receive, more or less regularly, a soldiers' paper. They were to circulate it through the Forces' communist " grape vine ", using the maximum discretion, make their organisational plans for seeing that men going overseas took it with them. Members in the Navy and Air Force were to act as distributors to other parts.

Forces members were to keep the contacts even more well-informed of all " agitational issues " among Service men and women so that the paper might publicise them and adequately reflect prevailing discontents.

It was a period of frustration and suspense, and it was not difficult to find agitational issues and to exploit them, not only in the Armed Forces but among all sections of workers.

We were just assembling for a meeting of the London Secretariat of the Party one morning when a Civil Defence worker arrived in uniform to report some discontent among the Air Raid Wardens, Heavy Rescue and First Aid workers in his area. He said he thought that if we sent someone down to address them we might " get something going ".

One of our number was told to miss the Secretariat meeting and to see what he could do. We were not half-way through our agenda when we heard the sound of tramping feet outside and looking out of the window we saw a small army of Civil Defence workers marching by, headed by our man who had already brought them out on strike and was taking them to the Town Hall to demand their rights. It was just as well no air raid occurred in their absence.

My Industrial and General Information news agency was making useful progress. It was by now recognised by most of the great national papers as a source of a particular type of news —what in newspaper jargon were called " grouse " and " nark " stories.

When War Minister Margesson's student daughter supported the People's Convention, which was known to be working against the war, we got a scoop which raised our standing with the " capitalist " Press.

And when some of the more popular types of papers began to interest themselves in production scandals in the factories we came into our own. Anything which suggested that the war was a racket and which lowered the confidence of the people in the war leaders and in Britain's war effort was grist to our mill. I found plenty of such stories and fed them regularly to selected national dailies and Sundays—especially to the widely-read tabloids, some of whose representatives I was now meeting regularly for this purpose.

In the factories the Party had grown strong to a point where our groups not only provided me with important news, but made it too. Events were playing right into the Party's hands and we made the most of it.

In Napiers aircraft works, situated in the area for which I was responsible, we had by the spring of 1941 got twenty-five per cent of the workers organised in the Party. The shop stewards, the majority of whom were communists, strengthened their

position in the factory to the point where each was a dictator in
his own department.

"I could get a strike over a cup of tea," a shop stewards'
convener in one aircraft factory told me. I accused him of
boasting, challenging him to prove it. He won.

He called a mass factory meeting in working hours to protest
at the quality of the tea, moved a resolution that no more work
be done until they had received an undertaking from the management that there would be an improvement. The great works,
engaged on producing bombers, came to a standstill, and the
power of the Party in general and of the shop stewards' convener
in particular was effectively demonstrated.

All over the country our people had succeeded in getting such
positions. "Capturing" is the word commonly used by anti-
communists. But in most cases no "capturing" was required.
The non-communists were too indifferent or too lazy to take on
jobs which involved giving up some of their spare time and the
risk of becoming unpopular with the management.

Our people had the drive, the fight, the training in leadership
to fit them for taking on such jobs and putting up a good show.
They did it for communism, saw a grand opportunity and seized
it with both hands.

The Party had said that its members must go into jobs which
could be used for the Cause and so those who were not conscripted
streamed into the factories. Equipped with the Party's training
in leadership and self-expression, and their own drive and zeal,
they invariably sky-rocketed into office in either the trade union
branch, the workshop organisation or both.

Between them they succeeded in making plenty of the sort of
news in which I.G.I. was interested, and in return for our daily
bulletin they kept us provided with reports on what was happening. Those reports, suitably sub-edited and polished up, frequently appeared in the national Press.

Particularly useful to us, of course, were the Communist
Party members employed in the editorial departments of Fleet
Street, who were often able to get an I.G.I. story published which
might otherwise have finished up in the waste-paper basket.

We had members working on most of the well-known papers

and for a while the Party actually had an office and full-time
organiser in Whitefriars Street—right in the heart of London's
newspaperland. The organiser was responsible for both the
communist print-workers and journalists, who between them contributed enough cash to keep him and to maintain the office.

He was a former International Brigader who had fought in
Spain and who had suffered for his communism. But one night
in the blitz he emptied the office of its equipment (typewriters
were fetching fantastic prices at the time), loaded it all into taxis
and disappeared into the night. We did not see him again.

So again our journalists and other newspaper workers paid out
and the office was refitted. But this time the work was done by
volunteers.

We decided that it would be useful to have a meeting of all our
most important Fleet Street contacts in order to discuss how the
Press might be used still more to aid the Party's campaigns.

One by one our most " hush-hush " people, using the black-out
as their cover, came into our top-floor premises. The atmosphere
was conspiratorial; the discussion was as brief as possible, since
it was obviously indiscreet for them to remain there together for
a minute more than was necessary.

An air-raid alert sounded. It was the signal to go, for we had
previously agreed that it would be necessary to disband at once
in the event of a raid, for fear that by some unlucky chance we
should find ourselves in any sort of " incident " and so be discovered together.

As the sirens wailed, we all crowded together into the little lift.
But the lift, hopelessly overloaded, stopped midway between
floors. We pressed the button furiously. We jumped on the
floor. But all to no purpose.

Stuck there between floors, with the gates jammed, we could
hear the bombers buzzing overhead. We held a conference to
decide what next. At all costs we must not be " rescued ", that
was clear, for we included in our number the chief sub-editor of
a daily paper, the night news editor of another, a well-known
financial journalist, a couple of leading columnists—all in the
company of such notoriously " red " characters as myself and
Reg Bishop, editor of *Russia Today*.

Reg, who was Chestertonian in size, was given the task of using his mighty weight to break the gates, the floors, the ceiling —anything that would enable us to crawl out.

At last, by means of a united effort with our heels, we smashed the steel gates sufficiently to make a small gap through which I, as the thinnest present, proceeded to climb.   From outside I was able to release them, and as we parted we passed a resolution that never again must we meet officially in our Fleet Street premises.

X

WORKING FOR VICTORY

WE did not, in any case, need to meet again for the purpose of discussing how to slip anti-war news into the Press.   For in time our line began to be modified until we were concentrating mainly upon attacks on inefficiency and upon " pro-fascists " in high places.   Secretly and unofficially it was being put around the Party that since the withdrawal from Greece, in May 1941, the war had become " just " in parts.   With the fall of Crete the discussion became more widespread in the Party's ranks.   But officially the " line " remained as before.

Nor did Bill Rust have to go to the woods whilst the print-workers and myself went to jail.

Fleet Street started humming with rumours of a possible Nazi attack on Russia.   As usual we took our news and views on the U.S.S.R. from Soviet sources and these denounced those who spread such stories as anti-Soviet warmongers who were indulging in wishful thinking, and so we did too.

Said a statement from *Tass*, the official Russian news agency: " Despite the obvious nonsensical character of these rumours, responsible Moscow quarters have still found it necessary, in view of the persistent and intense dissemination of the rumours, to authorise *Tass* to state that these rumours constitute clumsily-concocted propaganda by forces hostile to U.S.S.R. and to Germany and interested in the further extension and unleashing of war."

The Soviet Union, with considerable Marxist ingenuity, we felt, had so far succeeded in keeping out of the war whilst the capitalist world bled itself white. It was a state of affairs we hoped would continue. But it was we who were guilty of wishful thinking. For on the morning of Sunday, June 22, 1941, came the bomb-shell. Russia after all had been attacked.

Anti-communists usually hold that the communist rank and file accept the Party's policy-somersaults without any understanding of their why or wherefore.

But on this, the occasion of the Party's most spectacular somersault, every communist who heard that the Workers' Fatherland had been invaded knew for certain that communists everywhere were on the side of Russia and so would fight to assist her.

But how could she best be assisted? That was the problem for British communists. For the German communists, we felt, the path of duty was crystal clear: sabotage by the workers in the factories, mass desertions to the Soviet Red Army by those in the Forces. We had often discussed doing the same ourselves when it seemed likely that the war might be switched.

The first leading communist with whom I discussed it that morning was an Amalgamated Engineering Union organiser, a foundation member of the Party. " This means world revolution," he said. He telephoned a national figure in the shop stewards' movement, who endorsed the view.

" If Churchill decides to make Russia an ally—and I don't see how he can avoid it," I said, " we shall find ourselves having to make an ally of him, too." But that was too much for the two old-stagers, who felt that this revealed an unexpected Right-wing deviationist tendency on my part.

I phoned the first member of the Political Bureau I could find. He said that the Political Bureau was due to meet at Party headquarters at once. I told him that I would make for my Fleet Street office and stand by for action.

After hours of discussion a statement was produced. The

Party would support those who supported Russia. The entry of the Soviet Union into the war transformed it from an unjust war into a just one. It was to be expected that within the ranks of the ruling class would be some who put their hatred of Russia before the interests of the nation. The " Men of Munich ", therefore, must go, along with all other anti-Soviet, pro-fascist elements. Upon every factory worker now fell the responsibility to increase production as never before. Inefficiency, slacking and racketeering became crimes against the people. The call was now for a united war effort.

We duplicated the statement as quickly as we could, along with reports which had already begun to arrive through our own Soviet sources, and got our bulletin into the post in time for all the leading Party members and contacts throughout Britain to have the new Party line served up with their breakfast in the morning, before they left for the factory, mine or union office.

The job completed, I outlined the new policy to a meeting of leading Party members who swore that the anti-Soviet Churchill would never support Stalin. We stopped our proceedings to hear Churchill's broadcast. His declaration that Britain would fight alongside Russia quickly ended that line of argument. But to support the Coalition in any shape or form was a bitter pill for them to swallow.

Just eight days earlier, William Rust had written an article for *World News and Views*, the inner-Party organ, headed " Unite to End Coalition ". And only the day before, in the same journal, William Gallacher, our communist M.P., wrote: " There never was a Government held in such contempt as is the miserable mixture of liberalism and labourism pathetically hitched to the Tory wagon and trying to dignify itself with the name of Coalition."

Now that very Coalition was going to collaborate in a common fight with Stalin and the U.S.S.R. It was all very difficult.

From the propaganda point of view, and from that of our own members, too, what saved the new line and made it tolerable was the presence of the Men of Munich, the anti-Soviet elements and the pro-fascists.

The fight against them and the effort to expose and counter

their influence, the calls for vigilance lest even now the war should be switched, stopped it from seeming a complete abandonment of the old fight. There was still someone to attack in Britain. Still the traditional enemy in his most blatant and reactionary form.

Once the Party members understood the line they took it up with enthusiasm. To those sectarians who protested that Churchill was still the same old enemy of the working-class we replied: " Yes, of course, he is. But at the moment he believes that he is using Russia to help British capitalism defeat its imperialist opponents. But Uncle Joe knows quite well that he is using Churchill. We can use him, too, and later on, when the Nazis are defeated in Germany, we shall get round to dealing with our own class enemies at home. A working-class which is strong enough to defeat Nazism may well prove strong enough to defeat its own reactionaries, too."

By that means the members were brought to see the Party's new campaign as being in the long run for our own Soviet Britain as well as for the more immediate task of defending the one great stronghold of communism upon which all our hopes must necessarily depend.

Life at I.G.I. became hectic. Few papers boasted a Soviet expert and suddenly, it seemed, everyone remembered that the *Daily Worker* had always given a large amount of its space to Russia, that all its staff were by way of being Soviet " experts ". And, since we were all that remained of the *Daily Worker*, they turned to us.

The Communist International had always maintained its own International Press Agency, " S.U. Press " (Soviet Union Press), which supplied a free service for communist papers throughout the world. Now it began sending us long cables every few hours which, backed by adequate files of pro-Soviet publications and our own specialised knowledge, put us in an unrivalled position to meet the new demand for Russian news and features. From morning till night, day after day, we worked at " exclusives " for the various papers, in addition to issuing two and three bulletins daily.

Sometimes the thirst for " exclusives " on the part of the editors of papers specialising on stunts became embarrassing. One sweltering day in August, for example, the London editor of a provincial Sunday paper phoned to say that he was sending round a reporter for an interview. Their sub-editors, he said, would write it up as a feature in the way the readers liked best.

Supposing, the reporter asked me, the Soviet forces are driven right back to the Arctic Circle or to Siberia, will they go on fighting?

" Assuredly so," I said.

Would life be very tough in those cold parts? he asked. I told him it would indeed.

" What would be the lowest temperature? "

" Forty degrees below is quite normal."

" What happens at forty degrees below? Does anything queer occur at such low temperatures? "

I thought hard. I could recall reading nothing from Russia which had given such details. But like every good communist I knew my Jack London. I thought of his descriptions of life in the Klondike gold rush; Dawson City; the Yukon; fur-trading inside the Arctic Circle. Obviously forty below in Russia would be the same.

" Great pine trees split from top to bottom and fall crashing in the night," I said. " Hinges fly off doors, screws shoot out of the woodwork. A man who puts his bare hand on the barrel of his gun leaves the skin behind."

On the Sunday the article appeared, a centre-page spread, head-lines of which read somewhat as follows: " Red Army will fight with flayed hands inside the Arctic Circle ". It was signed " Ivan Ivanovitch ".

In another article which appeared in the following week's issue, based this time on material culled from our own Soviet sources and dealing with the part that women were likely to play in the Russian war effort, I was made Peter Petrovitch by way of a change.

The type of reports we were circulating to the Press from the home front became popular, too, making our agency doubly in demand, for by the time that the British-Soviet Mutual Aid

Pact of July 12 came along, Communist Party members were working wonders in the factories.

On July 19, the Party leader, Palme Dutt, wrote in *World News and Views* : " On the home front we work for the most effective measures of reorganisation in the field of industry and production, as well as in food distribution and agriculture.

" The industrial workers must, and will, take the lead in fighting for the maximum production, for the most effective utilisation of manpower and resources. . . ."

Soon, pledges of increased production were coming from mass meetings in the factories, moved by Communist Party shop stewards, planned and prepared for by the Party groups with the same care and enthusiasm which had previously gone into the calls for strike action.

There was nothing phoney or mechanical about that enthusiasm. If our emotions during the imperialist war phase were those of hatred and of hope, now they became those of anguish at the Soviet losses and determination to do all possible to keep to a minimum the destruction of Soviet lives and resources.

We were filled with apprehension at the way in which the Nazi armies were eating deep into Soviet territory, bastion of all our hopes, reaching the gates of Moscow and Leningrad; filled also with pride at the Soviet military and civilian resistance. When Soviet peasants " scorched " the earth and their homes along with it, pride at their sacrifices mingled with rage at the loss this represented to socialism. When the Russians destroyed their Dnieper Dam, about which in the past we had done so much propaganda as the greatest of Soviet constructional achievements, we angrily demanded speedy relief action by our Government.

These things became a colossal driving force behind our members and many other workers, too, in the factories. The post-war world, despite all its shortages and crises, has produced no dynamic to compare with it.

Our shop stewards, who had won their positions in order to make mischief, now used them to get more guns, tanks and planes by urging improved technical methods, by better planning, by propaganda and by personal example.

Reporting a " Production Conference " called by the National

Council of Shop Stewards, first of many and increasingly larger ones, I wrote on August 30:

" If the employers cannot end the existing muddle in industry, then the workers can—and will."

That was the temper of our own people in the war industries and was quickly becoming that of the workers whom they led. The fact that we had for some years worked to create that " existing muddle " did not lessen our determination to get rid of it now.

On the following day, August 31, I covered an event which stirred the imagination of people in the democracies throughout the world and which demonstrated, perhaps more clearly than anything else could, the ability of the communists to influence others, the distance we had travelled in less than three months and the loyalty and discipline of our members.

At Feltham, in Middlesex, home of the big General Aircraft works, some communist shop stewards planned a demonstration. But it was to be no ordinary one, although it was the prototype of others which became common enough in time.

The Party was talking a great deal about national unity. In Feltham they would at least achieve local unity. We talked of unity with our great ally Russia. They would demonstrate that as well. The Party had said its members must be prepared to back Churchill. They would do it with no public inhibitions at all. The Party had said that they must make concessions. They would make them on the grand scale.

When I got to Feltham Green a military band was playing " God Save the King ". Standing respectfully at attention between twin flag-poles from which flew the Union Jack and the Red Flag were Mr. Maisky, the Soviet Ambassador, the local city fathers, clergy, the Conservative M.P., a leading communist shop steward and others.

After " The King " the uniformed band played the " Internationale " and the local good and great stood bareheaded to attention for that revolutionary " hymn " as well.

Before great pictures of Churchill and Stalin, the representatives of the various sections of the community and conflicting political and class interests made their speeches. And the speech that got the biggest cheer from the 6,000 people present was that made by a communist.

My descriptive report went out to almost every free country in the world and before long the unique event was unique no longer.

Here was a popular front forged under unforeseeable circumstances such as we had never dreamed of. Here were chances for spreading our ideas; familiarising the public with communists and communism, building up interest in Russia and her leaders, and enthusiasm for the achievements of the Red Army, became one of the most revolutionary things we could do.

Soon St. Pancras was organising a great Anglo-Soviet procession; prime movers were again Communist Party members. But this time the foot procession was preceded by bren-gun carriers, supplied by the War Office, and military bands played Soviet songs. Representatives of all parties and organisations marched and not least among them were communists from all over North London; their hammer-and-sickle banners had become respectable at last.

We had no illusions about how long that respectability would last if we did not, after all, end the war with the " workers on top ".

I was covering the event for I.G.I. and for various papers. I fell in step with a Party member whom I knew, and who in the past had been a Bolshevik among Bolsheviks, hating the " capitalists " with all his heart. He was carrying a huge photo of Churchill whilst behind marched two men with a streamer-banner bearing the words, " Let us Go Forward Together— Winston Churchill ".

" How does it feel to be carrying a picture of Comrade Churchill? " I asked him.

" Lousy," he said. Then he added, cheering up again: " But we'll deal with that—when he's helped us to save the Soviet Union."

That summed it up.

But not all Party members had to carry pictures of Churchill. And even those who did had the pleasure of watching the leading local Conservative, maybe, carrying an equally large picture of

Stalin and feeling, no doubt, even more embarrassed. I thrilled as I saw this new type of unity in action—and saw its influence, and ours, spreading wider and wider.

Soon Anglo-Soviet " Weeks " were being organised under the patronage of the local authorities, with official programmes, which invariably included pictures of Churchill and Stalin and the words of the " Internationale ".

One, produced, as usual, under the guidance of a Party member, filled its two centre pages with the now familiar portraits of Winston Churchill and Stalin.   Under them was a caption which read: " What God hath joined let no man tear asunder ".

When a member of the local Communist Party suggested that wording none of the other members thought the city fathers would sanction it.   But, such was the mood of the period, it got past them without comment and the resulting cynical laughter could be heard in every Communist Party branch in the London area as copies of the programme went from hand to hand.

Here is an example from my own experience of how such Anglo-Soviet Weeks were organised.   It follows a pattern with which every communist is still familiar.

On my suggestion a London Communist Party branch for which I was responsible decided to force the local authority into organising a " Week ".   The local Borough Council was a Conservative one, the Mayor was a " reactionary ", well known for his anti-communism.   It was known, too, that he privately disapproved of Churchill's alliance with Stalin.

We instructed the secretary of the local Trades Council, a communist, to propose at their next meeting that they should organise an Anglo-Soviet Week.   We briefed all the other delegates who were Party members to support him, but arranged that after the idea had been accepted in principle, they should urge that, in order to broaden its character and appeal, the Trades Council should ask the Mayor and Borough Council to take it over and to be responsible for it.

Because of its links with the Labour Party the Trades Council secretary would be mandated to approach the Labour Councillors to press for acceptance of the idea from within the Council Chamber.   But they, too, had to be persuaded of the need for a united effort, since, if they or their party decided to organise it themselves, the Communist Party would automatically be excluded and so half the point of the thing would be lost.

After innumerable " fraction " meetings and much pulling of strings the proposal was accepted by the Trades Council and by the Labour group on the Borough Council. Then a deputation was formed, consisting of members of the two bodies. It was arranged during working hours, as we guessed that none but the communists among the Trades Council members would be prepared to lose their wages for time spent on the deputation.

At the last minute the Labour Councillors were persuaded to agree to the deputation including one or two people who were not members of either organisation " in order to broaden its character ". These were crypto-communists and fellow-travellers.

The line to take with the Mayor was clear. Make it clear that all patriotic mayors were already organising such events, that if he did not do the same he would be in danger of appearing hostile to our great Soviet ally and, indeed, in conflict with the policy of his own party in general and of that great war leader Winston Churchill in particular.

If he hedged, the under-cover communists on the deputation would, in the last resort, say that they had no alternative but to spill the whole thing to the Press and leave the public to form its own conclusions. Again it worked.

When the Mayor said that he could not spare the time for organising such an event, the Trades Council delegates helpfully suggested that he might call a representative meeting of all local bodies, from which could be formed a working committee to see the thing through. He fell for it. The communist Trades Council secretary, again to be helpful, promised to supply him with names of working-class organisations of which he might not be aware and which were vital to such a project, since its main purpose was to raise the morale of the war workers in particular.

We then listed all the shop stewards' committees, trade union branches and other bodies where we had supporters, re-creating in some cases bodies which had been out of existence for years, turned in their names and primed up their delegates in advance.

The invitations went out from the Mayor's Parlour, describing the meeting as one called to set up an Anglo-Soviet Committee. That was just what we wanted. The situation being what it was at that time, no one who secretly disliked the idea, apart from the Mayor himself, would go to it, which made things all the easier for us.

The invitations were, in the end, actually despatched by the Deputy Town Clerk and the Trades Council secretary working together. And together they prepared the agenda. The Party was in on the ground floor.

The Communist Party branch, of course, had a copy of the agenda in advance, discussed it far into the night and carefully planned every move we would make at the coming meeting.

On the night itself things did not go entirely as we had planned, since one or two of the religious bodies sent delegates who, although themselves influenced by the prevailing pro-Soviet mood, were nonetheless anxious not to be associated with anything which was openly communist.

In view of this, I got up to urge that the help of the Ministry of Information's Russian Department should be solicited and that some of their Soviet films and exhibitions should be used. This met with the complete approval of all the doubting ones, who now felt that the thing had been put on to a respectable footing. If the trade unionists and other working-class delegates present wanted other films and exhibitions from suspiciously communist-sounding organisations let them have them by all means.

I made myself the spokesman of those who wanted sweet reasonableness—and I talked nothing else, but some of the "compromises" I pleaded for were in fact in advance of what we had originally hoped to get. Since the provisional arrangements had gone so smoothly, it was agreed that the Trades Council secretary and the Deputy Town Clerk should function as joint Hon. Secretaries.

In practice our own man was left to arrange things pretty

much as he (and we) wished, with the Mayor giving formal approval to all major decisions.

When it came to nominations and votes we got nearly what we wanted. Actual Communist Party members were in a minority, but, with fellow-travellers, sympathisers and people who clearly knew nothing about the question at all adding up jointly to a majority, we knew we could control the whole organisation.

The programmes carried a message from the Mayor and a list of patrons who included the two Conservative M.P.s, the local leaders of the other parties, Mrs. Churchill and Madame Maisky, wife of the Soviet Ambassador.

The " Week " began with " Services of intercession in all churches ", also to make it easier for us to get support for other things about which we were really concerned, and events included an orchestral concert by the Unity String Orchestra (one of " ours ") at which Soviet music was played, and a choir (one of " ours ") conducted by Alan Bush (one of " us "). A women's meeting (speaker, one of " us ") was held in a Congregational Hall to bring in the Nonconformists. In addition to Ministry of Information films there were films presented by the Workers' Film Association (one of " ours "). And there were other and sufficient events of no political significance to " balance " the programme for the non-communists.

The " Week " ended with a great procession supported by the W.V.S., Red Cross, A.T.C., St. John Ambulance, Civil Defence, trade union branches, political parties and all local organisations, banners, tableaux and bands.

And that was where we came into our own. The trade union branches turned out well, the Labour Party moderately well, the Liberals poorly and the Conservatives (apart from the Mayor, who took the salute) hardly at all. But the Communist Party turned out with the biggest and most disciplined contingent, the largest banners and the best tableaux. Along the route hammer-and-sickle badges were everywhere.

The procession ended at the largest local hall, where we had a mass meeting, speakers at which included a shop-stewardess " Heroine of Labour " (Party member) and myself.

They were supported on the platform, said the programme,

by " the four political parties ". That word " four " was an achievement in itself. Always in the past the Communist Party had been left out of such things; city fathers and others thought only in terms of " the three political parties ". We had insisted that the communists should be officially included, and, since it was ungracious to keep us out when we were far and away the most helpful and active supporters of the event, we won.

From our point of view the " Week " was a great success. We made a number of new Party members, sold large quantities of open and concealed communist literature, did a great deal of Soviet, and therefore communist, propaganda, put the Party " on the map ", made scores of new contacts and, last but not least, used a Conservative Mayor and Council and members of the Armed Forces in the cause of communism.

To suggest that the " red haze " which covered Britain throughout that period of the war was entirely created by the British Communist Party would be absurd. Apart from anything else the gratitude of the public when Hitler's bombers turned East and away from British homes was likely to ensure interest in the Russian people. The hard-won battles, sharply contrasting with the early Continental collapse, were a further guarantee of sympathetic interest.

But it was by such means as those I have described that that interest was deepened into a great emotional enthusiasm and broadened to include nine-tenths of the population. It was by such means, too, that it was given a political content, canalised into political channels, and an atmosphere was created where criticism of Russia became tantamount to treason; failure to bow down and worship Stalin was seen as evidence of fascist sympathies.

Simultaneously the Party was running three major campaigns, for production, for Anglo-Soviet unity and for the raising of the ban on the *Daily Worker*.

Like most such campaigns the third had small beginnings. After cocking a snook, as it were, at the Government in general and at Mr. Herbert Morrison in particular, with our little cyclostyled paper, we got down to serious business.

In trade union branches where we were sure of a majority

Party-sponsored resolutions were moved, demanding that, in the interests of freedom of the Press and democracy generally, the ban should be raised at once. The resolutions urged that trade union district committees and National Executives should make similar demands.

Soon such resolutions were coming spontaneously from trade union branches and Trades Councils in various parts of the country. Every communist holding an influential position in the trade union movement was pressing for similar action by his organisation.

The campaign went slowly whilst we were still opposing the war, but when Russia came in and we started supporting the war effort it became possible to get wide non-communist support. Within a few days of the attack on the Soviet Union the editorial board was renewing its demand that the Government should lift the ban.

In those organisations where resolutions had already been passed, new ones were pushed through. The support of influential non-communists was sought and, in most cases, obtained. The list soon included leftish university professors, artists, musicians, actors, writers, clerics—anyone who could be brought to say that the ban was an affront to democracy—even though we knew quite well what we would do with freedom of the Press and democracy when the revolution came.

Great demonstrations were organised, with platforms well lined with people with " names ", regardless of what we thought of them personally. Everything possible was done to give the campaign an appearance of respectability and breadth of support.

People whom we had derided or opposed for years were invited to speak from our platforms, but always among the long list of speakers was a sufficient number of fellow-travellers and crypto-communists to ensure that the general tone remained as we wanted it. The last speaker was always William Rust or some other leading member of the staff, so making it certain that it should finish with a demand that all present should go back to their organisations and build up pressure along the lines we wanted.

Trade union leaders began to join the campaign as they received more and more resolutions from the rank and file, along with Labour Party organisations and some well-known Labour figures; then Labour and Liberal M.P.s followed.

The Press took up the demand, with every communist and fellow-traveller inside the newspaper offices giving a hand.

By the time that the ban was finally lifted, twenty months after it had been imposed, organisations speaking in the name of millions had gone on record in support of our demand.

From first to last every possible string was pulled, the campaign was conducted as a military operation. Directives went out week after week from the special office we had set up; months before each trade union conference was held a plan was thrashed out with the leading Party members within the union to ensure that a majority vote should be obtained. As those who moved or supported the resolutions at such conferences were usually lacking in the necessary background as to the history of the ban, the best line of argument to pursue and the extent of support so far won, we obligingly provided all this in the shape of confidential documents and personal briefings. Often non-communist trade union leaders would make speeches which we had prepared in all but the least important details.

On the eve of a *Daily Worker* resolution being debated at the Labour Party's annual conference we had a " briefing " meeting at the St. Ermin's Hotel, in Westminster. Present in addition to William Rust and myself were crypto-communists and fellow-travellers who were members of delegations from trade unions, local Labour parties and affiliated organisations. Present, too, was one man who at the next General Election blossomed out as a Labour M.P. He has since been expelled as a fellow-traveller and has lost his seat in Parliament—but it took years for the Labour Party to catch up with him and to deal with him.

By the time the Trades Union Congress was due to meet in the following autumn it was clear that so many of the affiliated organisations were now committed in our support that we were assured a majority vote. It was, apparently, equally clear to the Government, and on the eve of the Congress the ban was lifted.

It had been the biggest and most successful campaign of its sort that the British Communist Party had ever conducted.

Thousands of resolutions had been passed, committing probably some six to eight million people. How many had actually voted on the question it is impossible to say. It is unlikely that they exceeded 100,000. Twenty people at a trade union branch can pass a resolution in the name of hundreds or even thousands of members; a couple of dozen active co-operators may vote in the name of, maybe, 20,000 members whose activities are limited to the purchase of their groceries, meat and milk at a Co-op. store and the quarterly collection of their dividend. But who can blame the communists for exploiting such a situation?

The votes, as is usual with such campaigns, were duplicated over and over again. A trade union branch with 2,000 members would go on record against the ban. That figure would then be added to our much-publicised records of the numbers already supporting. Then the district committee would also be prevailed upon to support. They, perhaps, represented 20,000, and that figure would be added to our total, although by the time the vote was taken it was likely that the majority of branches covered by the district committee had already voted favourably and had already been duly recorded.

Then the district committee and branches along with others from all over the land would vote at the annual conference and our total would leap, say, by half a million. For more than half of those votes this would be their third recording.

Then the national executive of the same union would, perhaps, send delegates to a great Central London conference called by the *Daily Worker* itself or possibly by the National Council for Civil Liberties or some other such organisation. When the vote was taken the delegation would support it and the half-million votes would go into the grand total cast at the meeting—and into our records yet again.

But the figures sounded convincing, and trade union leaders, politicians and newspaper editors who were concerned to speak in the name of the " masses " were duly impressed and acted accordingly. And again, who can blame them? That is how democracy works, and if apathy and indifference exist at the bottom they must be reflected in farcical votes at every level.

In that campaign experience was gained which not long after came near to bringing about the affiliation of the Communist Party to the Labour Party. In addition, important new contacts were made in trade union and cultural circles in particular which are still being exploited to this day.

XI

BACK ON THE " WORKER "

WHEN, after twenty months' campaigning, the ban on the *Daily Worker* was at last raised we immediately announced that the first issue of the new paper would appear just ten days later.

The main emphasis of the Party's work and propaganda had by then been shifted away from increased production and on to the demand for a Second Front.

We were still, of course, pushing for increased output in the factories, but the demand for a new front in the West was considered to take precedence over it. We felt that without that new front which would take the strain off the Red Army the production campaign in the factories was only half as important as it might be.

The slogans " Tanks for Joe " and even " Joe for King " were still appearing on the walls, in the factories and on the weapons coming off the production line.

A " dummy " paper, prototype of what the new *Daily Worker* would look like, which we published and with which we armed members of a big deputation to Parliament just before the end of the ban, reflected our attitude.

Main story was the report of a Second Front demonstration in Trafalgar Square. Stories of support for Russia occupied the second position in space and prominence. Production came third. The new paper was, first and foremost, going to be a weapon in the fight for a Second Front!

The *Daily Worker's* works and offices had been destroyed in the blitz, our staff was dispersed, some were in the Forces, some in industry. Only a skeleton staff was available.

There was William Rust, the editor, who had headed the office from which the lift-the-ban campaign had been run. Claud Cockburn, the Diplomatic Correspondent (known to the readers as Frank Pitcairn), was working with me on I.G.I.; Walter Holmes, the columnist who had also at one time been with me on the agency, had gone to work for the Soviet Embassy and had still to be retrieved. George Sinfield, industrial-cum-sports writer, was editing *Challenge*, the organ of the Young Communist League. We had no sub-editors, practically no reporters and only a rump business staff.

The ten days which followed were hectic. First I wound up I.G.I., literally overnight. I wrote one last bulletin on the day following the Government's announcement, locked my office and never went near the place again.

The last issue consisted of a letter to those who had been receiving our news service. To keep within the law I had had all along to pretend that it was not a continuation of the *Daily Worker*, that it had no official connection with it. In that last bulletin the mask was dropped to some extent, although some of the pretence was still maintained.

" This is the last issue of the I.G.I. *Bulletin*, but we announce it with no regrets," I wrote. " The closing down of a publication today usually represents a journalistic or business defeat. The closing down of I.G.I. reflects a smashing victory for the working-class, the victorious conclusion of the great united campaign for the raising of the ban on the *Daily Worker* in which I.G.I. is proud to have played a not insignificant part."

I went on: " Hampered by lack of staff, restricted by the paper shortage, I.G.I. nevertheless has succeeded, by means of its bulletin, in bringing the urgently desired daily lead to several hundreds of workers' leaders, and through them, to tens of thousands of Britain's key war workers in factories, mines, shipyards, docks and depots in all parts of the country. In addition, through

Facing pictures: 1. A Communist-sponsored meeting attracts the intellectuals.
2. . . . and the proletariat as well.

its work as a news agency it from time to time has succeeded in bringing to millions, through the medium of the general Press, stories which, had it not been for the ban, would have reached the public through the columns of the *Daily Worker*."

After recalling our first police raid and the eventual return of our documents, I continued : " A new issue was, however, raised within a few days by the Paper Controller, who took exception to the publication of I.G.I. *Bulletins*, which finally resulted in publication of the Agency's weekly printed bulletin being dropped. From time to time attempts were made by the Ministry of Supply to establish a case against I.G.I.'s daily publication of the service bulletin, but these were finally dropped when I.G.I. established its right as an agency to issue such material.

" No other news agency has published so many stories of the work of Production Committees, of their difficulties, their failures, their successes. When these vital instruments for releasing the pent-up initiative of the workers were first conceived by shop stewards on the job, I.G.I. immediately publicised their formation and pooled the experiences of their members. We believe that by this means an invaluable service has been rendered to the people's fight against fascism."

I retold the story of the agency's part in the campaigns against the *Daily Worker* ban and for the Second Front, and ended :

" I.G.I. is proud to have served in its own small way the British workers in this the most urgent and yet most glorious struggle they have ever waged. Today one great need above all else faces the liberty-loving people of this country—the need for a Second Front in the West. I.G.I. believes that it has assisted in building up the great public demand on this question which now exists. Our job is now being taken over by the *Daily Worker*, in whose strong hands the weapon of working-class journalism can be used on a scale impossible to I.G.I. and which can carry the fight for the Second Front on to a new and victorious plane."

I submitted a draft to Rust, since discretion was still needed and I wanted to do nothing which would embarrass the new *Daily Worker*. He made just one alteration. In the last paragraph the words " in its own small way " had been deleted when it came back.

Facing pictures: 1. The Communist Party Executive Committee in session in London.
2. Party Leaders. *L. to r.:* The late William Rust, editor *Daily Worker*; school teacher Annie Powell; Elinor Burns, leading co-operator; Phil Piratin, former Communist M.P.; Bill Brooks, leader of the Y.C.L.; Prof. George Thompson, Birmingham University; William Alexander, former International Brigader.

E

For twenty months people at meetings all over the country had contributed sums of money for the lift-the-ban campaign and for the new *Daily Worker*. Our followers, who had in the past subscribed week by week to maintain the paper, so bridging the gulf between expenditure and receipts, had continued to do so even though they got no paper in return.

The result was that although the campaign had been an expensive one, we still had some £60,000 in hand when it ended. A print works was found, and a rotary machine which had not been used for twenty years was tried out and proved to be just barely capable of producing a daily paper of our size.

Our first issue was to appear on Monday morning. On the Sunday the staff which was to produce the paper assembled. More than half were volunteers from other papers who had come along to give a hand.

There was a man holding an executive position on the Liberal *News Chronicle*, another from Lord Beaverbrook's *Daily Express*, a third from one of the financial papers, others turned up from the *Sunday Pictorial*, *Reynolds News*, Reuters and the Press Association. One or two of the former members of the staff who had been called into the Forces obtained leave or just took it and arrived in mufti.

The office which was to be ours was full of uncleared junk, and for the first few days we had to use as our editorial department a corridor which later accommodated the tape machines.

The available space was so overcrowded, so many people were coming and going, some doing an hour or two's work before going on duty with their own papers, that I, the chief sub-editor, had only the haziest notion of what was being done and who was doing it.

But somehow it *was* done and the paper appeared next morning, winning approval from the rest of the Press for its technical and journalistic standards. As chief sub-editor I had worked fourteen hours before that first day was through, and those hours continued for day after day throughout the first week, with none of our editorial staff working for less than twelve daily.

We told ourselves that these were exceptional circumstances.

But the voluntary help dropped off, those who had obtained leave from the Forces returned to their units and soon we were faced with an acute man-power shortage.

A rota was started of all the Communist Party members employed in London journalism, each giving a couple of hours weekly. They came from the weekly magazine press as well as from the daily papers. One or two came from the B.B.C.

The staff of most daily papers includes a lawyer whose job it is to keep a watchful eye on legal points, such as possible libels. On the *Daily Worker* this was particularly necessary since we spent so much of our time skating on thin ice. Moreover, war conditions made it necessary for a lawyer to censor every word we wrote to ensure that the various security regulations and directives were observed.

A Party member who was a lawyer was brought on to the staff, sacrificing a good deal to do so. He was supported by a rota of some ten or twelve other communist lawyers who relieved him in turn each evening and at week-ends. Two of these later blossomed out as Labour M.P.s, but were in due course expelled by the Labour Party.

To our daily appeals for money to keep the paper going our readers responded magnificently, sending in £3,000 to £4,000 each month.

There is nothing fake about that fund total and those who try to convince themselves and others that the continued existence of a communist daily paper in Britain is made possible only by Moscow gold simply under-estimate their opponent.

It is far more significant that 40,000 communists and their sympathisers are able to maintain it on the basis of very real sacrifice.

Often during the years that followed, I went through the letters which accompanied the contributions, looking for ones to quote in our daily appeals, and I know the genuineness of the sacrifices made.

There were old age pensioners who made regular monthly contributions from their tiny incomes. Sometimes quite sizable windfalls would come from unexpected quarters. A reader would send, perhaps, £25 or £50. The accompanying note might be all but illiterate, but there was no doubt about the extent to which we had succeeded in winning its writer.

I remember in particular one which read somewhat like this:

" My old Aunt Maudie died the other day, left me £50, i never knew the old girl had so much. There are dozens of things we need for the children and ourselves because i am only a labourer, so i am sending off the whole of the money to the good old *Daily Worker* before we spend it."

That is one side of the picture. The other is not so elevating, for the Party and the paper both maintain people whose job it is to " milk " the wealthier fellow-travellers.

At one time we used on the *Daily Worker* a seductive young woman communist who would switch on the charm and go to any lengths in order to obtain fat cheques.

The Party, of course, does not hesitate to make big demands of the fellow-travellers, for it knows that most of them have uneasy consciences. They know, though they will not admit it, that what prevents them from joining the Party is a lack of moral courage or their preoccupation with a career. And so they subsidise communist causes in order to salve their consciences.

If they are not prepared to do so, the Party has a hold on them which it does not hesitate to use. The man who has at some time secretly associated with the Party is in a vulnerable position. He knows the fate of those who play with the Party and then drop away, how they are singled out for particularly vicious public attacks. And so he is likely at all costs to avoid the same happening to himself.

Among such regular contributors are Left-wing politicians; ministers of religion; university professors; business men; people on the Stock Exchange; industrialists; some Jewish factory owners, non-communists who see a regular subsidy to the *Daily Worker* as being an insurance premium against fascism. These latter do not want communism, which might mean the end of their position as capitalists, but still less do they want fascism, which would probably result in their physical extinction.

The main basis of the paper's funds is the steady flow of small sums coming from the skilled artisans in the factories, from miners, building workers and others, and the rather larger ones

from communists and sympathisers in the professions, and among
the intelligentsia.

Not long after we restarted we found that the paper was, for
the first time in its history, making money. With the ending of
the Government's ban had gone a number of others besides,
among them that of the advertisers. Communism in Britain had
become respectable, made so by the Red Army. In particular
we were able to get large numbers of advertisements from
Government departments, most of whom were buying advertising
space at the time.

A special business meeting was called to discuss the position.
Should we continue to ask our readers to sacrifice for the paper,
or should we tell them the truth and wind up the fund, at least
for the time being?

We decided to go on tugging at their heart-strings, pleading
poverty and impending financial crisis, and after putting aside a
considerable sum for the larger building we hoped one day to
be able to purchase, to pass a further sum to Communist Party
headquarters each month.

Our decision was based first and foremost on the belief that
it is good to make people sacrifice for the things in which they
believe; that in doing so they come to believe in them all the
more. The man who gives a copper to a cause may feel no great
ties with it, but persuade him to give until it hurts and he will
see the cause as his own and be prepared to make even bigger
sacrifices for it if necessary.

It was the sacrifices of the staff, sympathetic journalists and
readers combined, which made possible the republication of the
Daily Worker and its immediate success.

So urgent was the paper's need for staff that Carol went to
work on it only ten weeks after the birth of our first child, Rowena,
whom we put into a nursery.

The ban and the associated publicity had done us good. The
paper was in great demand and was popular.

The newsprint on which newspapers are printed was rationed.
We were printing as many copies as were permitted and there was
no hope of getting round the regulations to any great extent.
We started a campaign to persuade our readers to pass their

copies on. An instruction went out to all Party members to the effect that they must see that their own copies were passed on to the maximum number of non-communists.

Soon we had ample evidence to show that, on an average, each copy of the paper was passing through at least five different pairs of hands during the course of the day. We knew that our one hundred and twenty thousand copies were being eagerly consumed by at least half a million people daily, most of them at that time in key industries or in the Forces.

Copies would sometimes come back to us from engineering works, black with the oily thumb-marks of dozens of people who had read them. Sometimes each reader in turn would pay a penny for his copy and then initial it. Some bore as many as two or three dozen names before they came back to us along with the money subscribed to the fund.

I never failed to be stirred by the torn and well-thumbed copies which came into my hands in this way. They helped to maintain the feeling that one was engaged on a mission. The oily thumb-prints took on an almost mystical significance. There is nothing better for the communist cause than for its members constantly to be reminded that they are fighting against odds, with the scales weighted against them.

Six months after the paper restarted I was still working some fourteen or fifteen hours daily for six days of each week. I would start at between nine and ten in the morning, see each edition to bed and wait until the Soviet midnight communiqué came from the Eastern Front before passing the last page to the printer.

War-time London was by then all but dead and I would walk two or three miles home through the darkened streets. Once in a thick pea-soup fog I lost my way. Too exhausted, both mentally and physically, to carry on, I spent the rest of that winter's night sitting on a seat somewhere in Regent's Park.

After six months as the paper's chief sub-editor, I was made chief reporter and, soon after, news editor. As such I was in charge of the reporting team and of the whole of the paper's campaigns on the home front.

It is an axiom in Marxist journalistic circles that a communist paper lives on its campaigns. Remembering this, I determined, as soon as I took on my new responsibility, to find some issue on which I could campaign continuously and which would assist the paper to become the leader of a broad agitation.

A week later I heard of a meeting which was being held to protest at the continued operation of Regulation 18B (under which the police had earlier in the war hoped to intern me for the duration). Those against whom the Regulation had been operated in practice were mainly alleged fascists of one sort or another.

I sent a girl reporter to cover it, with instructions to look for anything which smelt of fascism. At the meeting were a number of people with undoubted fascist sympathies. We carried a report of the meeting that night.

Going from my Maida Vale flat to the local Underground station next morning, I saw a large fascist slogan painted on a wall, along with the Mosley " flash in the circle " sign—or as we irreverently called it " the flash in the pan ".

I had not the time to stop and examine it, but all the way to the office I was thinking about it. Had we been banned as the fascists had been we should have continued to propagate our policies and slogans by stealth, I reasoned.

We should have painted slogans on walls by night, circulated illegal leaflets, set whispering campaigns going in pubs and queues. Surely the fascists might be expected to do the same.

I followed up the report we had published of the previous day's meeting with a story on the possibility of the fascists starting their propaganda once again; even whilst fascist bombs were still dropping on Britain they would dare to come out of their holes and already their slogans were appearing on walls in some parts of London.

Before the next day was out I had received telephone calls from many parts of London about fascist slogans seen on walls and had received the first resolution passed by a meeting of East London clothing factory workers who called for vigilance against a rebirth of fascism and the immediate reinternment of those fascists already released.

Day after day the resolutions came in; Party members everywhere took up the campaign, and soon I was writing a daily piece

on the question. It was exactly what the paper and the Party
needed. Our pre-war anti-fascist record had been tarnished by
the Soviet–Nazi pact and by our earlier anti-imperialist-war
activities. Here was the chance once again to come out as the
great anti-fascist fighters.

At the beginning of the campaign it was very much a question
of bricks without straw. When I one day inspected more closely
the slogan which had given me the initial idea I found that it was
quite definitely of pre-war vintage. It was no real proof of first
steps towards a fascist come-back at all. And when I checked up
on a good many of the others which had subsequently been
reported to me it was clear that they were of the same period.

But there is only one test for a communist campaign. Does it
serve the cause or does it not? If it does it is right. This one
most certainly served the cause and so I kept it going.

I unearthed obscure neo-fascist organisations, published attacks
on their leaders and any sinister-sounding quotations from their
publications. Their intentions, usually well concealed, were in
any case unhealthy at a moment when Britain was preparing a
Second Front against the Nazis with whom most of them had
a good deal in common. I began to believe in the campaign itself
and to feel inwardly happier about it.

Then fascist slogans, mostly scrawled in crayon, appeared all
around my Maida Vale home. The anti-semitic P.J. (Perish
Judah) was painted on the gate-posts of houses in which Jews—
most of them refugees—were known to live and it appeared
regularly on my own. I hotted up my campaign.

Occasional threatening letters came by post. Sometimes they
threatened the paper. More often they threatened me personally
with anything from a beating-up to an unpleasant death. My
fascist enemies seemed to be agreed that I must be a Jew, and
many of the letters were addressed to me as Douglas Hydinsky.

Our members in the National Council for Civil Liberties urged
that body to organise a conference on the question. Their
suggestion was discussed and an executive member was sent to
ask me to provide evidence. I took her, late one evening, up and
down the streets of the Maida Vale area, showing her the slogans
and the " P.J.''s on the door-posts. She was suitably impressed.

But I noticed, as I accompanied her, that the majority had obviously been done by the same hand. One man with a crayon, a stick of chalk and a white-wash brush could, it seemed, do a great deal. Maida Vale quite obviously housed one active fascist at least.

The Civil Liberties conference was a packed one. Delegates came from all over England. Great trade unions sent delegations. Millions were represented—in so far as the millions are ever represented in that way. Our own people set the pace, and indignant resolutions were passed demanding an end to anti-semitism and all fascist activities. It was also decided that similarly representative district conferences should be held throughout the land.

The conference was widely reported and, in due course, the Labour and Liberal Press began to take up my campaign.

An obscure and in itself unimportant body on the idiot fringe of the Fascist Movement, calling itself the British National Party, provided me with more ammunition. Its literature was always quotable, and when one day a man describing himself as one of the Party's members was convicted of treachery my campaign went forward by leaps and bounds.

New members came rolling in to the Party, subscriptions from East End clothing and furniture manufacturers sky-rocketed and my daily piece became the most popular in the paper.

In the middle of it all I received one day a visit from two mysterious individuals who said that they were interested in the fascists' activities too. They wanted to help but lacked information. After much sparring I got them at last to come to the point. They were Special Branch detectives engaged in keeping a check on subversive activities. They had, they admitted, practically no worth-while information on the neo-fascists and neither had M.I.5, despite the fact that the Government had thought it necessary to detain the active fascists and was still keeping them in jails and camps.

I was not surprised, for all our experience indicated that they knew very little about us either. They had never come near to understanding the way in which the Party worked and still less how it thought, and their attempts to keep the communists out

of the Armed Forces were little short of pathetic. The little fish
had occasionally been stopped, but most of the big fish got in
easily. I wanted to see just how much they knew.

I told them that we would work together. I would give them
information if they in turn would check on some things which
it was impossible for me to follow up. This they agreed to do,
and for a time I got some little help from them, for they eagerly
followed up every smallest clue I gave them, gratefully sharing
with me what they discovered.

In return I gave them information which had in fact already
been published in the *Daily Worker*, which I had earlier ascer-
tained they did not even read despite their interest in subversive
movements.

I told the editor what I was doing and he gave it his approval.

They must after a time have got around to what I had done,
for only one continued to visit me, and he became less and less
co-operative.

When I left the *Daily Worker* there were still some of the
carbon copies of " confidential " reports there which they had
passed to me and the contents of which I had published in the
paper as " exclusives ".

The little bit that was genuine in the campaign was just
enough to enable me to believe in it and so to be at my
best, for I, like most communists, had always found it easier
to campaign well on those whose declared aims I believed
in, even though as a Marxist I believed that their truth and
falsity were subordinate to the over-riding interests of the class
struggle itself.

XII

SPIES AND CONFESSIONS

WHEN the vote on the question of communist affiliation was taken
at the Labour Party conference in the following year, Mr. Herbert
Morrison swayed the waverers with a reference to some of the

" wicked people " behind the scenes in the Communist Party. He told delegates that if they knew what he, as Home Secretary, knew but could not disclose, they would never cast a vote for anything to do with the Communist Party.

A few days later " Dave " Springhall, our National Organiser, was arrested under the Official Secrets Act, tried and given a seven-year sentence for passing information to a foreign Power. Everyone knew that that Power was our ally Russia. Several other Party members during the same period were sentenced on similar charges. A vastly larger number who were guilty of the same activities were never caught.

As soon as Springhall was found guilty the Party expelled him. He was expelled, not because the Party disapproved of his activities as such, but for two quite different reasons: first, because we had no desire, least of all at that moment of growing popularity, to get the public reputation for condoning spying by our members (for this reason his wife, who worked on the *Daily Worker*, was sacked at once); second, because, viewed from any angle, it was a major indiscretion for the National Organiser, of all people, to take such risks at such a moment.

A great deal of information which was thought by Party members to be of possible use to the U.S.S.R. was flooding into our headquarters and other offices. Under the circumstances, a National Organiser might be expected to divert it to some of the Party's less prominent figures who could see that it safely reached the Russian Embassy.

Some of Springhall's colleagues guessed that he was passing on material to the Embassy and he was warned that this would be a major indiscretion, bearing in mind his position. His answer was a complete denial. But suspicions continued and he was warned again. A few days later, when the police raided Party headquarters and Springhall's home, they found documentary evidence in both his office and his rooms. The Party membership was outraged by his indiscipline and his indiscretions. Only the rawest and greenest were disturbed by the nature of his activities as such.

The Party still believed that our military alliance with Russia was not fully being carried into effect. We all believed that it was necessary to be watching for signs of a " double-cross " the whole of the time.

The reaction of the average member was : " If they won't supply the information to Russia, we will." The spying which had gone on during the " imperialist war " phase was nothing to that which followed. The information came from factories and the Forces, from civil servants and scientists. And the significant thing to recognise is that those who did it were not professional spies ; they took big risks in most cases, received no payment whatsoever, and, this is doubly important, did not see themselves as spies and still less as traitors. As Party members they would have felt that they were being untrue to themselves and unworthy of the name of communist if they had not done it.

An example from my own experience will perhaps convey what I mean. Anyone in a leading position in the Party at that time could give dozens of others.

Not long before the *Daily Worker* ban was lifted I was acting as " political commissar " to a London branch of the Party, or, in the Party's own jargon, I was " politically responsible " for it. In my spare moments I gave political direction to the local leaders and tutored classes for them from time to time and was available for advice.

I returned to my flat late one night to find one of them waiting for me. He was very tense and obviously nervous about what he wanted to discuss with me.

He was one of the Party's more likeable middle-class types. He had joined in his student days at university, when it was fashionable to do so ; when he came to London he dropped out of activity for a while, but was later contacted by the Party and brought back into action. By the time Russia came into the war he was a local leader and, in addition, had had the good fortune to get work as a temporary civil servant in the War Office. His social background was right and no one there suspected him of being " Red ".

He had, he told me, recently been given a position of greater responsibility, as a result of which much more information, mainly concerning the Middle East, now regularly came his way. It seemed, he said, to confirm the Party's worst suspicions. Recent movements of men and materials in some parts of his department's area might, he thought, possibly be connected with future hostile action against Russia. " I don't know how important or significant it may be, but I feel that the Party ought to know about it," he said.

I told him that it would assist the Party greatly in our analysis of the political and military situation. He promised to pass on anything which seemed significant. I passed him, as was our routine, straight on to a member whose job it was to keep in touch with such people. He was instructed to drop all local activity at once. " This is far more important ", he was told, " than anything else you can do for the Party." He had grown accustomed to the idea of passing on secrets " for the Party ". Now he was urged to remember everything in greater detail so that it might be of use to Russia too. Then he was passed to a colleague who was in touch with the Soviet Embassy.

" I rather feared this would happen," he told me. " I know I ought to help but I'm nervous. I'm hoping to get married soon and I don't think that, in any case, I'm the type who could settle down in jail." But he pulled himself together and added: " I know that I'm privileged to be able to help Russia in this way and in my heart of hearts I'm proud to take the risk. I'll do whatever is needed."

I reminded him of what we both knew to be true, that thousands of Party members would give all they had to do such a job for communism.

The clandestine meetings took place with increasing frequency as he learned to note what was useful and what was not, training his memory so that he might accurately report conversations overheard between departmental heads, visiting generals and others.

I knew him well enough to be able to say with certainty that he never ceased to be scared of what he was doing and that to see it through called for a high degree of misapplied heroism.

I know, too, that his conscience had troubled him for a long time before finally he came to talk to me about the matter, and that until he started spying he felt himself to be less than a man for not doing what seemed to him as a Party member to be so obviously right and necessary.

One spy of that sort is worth scores of mercenaries. And
Russia has forty thousand such potential spies in Britain in the
ranks of the Communist Party, and millions more throughout the
world.

At no point did the question of its being unpatriotic enter
into our thoughts. We were, after all, agreed that a communist
Britain would be a better Britain, that we should not see communism here in our lifetime if Russia was allowed to be crushed
and that, therefore, in defending Russia from her class enemies
and ours we were fighting for " our " Britain. The conventional
attitude to patriotism and love of country was easily dismissed
with the question: " Whose country—theirs or ours?"

The newer the Party member the more he would *consciously*
think in terms of Britain in that way. To the seasoned Marxist
the axiom that " the workers have no country " is sufficiently well
absorbed for such considerations not to enter into his conscious
reasoning at all. For him there is one war front stretching across
the world, with the working-class and its allies, led and moulded
by the Communist Party, on the one side and the class enemy
on the other. Any part of that front is as important to him as
another and he will work or die as readily for a communist Spain,
China, America or Britain as the need may arise.

In time the War Office caught up with our local spy, but only
to the point of discovering through M.I.5 that he had been a
student communist at Cambridge. He was questioned about
this, admitted it (since there was nothing else he could do in the
circumstances) and said that he had since ceased to be a communist.

He was not questioned further but some weeks later was
suddenly dismissed. His call-up to the Forces was equally
sudden and he soon found himself drafted to the Far East.

One other story about him remains vividly in my mind.

The sexual freedom in his Party branch was much what it
was in others and members took advantage of it or not according
to temperament.

I went with him one night, before he had been withdrawn
from local activities, to a social the branch had organised. We
were joined at the door by another local leader, an ex-Inter-

national Brigader who had lost an arm in Spain and who was of the type which likes to publicise its " conquests ".

" My God," he said, as he looked around the crowded room. " Do you know, there isn't a single woman here I haven't been to bed with."

I saw my companion look agitatedly around the room and then turn slightly green. Later, alone, he talked to me about it.

" Of course, I agree with all that Marx and the rest have written about morality," he said, " and I've practised it all myself. But I absolutely hated him when he bragged in that way. I know it was damned silly of me, but, you see, I got secretly engaged to —— only the other night and I prefer not to be reminded of his conquests at the moment." The girl he named had, of course, been among those present in the room.

He was discovering in his own experience, for the moment at least, that there is a lot of Marxist teaching that runs counter to human nature itself. As a postscript I should add that his marriage did not survive the war.

As a member of the London Secretariat I was one day given the job of conducting the trial of two members of a West London Party branch who were alleged to be guilty of Left-wing deviations, and whose expulsion was being demanded by the branch.

The man and woman whom I was to " try " joined the Party at its foundation and had spent years working at the great Communist International headquarters in Russia. Both were members of the Ealing branch, but the man was also a member of an aircraft factory group in Hayes and as such was linked with the Hayes branch as well.

The woman turned up to face the music; the man sent an excuse for not being present. Since, however, they were charged with much the same offence, I agreed, at the man's request, to accept the woman's evidence on behalf of both. Present were the local Party committee and others who wished to give evidence.

I followed what were the customary lines and which had been endorsed by headquarters. First I made a lengthy " political statement ", which took the form of a comprehensive analysis of the political and military situation throughout the world, with particular reference to the rôle of the Soviet Union, and Stalin's rôle both within the U.S.S.R. and as the leader of all peace-loving peoples. This last point was important because the deviations of the two " accused " arose from their attitude to Stalin and the U.S.S.R.

I emphasised the rôle of the British political leaders, the way in which their plans for war against Russia had so far miscarried and the fact that only the vigilance of the working-class had stopped the attack from being switched from Nazi Germany to the U.S.S.R.

By this means what would otherwise seem a trivial offence was revealed as a piece of treachery, a going over to the enemy camp at a critical moment. Those present by now felt even more strongly than before about what had been done by the accused.

The woman herself sat on a chair in full view of everyone present. She was a highly strung, neurotic type whose moods, as I talked, seemed at first to alternate between impatience and defiance. But the rest of those present saw the political significance of my long build-up, and before long she, too, was listening intently and with increasing shame.

That, of course, is the purpose of the " political statement " which forms the opening of all such " trials ". The sabotage of the guilty two had been purely on the ideological plane and so, if they and all present were to see the full seriousness of the charges, it was necessary to ensure that all felt that an attack on, or even lukewarm support for, Russia and its leaders amounted to an attack on the peace-loving peoples everywhere, upon the cause of communism and upon the British communists themselves. That meant that those who were disloyal to Russia sabotaged the cause for which our own Party members were living and for which in other parts of the world they were dying, too.

My " statement " had clearly registered, but the woman was still anxious to put up a show in front of so many people she knew so well. As I finished, without waiting for her turn, she began to question some of the policy as outlined by me and to declare that she thought that flattery of Stalin was overdone by the Party and we might as well have our eyes open about Russia. I let her run on, as she was now saying precisely those things with which she had still to be formally charged. As she talked with increasing excitement, those present began impatiently to interrupt her. Finally the local secretary, an aggressive, intolerant man with a club-foot, angrily stopped her, demanding that he should be allowed to proceed with his charges.

He first recited a list of her " crimes ", whilst she interrupted hysterically at every point. She had, it seemed, been instructed by the Party to work inside the local Co-operative Women's Guild, which she had from the start only done under protest and with an ill grace. But in that Guild, unknown to her, was another Party member who had reported that she had several times told the assembled women Co-operators that she had lived in Russia and knew from experience that there were still imperfect social conditions there, and that the worship of Stalin had been carried a great deal too far.

The branch secretary went on to relate how the local executive had taken this up with her. She had, however, defended her actions and had, despite warnings, continued them for some time. She had then been told that she would be reported to the local executive and there she had found a defender in the second accused, who had supported her.

When warned by the executive that she would be reported to the Party District office and that her expulsion would be urged, she had dropped out of her work in the Co-operative Guild, stopped talking in public about the shortcomings of Stalin and the Soviet Union, but had privately maintained her point of view and still persisted in doing so.

He ended with a bitter description of her as a Trotskyite, a petty-bourgeois deviationist and a saboteur who should be expelled from the Party's ranks. His recital of her crimes had raised the anger of those present and his demand for her expulsion met with loud and sustained applause.

Then others gave evidence along similar lines, showing a degree of hostility greater even than that normally reserved for capitalists and fascists. Time after time their evidence was interrupted by the accused woman and angry recriminations and personal abuse would follow from both sides. She maintained her mood of defiance and self-justification when she began her evidence, stressing the years she had spent in the Party, her Moscow experience and her conviction that the branch's instruction that she should work among "a lot of women" in the Co-operative Guild was absurd since she had no interest in such activities. But then she weakened and confessed that she had been indiscreet, and that the strictures of her comrades had driven her into a mood where she had said things which were inexcusable. She ended with an impassioned plea that those present should understand that she had not intended to betray the cause to which she had given her life. She would, she said, accept whatever punishment the Party considered necessary, but wept as she pleaded against her expulsion.

In my summing up I said that the issues had been obscured by the fact that "personalities" had featured far too much in the case, and in this the branch committee, and in particular the secretary, were also at fault. But, since the accused did not deny the main charges, I should have to report that in my view both she and her partner were guilty and my decision as to punishment would be made known at a later date.

As I presided over the proceedings I had, in fact, felt a certain sympathy with her, even though "deviations" on the part of one who had had such a long experience of the Party shocked and angered me. The sight of this obviously highly neurotic woman being baited by everyone in that crowded room seemed almost indecent to me and this influenced me when I came to recommending appropriate punishment.

In due course I handed in a full report to the Secretariat, along with the recommendation that her membership and that of her accomplice be suspended for twelve months, during which they were to accept full Party direction without having the rights of members, to be followed by twelve months' probation and then re-admittance to full membership of the Party.

My recommendations were accepted and carried into effect. But I later learned that it was felt that I had shown more leniency than the circumstances warranted. I was not asked to preside at any more such "trials", those chosen usually being leaders who prided themselves on being as ice-cold in their approach to people as they were to policies.

XIII

PARTY PEOPLE

IT IS difficult, I suppose, for anyone who has never been a Marxist, to understand how people who pursue immoral policies can in most cases nonetheless be likeable, intelligent and, at any rate when first they come to the Party, well-intentioned as well.

It is difficult, maybe, to believe that the hard, cold materialism of the Communist Party can really appeal to idealists and can be something for which men are prepared to die. Yet there is ample evidence all over the world to show that this is so.

What are the communists really like? Why do they come to communism? What were the people like who were running the various campaigns which I have described? Let me introduce you to a few.

First, the *Daily Worker* staff, the people who were my comrades and colleagues; who worked sometimes until they collapsed, who were prepared to be jailed for the paper at any time and, if necessary, to die for their communism. They were a mixed crowd. Starry-eyed idealists were in a minority. Most were seasoned Marxists.

It is not the purpose of this book to smear old friends who now see themselves as my foes. For that reason I shall use no names except where those I name cannot possibly be hurt by what I write. Some may be recognisable by their friends, but communists always make their friendships within the movement and so their friends will not be the type who will think less of them for practising their communism. At the worst I claim only that they were good Marxists.

There was, of course, the editor, the late William Rust—" Bill " to everyone from the messenger-boy upwards. But that was something of a piece of window-dressing. Bill Rust was not, in fact, very approachable. He made few friends and very few established any warm relationship with him.

He was by nature cold. He was all but incapable of warmth even though he could generate great heat. This was both his weakness and his strength. It enabled him to initiate and support policies without regard to what might be their human consequences, provided only that, on the basis of cold reasoning, they served the cause of communism.

He had been jailed more than once for his communism and had from his late 'teens been a Party functionary. He went to pains to perfect himself both in his journalism and in his study of Marxism.

He was well informed but had little culture. In some ways he was curiously adolescent. When complimentary tickets for the first nights of West End shows came to the office he claimed them and got there at all costs. He would boast of the number he had attended and of the actors and actresses whom he had met back-stage.

He would always be at the top of the Party but would never be a popular figure among those who knew him best. He had his followers, but they were usually among the place-seekers. Among the rank and file he was feared by some and respected by others. There was little love lost between Bill Rust and Harry Pollitt, the Party's General Secretary—so much so that Pollitt hardly set foot inside the *Daily Worker* building for years at a time.

Pollitt made mistakes. Rust hardly ever did. By carefully keeping an eye on Moscow, by caution and by playing off one leader against another he succeeded in holding his position in the Political Bureau and never losing it. The " P.B." is all-powerful in so far as it has to answer to no one below it. It answers only to Moscow—and Rust was a Moscow man.

I do not doubt his belief in Marxism. He was intellectually convinced that it was right, and emotionally, as a proletarian, was attracted by it. But he was also determined to get on. And having arrived at the top he was determined to remain there.

His Marxism told him that the revolution for which he worked must come. It would come in his generation. After it would come the dictatorship of the proletariat.

If he remained in the leadership, therefore, it mattered little what indignities, what sacrifices, might be demanded of him.

Sooner or later communism would triumph and he would be one of the mighty. He would have power. He would have the chance of retribution.

His very belief in his Marxism, as with some of the other leaders, was precisely what made him, in one sense, a super-careerist. But death got there first and he died heading a Party still far from making its leaders into British Stalins and Dimitroffs.

Then there was Cuthbert, a very different type. Public-school-and-university educated, his was a colourful personality. He loved intrigue, took a keen delight in debunking all and sundry, particularly the members of his own class. He made no attempt to disguise his class origin—as do so many bourgeois communists—but used it for the purposes of communism.

With an unshaven chin, two ancient overcoats worn one on top of the other and holes in his socks, he could, and did, still mix with Cabinet Ministers, aristocrats, even Royalty. And they all knew that in due course he would " blow the gaff " on them. But they mixed with him just the same.

Everything he did was unusual and so, of course, the way he came to the Party was unusual too. As told by himself it ran something like this:

He was working as a foreign correspondent in Berlin in the nineteen-twenties when he decided to take a week-end in an out-of-the-way hamlet in Bavaria to get away from it all.

He had booked at an obscure *pension*. When he got there it was raining and it never stopped for one moment the whole week-end. Stranded, and an inveterate reader, he looked for something to read. The only book he could find in the whole place was a tattered copy of a German edition of Marx's *Das Kapital*. Since there was no choice he sat down and read it. And it made him furious. Its forecasts, its conclusions seemed to this young member of the " ruling-class " outrageous.

But when he got back to Berlin he began to see the German capital through different eyes. There was a good deal that was unpleasant in post-war Berlin, and its decadence, which had missed him before because he was too close to it, now became apparent to him.

Once he turned away from his own circle there appeared to be signs in plenty of the pending collapse of German capitalism—millions of unemployed, appalling poverty side by side with blatant racketeering and also rapidly-growing revolutionary movements. Could that outrageous old bore Marx be right after all?

He put his question to his friends, then to his colleagues. He read other Marxist works.

The news that Cuthbert was going " Red " reached his London office. He was switched to the United States. " That will show him whether capitalism is collapsing," they said.

But he had only just arrived in the land where every bricklayer was said to have a car when the Wall Street crash came like a bolt from the blue.

" I had only to look out of my office window", he told me, in characteristically colourful terms, " to see stockbrokers and financiers jumping out of windows on to the street below all day long."

This was it. This was the collapse of capitalism. After this should come the Revolution. Old man Marx was right after all. He threw up his job—and a promising career—to return to England and there to join the Communist Party.

He took a job on the *Daily Worker* at not more than one twentieth of what he could earn on Fleet Street.

He fought recklessly in Spain, showing not the slightest fear of danger at any time. He worked night and day for the *Daily Worker* and enjoyed every minute of it.

He did not become a fake proletarian. He did not behave like an idealist. He just believed that his class was decadent and done for, that there was adventure and victory ahead for those who were today the scorned and rejected.

Or, by way of contrast, meet Richard, who came to the *Daily Worker* from a provincial paper. Richard was not one of the " names " on the paper. He was essentially anonymous. The only thing he shared with Cuthbert was a public school education. His parents all but disowned him when he became a communist. He was invalided out of the Army as a neurosis case.

He was an idealist, eager, naïve, and of the type that gets its leg pulled mercilessly yet never takes offence. At twenty-five years of age he seemed like an unsophisticated eighteen-year-old. I found him lovable, one hundred per cent decent—and exasperating in the extreme, for he would never make a good Marxist, lacking as he did any sort of subtlety or capacity for duplicity.

His early home background, as he recalled it to me, was one in which there was little happiness for him. It was a broken home. One of his parents had remarried and when he came home from school at holiday time he believed himself to be unwanted. He was sensitive and yearned for friendship. It was that, I should say, which drove him very young into the Party.

When he joined my reporting team he was the junior in the office and so was given the " cub " reporter jobs. For him the humdrum and the mediocre. The plums were for the people with " by-lines ".

When the V-1 flying-bombs began to fall on London, with many dropping in the immediate vicinity of the *Daily Worker* building, the covering of the resulting " incidents " became a daily part of his work.

But censorship was heavy and the stories came in time all to look very much the same. I had a heart-to-heart chat with Richard. The only hope of getting good stories, I told him, was to get something different. Get heroic stories of the way in which London's workers were standing up to the V-1 attack; stories which showed how the Civil Defence workers, ambulance men, wardens, rescue squads responded. Such stories would raise the standing of the paper with the common people, raise morale and at the same time help us to increase sales of the *Daily Worker* and so to spread the influence of the Party.

We agreed that the best way to get them would be for him to aim to be on the spot where the bombs fell before the defence services themselves arrived and, if possible, personally to assist with the rescue work.

We put the new policy into action at once.

When a V-1 was heard buzzing its way towards us he would make for a fanlight in the tape-machine room and scramble out on to the roof. As the bomb cut out and dropped he would watch for the smoke. If it was light in colour and hung about in the sky, the bomb had dropped on an open space. If it was dark and quickly disappeared, it had fallen on a built-up area, for its darkness was made of pieces of timber and stone—pathetic bits of people's homes, which quickly dropped to the ground again. And that meant a job for Richard, who would race to the scene of destruction.

The result was the best stories he had ever done. Time after time he came back covered with dust and plaster, sat down at his typewriter and produced stories which conveyed the action, the stoicism and the tragedy that he had just left behind. I told him that he was doing a good job. That, for him, was enough.

But I had no idea of what was actually happening until, one night, a group of Civil Defence workers came to see me. They wanted to pay a tribute to the courage of my young reporter. He was, they said, always on the scene before them, and so saw everything with all its initial horror.

Time after time when they had arrived they had found that already he had made his way into the wreckage bringing out the injured and the dead. His heroism had become almost a legend among those blitz-toughened workers.

Then, one night, he came back badly shaken. I had difficulty in getting him to talk, but at last got his story out of him.

From the *Daily Worker* roof he had watched the bomb cut out and fall in a nearby square. He had dashed to the spot and there found what had been a large tenement house thrown up, by a curious trick, into a huge cone, at the point of which he could see a human head protruding.

He scrambled to the top and grabbed it with both hands. But the head came away in his hands and he hurtled backwards down the rubble. It was just a head and no more, thrown there by the explosion. That incident was the last straw. His nerve cracked completely and I switched him to other work. But he had done the best job he could for communism. He had no regrets.

Michael, another of the anonymous reporters, was Irish, full of terrific enthusiasms, irresponsible and utterly undisciplined.

Brought up a Catholic he " lapsed ", for what are known as " confessional " reasons, having offended in some way against the Church's law on marriage.

In the Party such an action was not likely to bring condemnation; indeed, its theories on the home and family more than justified him in what he had done. For the militant atheist-communist no vows taken in church are binding and the Marxist theorists have laid it down that modern bourgeois marriage is no more than legalised prostitution. Yet I know, such was the influence of the home, the school and the Church from which he had come, with their constant emphasis upon the sanctity of the home, the family and the marriage vows, that he never managed to lose his sense of guilt even after he had joined the Party. The Party was to be an escape from all that. In practice, it could not efface the recollection of what he had done.

The more it forced itself into his consciousness, the harder he worked for the creed which said that everything sacred was so much nonsense. Yet, through it all, conscience would not die, and when he told me of it we agreed that it was proof of the appalling things that Catholics could do to the minds of men.

The editorial executive, of which I was a member, met each Wednesday morning to review the work of the past week and to plan for the coming one. A regular attender there, as representative of the Political Bureau, was R. Palme Dutt, vice-chairman of the Party. The Political Bureau was already represented in the persons of the editor, William Rust, and the assistant editor, J. R. Campbell, so that we had almost half of the P.B. present, with only that Party's National Organiser, the assistant secretary and the leaders of the industrial and propaganda departments absent.

But Dutt was the man with the greatest influence, whether it was at *Daily Worker* executive meetings or at the Political Bureau itself. Over many years he had been the man whom Moscow trusted and, no matter who might deviate from the Party line, Dutt never went wrong.

When both Pollitt and Campbell " went off the line " early in the war it was Dutt who stepped in, with the whole weight of the

Comintern behind him, and took charge. He was the most powerful man in the Party both by virtue of his ties with Moscow and his own personal qualifications too.

Like Rust, he was lacking in warmth, but unlike him he was almost entirely without humour. Almost, but not quite. For I have often seen him sitting in the low arm-chair which was reserved for him in the editor's room, long arms hanging down on either side so that his hands all but touched the ground, his shoulders shaking with silent laughter. But it was always at the expense of those whom he saw as his political opponents, and often enough they were those who thought they were his political friends.

Temperamentally he was the perfect Marxist. To him Marxism was a science, human sympathy and idealism appeared not to enter into his make-up at all. The changing world situation was something to be analysed with an ice-cold, scientific mind, and the necessary policies initiated with equal coldness. If the cause of communism was best served by a campaign on some humanitarian issue he would launch it with the appropriate words used to convey an emotional appeal.

If the need was to work for policies which in the event of their success would result in widespread suffering for millions, he could still make his decision and expound his case to the leaders with not a thought for the human consequences.

Rust would open an editorial discussion with a policy statement; for half an hour, perhaps, all present would put forward their views or, more probably, apply Rust's outline to their own sphere of work. Then Dutt, if he thought it necessary, would take his pipe out of his mouth and quietly and with an air of finality lay down the Party line. It might cut right across the editor's opening statement and make nonsense of all that had followed, but his contribution to the proceedings was never contradicted, never discussed.

His encyclopædic knowledge of Marxism was respected, but still more was the fact that Dutt's sources were of the sort which could not be questioned.

His intervention was not resented. It was recognised that he was right to let discussion remain " free " for as long as possible in the hope that those present might themselves arrive at the correct Marxist interpretation of events—which was usually the case. His interventions occurred only on occasions when the executive failed to see the line for itself, and all recognised that he had " sources " which they had not.

Dutt was one of the few who had reached communism by the purely intellectual path, with neither emotions, idealism nor even a real humanism playing any part in his evolution.

Harry Pollitt, the Party's General Secretary, is of a very different type. He is, in many ways, the proletarian " front " behind which Dutt operates, just as in France the proletarian Thorez screens the intellectual Duclos.

Dutt makes basic policy, in so far as he takes the Moscow directives and relates them to his analysis of current British conditions. Pollitt applies them to the every-day work of the Party, and, in particular, to its propaganda. Dutt initiates, Pollitt applies.

That does not mean that Pollitt feels himself to be a mere puppet. Once the line is " laid down " he has a wide range of initiative left open to him, applying policies already agreed upon and to defy which would mean resignation or expulsion, as he found in 1939.

Capable of terrific hatred, a characteristic which, like most Marxists, he has deliberately cultivated as necessary and desirable, Pollitt is also warm and human. Yet no matter whether a campaign is genuine or for purely propaganda purposes, he gives the same appearance of absolute conviction, and it is not easy to know just which is the real man behind it.

I recall, for example, how during our campaign for the Second Front a stick of bombs was dropped across a school in Kent, killing large numbers of children. Pollitt used that incident over and over again in his propaganda and brought tears to the eyes of thousands at great demonstrations in Trafalgar Square and all over Britain, by his reference to the children's " little velvet bodies ".

It was the type of demagogic phrase which is so useful in communist propaganda, but the seasoned Party members became utterly cynical about it. "Pollitt's little velvet bodies " became a joke in the Party. When groups of communists were heading for yet another demonstration called to demand that we " strike now in the West " someone would groan: " I suppose we shall have to put up with another dose of Harry's little velvet bodies."

I remember, too, how that campaign arising from the bombed school was first launched. On the *Daily Worker* we had had a more-than-usually uneventful day for such times. No important news had broken. There was nothing which really justified the conventional big headline types used to make the main story of the day appear important. Little reason really, I suppose, for producing a daily paper at all (which is not so unusual).

Then, at the last moment, the chief sub-editor came racing down to my office shouting, " Come along to the editor's room." When we got there he planked down before the editor a long strip of copy from the tape machine, saying, " There's an absolute god-send here. It's a marvellous story. Stick of bombs dropped on to a kids' school down in Kent. Scores of them killed. It's saved the edition, and if it doesn't make the customers fighting mad I'll eat my hat."

Within a few hours the Party's London district office was rushing out a leaflet exploiting the incident in the interests of the Second Front campaign.

Pollitt has children of his own and I would not for one moment suggest that he cared nothing for the deaths of those small children in Kent or for the mutilation of their little bodies. But, as a good Marxist propagandist, he would have to be equally willing to popularise policies which might lead to many other children being killed in the course of a British civil war, provided only that they served the cause.

It is Pollitt's warmth which makes him a good propagandist. He believes in his campaigns at the time, and so the genuine idealism and humanity which are in him find a channel for expression even though in the back of his mind all the time is the knowledge that such campaigns must not be made an end in themselves but must simply be made a means to the communist end.

That, I think, goes for a good many communists who were

brought in the first place to communism through a desire for social justice but who, after undergoing Marxist training, come in time to believe that it is not social justice but communism which should be their goal.

The colour and drama of the Spanish civil war brought many members into the Party, particularly from among the intellectuals who are well to the fore among the *Daily Worker* staff and in the leadership of the Party. There are certainly not many real proletarian types on the paper's staff, and they are in a minority in the top ranks of the Party too.

To see a cross-section of the Party's membership one had to go to the Annual Party Congress. There, although there were a disproportionate number of full-time officials and functionaries, the factory and trade union delegates were much in evidence too.

Most of these had come to the Party attracted by its social, economic and industrial campaigns but had, in the Party's jargon, been moulded into " steel-hardened cadres ", ready to lead strikes, hunger-marches or revolution as the opportunity occurred.

Most people who joined the Party did so because they were already in revolt. It might be against their own class, or against bad social conditions experienced in their own lives or observed as spectators with a sense of social guilt. It might be against religious or other restraints which they knew deep down to be right but against which they had kicked or wished to kick. It might simply be against a sense of inferiority or aspirations unfulfilled which made them seek personal power or the strength which comes from collective discipline. Or, quite often, it would be because they were good enough and intelligent enough instinctively to revolt against drifting along with no sense of purpose or direction, and the Party was able to draw simultaneously upon their reserves of both good and bad, utilising them for the cause of communism.

So with the women members, too, there was that same blend of idealism and careerism; that same curious admixture of good motives and evil practices. But women members are much fewer than men, and the woman, when she stays the course for any length of time (which few do), tends to take on the outward

impressions of the Marxist mould much more obviously than
does the average male member.

Go to any Communist Party Congress and watch the hard-
faced women who go to the rostrum. The hatred which the
Party kindles and uses is often quite shockingly apparent in eyes
as hard as those of a Soho prostitute and lips as tight as those
of a slumland money-lender. One does not need to go to
Rumania to see Anna Pauker.

It is something of which the Party leaders are themselves
painfully aware. Always they are seeking to attract to the Party
" typical working-class housewives ", but few of those who come
to the Party are in that category at the start and still less remain
in it for long.

" We get women into the Party, and they are all right for just as
long as they remain obscure," one Political Bureau member
complained to me, " but within twelve months of our turning
them into Marxists they are about as attractive as horses."

The Party aims by its training to produce " men of steel ". But
" women of steel " attract neither other women nor even the men
of steel themselves. " Steel-hardened cadres " may become good
leaders—but they are not the sort you fall in love with. Thus,
the working-class housewife or the fresh young girl who comes
into the Party is at once the centre of attention for a number of
reasons, personal and political. She is useful for breaking down
the suspicions of other women and so is seen as an effective
" front ", and at the same time she is a welcome relief from the
steely, hard-faced, betrousered women who have made their way
to the top and who are, in Party parlance, so utterly unbed-
worthy.

But the result is that, if the female recruit really develops as a
Marxist (and few do), she will soon be indistinguishable from the
others. It would, of course, be wrong to suggest that it happens
in every case. But it is general enough to be a matter of concern
to the Party leaders and even from time to time to feature on
agendas as a problem to be solved.

The woman rank-and-filer's career in the Party is often short
and sharp. I think of the starry-eyed attractive little middle-class
girl who came into the Party on a wave of enthusiasm for the

" Russian glory " and came up to London in order the better to be able to help the Party. For a short time she lived in a Central London hostel, connecting up with the local branch of the Party. Its membership was, as is the case in most of the Central London branches, made up of people of a variety of nationalities, all excessively sophisticated, all very bohemian.

Within a few weeks she was living with a bearded, " arty " intellectual, many years her senior; soon she was defiantly flaunting her pregnancy. I lost track of her for some time and then her parents got in touch with me. Contact between them appeared to have been very loose, but now, at last, they were trying to find out what had happened to her. I made enquiries and found that by this time she had had a second child and I had to tell them so. Very worried and even more scandalised, they went off to find her. She was still under twenty years of age.

It would, of course, be absurd to pretend that such things happen only to girls who are communists; indeed, one might say that the communist girls are more likely to have the fun and less likely to have the babies than most.

The story of the little girl coming from the provinces to the big city and there quickly becoming pregnant is as old as the big cities themselves. It happens to little Irish barmaids and servant girls from villages whose Catholic faith is too strong to give communism even the slightest foothold.

The difference lies in the fact that the little Irish girl, or even the English country girl from a home where religious influences are probably much weaker, knows that she has done wrong, feels guilty and so conceals it if she can.

The communist girl has been given a theory which tells her that she has done no more than defy outworn, bourgeois conventions and that in so doing she has demonstrated her freedom.

Communists have, since the days of Marx, ridiculed all attempts to establish communist communities within a capitalist society. The practice of the economic aspects of communism must wait, they have said, until the communist economic and social system has been established.

Not unnaturally, devoting their lives to the Cause as they do, communists have wanted to practise as much as they could of the teaching they have accepted but have been frustrated in most directions.

It may be a long time yet to the Revolution and still longer to the practice of full communism. But they have discovered that the theories of Marx and Engels on the home, family and kindred subjects can be practised right here and now.

There must have been many men who have quietly dropped their Party activities because their wives have sensed the threat to the home which communist practice represents and have confronted them with the ultimatum: " Either choose the Communist Party or me."

It is true that the communists' public propaganda is not today as outspoken on these matters as it was in the Party's early days.

But the same theories are taught as before and it is not, therefore, surprising that their practice continues much as ever it did.

Yet whilst this undoubtedly attracts some it also repels others. There is a great deal in communism which clashes with human nature and no one becomes more quickly aware of this than the ordinary working-class housewife.

The majority of women who come into the Party soon leave again when they see where they are going. Of the majority of those who stay, some remain uncorrupted but never become good Marxists, and others steadily lose their womanly characteristics as they climb the ladder of Party leadership.

The Party, too, has a human problem with its youth. Youths who have been converted into " steel-hardened cadres " become arrogant, excessively self-assertive and self-confident. They have been trained in leadership, hope one day to lead millions and expect it to be soon. They are equipped with invincible and infallible Marxist theories which enable them to explain everything. For them there are no mysteries, they have the solution for all things.

Those are, to some extent, the natural weaknesses of adolescence. But in a Communist Party youth those weaknesses are promoted into virtues, they are cultivated, developed, organised and become his strength as a Marxist. But they also make him unbearably unattractive to others.

Facing pictures: 1. R. Palme Dutt, vice-chairman, but the most powerful man in the Party.

2. A Staff Meeting in the *Daily Worker* office, showing the author on the left at the rear.

This tendency is also one of which the communist leaders are painfully aware and constant efforts are made to combat it. Organisationally it reflects itself in a chronically undersized Young Communist League and an over-youthful Communist Party. The reason for this is that when teen-age youths link up with communism they should, in theory, join the Y.C.L., whose job it is to train them in communism with a view to their passing into the Party when they are older. But the teen-ager who becomes a communist will quickly feel too superior by far to belong to youth clubs or to mix with other youths. He must join the Communist Party, the organisation of the dialectical materialists. And so into the Communist Party he goes, leaving the vital work among youth to take care of itself.

That, for example, is why, although communism in Britain has undoubtedly influenced youth very considerably, the Y.C.L.'s total membership remains at only a couple of thousand. It helps to explain, too, why the Communist Party membership's average age normally keeps well below thirty.

XIV

THE INTERNATIONAL IS DEAD

THROUGHOUT the first few years of my work as *Daily Worker* news editor, the paper's campaigns, which are, of course, always keyed to those of the Party, remained much the same: the demand for a Second Front, the fight against "reactionaries and anti-Soviet elements" within the Coalition parties, the constant exposure of fascist and anti-semitic activities, and the demand for increased production in industry, through greater effort and improved managerial efficiency and by means of joint production committees.

For the first time we were having seriously to think along constructive lines. Communist shop stewards were interesting themselves in how to increase factory output (which would have

Facing picture: Harry Pollitt, the Party's General Secretary.

F

been treachery in the past) and we were publicising what they did with the usual communist thoroughness. We had our heroes of labour, our Stakhanovites whom we built up in every way possible.

It is often said that the Communist Party organises only the malcontents, those incapable of making anything but mischief. It is true that in the Party are some who would be rebels in Paradise itself, and who are pathologically incapable of constructive thought. But they are a minority.

The way in which the bulk of the Party members adjusted their minds to the new policy in that period, giving leadership for constructive purposes and themselves setting the example, becoming first-rate members of production committees and initiating output drives, for as long as the Party dictated, proved beyond all doubt the latent qualities of many of those whom the Party attracts.

The communist campaigns of that period were fairly straightforward and little guidance from outside the country would have been required to keep undeviatingly on the International Party line. No great crisis therefore was precipitated by the widely-publicised dissolution of the Communist International.

The British and other Party leaders had, as usual, been kept in the dark about the Russians' pending move and we first learned of it from the same sources as those of the rest of the Press.

There were awkward points about it which demanded some explanation for the rawer Party members themselves. We had always publicly denied that the Communist International's policies were dictated by the Russian Party or the Soviet Government—although we realised that even if this were so it would be permissible, since at all costs the communist victory in Russia must be preserved.

Now, however, the Russians had dictated that the C.I. was to be brought to an end. If they could do that, then clearly the C.I. must all along have been their pawn. That was the bewildered reaction of a few of the rank and file.

It was a point which members of my staff raised, too, at our morning editorial meeting. But their concern was with the problem of how to provide convincing answers to those non-communists and communist sympathisers who posed this question.

The decision was to ignore that awkward aspect of the dissolution entirely, which is always the Party's propaganda tactic when some such situation arises.

People would want to know how it affected the war effort. We would show that the people of Britain would be tremendously helped by this because the Americans, who had been so suspicious of Russian motives, would now back the war effort more wholeheartedly.

And soon the Soviet Monitor was coming to our aid. It had already proved its usefulness. Now without the C.I. it would be indispensable.

Soviet Monitor is a department of the Soviet Embassy in London: it enjoys diplomatic privilege, is completely above board —and is one of the smartest things in its own way the Russians ever did.

Before the war the Communist International's own S.U. Press agency supplied the Communist Party Press of the world with news of Russian achievements and with items concerning the activities of communist organisations everywhere. It also put out in full the texts of all the major Russian policy documents and the speeches of Soviet and Communist International leaders.

Thus it supplied what amounted to daily directives for those who knew the jargon, could read between the lines and knew how to take " leads " from the examples quoted by it. The day-to-day messages received by the communist Press went back, in due course, to the Communist Party national headquarters as their day-to-day directives, too.

Then, when Russia came into the war, S.U. Press for a time devoted almost the whole of its cables to the progress of the war on the Eastern Front, to the calls to action issued by the Soviet Government and to the various Orders of the Day.

But as the Anglo-Soviet alliance developed at top-level, so S.U. Press was seen as being too limited and sectarian in its range and methods.

The Russians were no longer depending first and foremost upon struggling little Communist Parties as their allies. They now had the political leaders of Great Powers to operate through as well, who might not be enamoured of such hole-and-corner publicity methods. S.U. Press was suppressed.

Soon, in its place, came Soviet Monitor, a creation of the Embassy, approved at top British levels. It was installed in its own building with all the necessary staff and equipment for monitoring all Soviet broadcasts and for their duplication and distribution to the national Press.

As an Embassy undertaking it had, of course, no official link with the British Communist Party. True, most of those employed there were British communists, including some people well known within the Party's ranks. But that was easily explained by the fact that, regrettably, there was a past of hostility to the Soviet Union which had resulted in few Englishmen learning the Russian language. Only the communists had bothered.

There were, of course, White Russian emigrés equipped to do the work, but the Embassy could hardly be expected to employ them. Indeed, since attack is the best form of defence, the Embassy itself protested many times behind the scenes at the employment by the Ministry of Information's Russian Department of precisely such people.

And so a staff of Russian journalists and British communists (mostly with Communist International experience) began painstakingly to record and translate every Russian broadcast, and to issue them in bulletin form every few hours throughout the day. It was all part of helping Britain to get to know and understand the Russians.

Some of the broadcasts were of obvious world significance. Many were, to the average national newspaperman, of no possible interest at all: internal broadcasts in impossible jargon which might appear as a tribute to the thoroughness of the people at the Monitor building in taking down absolutely everything the Russians put on the air but fit only for the waste-paper basket.

And into the waste-paper basket of every national paper but one went the pages of duplicated material, morning, noon and night. That one exception was, at first, the I.G.I. agency which I was editing. The more obscure items from the Monitor went into the I.G.I. bulletin and so out by post each day to every leading communist, every Party trade union leader or prominent shop steward in the land. And a second copy of the full bulletin went to Party headquarters at King Street.

When the *Daily Worker* ban was lifted and I.G.I. was wound up, the one exception then became the *Daily Worker*.

A single issue of the Monitor might not appear to reveal a great deal. Taken over a period and followed by those with the necessary Marxist training it provided a clear picture of almost all the various trends in Soviet foreign policies, present and pending; it revealed the Marxist aims behind the propaganda and ensured that Russia's influence should be instrumental in determining the paper's line—and, in due course, the Party's policy on the questions of the day.

It might not be discreet for the Embassy to issue obvious communist directives to the national Press nor even to send them privately to the *Daily Worker*, but if a directive was needed for communists everywhere, then a highly doctrinal broadcast in impossible jargon directed to the toilers and peasants of some far-away Asiatic Soviet Republic would take care of that.

So, when the news came through that the Communist International was being dissolved, we were all the more grateful for the existence of Soviet Monitor and for the foresight of those who had brought it into being.

No immediate public result of the winding up of the international body was visible at all. Meetings were held at all levels of the Party, where its significance was explained. There two explanations were given which were, in fact, mutually contradictory but which could be used as need arose.

The first was the " doctrinal " one that the national parties, after nearly a quarter of a century, were now " mature " and at last capable of standing on their own feet. In the past, as struggling infant bodies, they had needed a world organisation to link them together.

But in the new world which the defeat of fascism (and with it world reaction) would bring to birth, each country would be mature enough, rid of its enemies from within and without, to develop its communism along its own national lines, taking account of national traditions.

The second explanation was that in any case the first job for communists everywhere was to see that the Soviet Union did not suffer military defeat. If that was to be the case, then the whole-hearted, unstinted aid of America would above all else be needed. The Yanks were proving " difficult " because of their suspicion of their own Reds and this clever move would dispel the last fears of the noisy but naïve backwoodsmen.

If the doctrinal answer sometimes failed to convince our own members, the second never did.

When the members had been " won for the new line ", changes began slowly to be made in the Party. We were to develop along new, " British " lines.

The good sense of this was obvious. The war situation, the terrific feeling for Russia, the new tolerance for communism at home, the new, constructive policy of the Party in industry, all gave us opportunities such as had never appeared possible before. The chance of building up a large mass Party had come at last if we used it aright.

There had undeniably so far been something " alien " about the Party. It was this which had proved one of the stumbling-blocks to mass recruitment in the past.

In the '30s, during the Popular Front period, we had tried to strike the national note. We had held great demonstrations in the big cities under the slogan " The Past is Ours " aimed at proving that we were really the most " British " of all Parties. We had claimed not only John Ball and Wat Tyler (the fourteenth-century peasant revolt leaders) as our natural ancestors, but Cromwell, Milton, Bunyan, Shakespeare and a host of others as well, carry-ing their enormously enlarged pictures through the streets in procession.

Now we would complete the process. We changed the Political Bureau into the Political Committee, the Central Committee into the Executive Committee. At headquarters we had had an anonymous Secretariat. Now we had a General Secretary and Assistant General Secretary. Our famous " cells ", the smallest but most important units of the Party, became " groups " in-stead. Party " locals " became " branches "; " aggregate meetings " became " members' meetings ".

Away with the narrow sectarianism of the past and on to a great mass Party, equipped to mould the post-war anti-fascist world!

XV

UNDERSTANDING THE ENEMY

BUT at that time the fascist enemy abroad was far from being defeated. A bitter war of attrition was being fought on the soil of the Socialist Fatherland. The lives and homes of Soviet citizens, inhabitants of our " Sovietland so dear to every toiler ", were being worn down in bitter, grinding battles.

Children who had had the incomparable good fortune to be born under Socialism were now starving in mid-winter sieges. The greatest achievements of the Soviet State, its crowning glories, such as the Dnieper Dam, were being sacrificed, the peaceful fields of the collective farms were being turned into battle-grounds, soaked in the blood of the citizens of our brave new sixth of the world mingled with that of the fascist cannibals.

And still there was no Second Front. In the office, in the Party branch meetings, everywhere where communists met together they were beginning to say : " If lives must be lost before this war is won why must they all be Soviet lives ? Better that they should be of those of the decadent old world of the West. Time it was British and American lives for a change." " They're talking of Britain and the U.S. providing the steel whilst Russia provides the lives—good Soviet lives," we said. " They're waiting for Hitler and Stalin to bleed each other white." As usual, there was sufficient substance in the charges to make the propaganda get across.

I felt a colossal hatred for the plotters. There was nothing phoney about it even though I might be using it for propaganda purposes. It coloured all my writings and so helped to increase the hatred of those who read them.

For years I had dreamed of what we would do when we had set up our Workers' State as the Russians had done. It would be different from theirs, no doubt, for our traditions and even our temperament were different. If I, by being in the leadership of the Party and amongst the moulders of its thought, could do something to fashion it after my own heart, then so much the better. But it was upon Russia that my hopes for the moment must be pinned.

Day after day I exposed the British fascists as the friends of Nazism. They were the focal point of a deep hatred which expressed itself in the bitter daily attacks which I wrote. The old slogan: " Smash fascism or fascism will smash you " took on a new significance.

I made it my business to learn about every little fascist and near-fascist body and built up considerable files on them all.

Into those files went details of over fifty different fascist, near-fascist and crypto-fascist organisations which sprang up at that time. Some were led by would-be Führers who were trying to cash in on the enforced inactivity of the big fascist leaders. Some were bodies started by the genuine Mosleyites whose policy seemed to be to create a multitude of small bodies whose importance and numbers would appear to be too small to bother with, but which, in fact, would in time add up to something of some significance.

Into the files, too, went material about several thousand individual members of the various fascist organisations, all carefully card-indexed, and constantly referred to. I submitted reports to the Political Bureau on the growth and development of the fascist bodies. The Soviet Embassy also asked for, and received from me, summaries of the situation from time to time. The growth of fascism in Britain would, within a week or two of receipt of my memoranda by the Embassy, be featured in the Soviet Press and on Moscow Radio.

Gradually the smaller fascist fry were being released from detention. And gradually the amount of political anti-semitism appeared to be growing as a consequence. More fascist slogans appeared on the streets by night. The little neo-fascist bodies of mushroom growth stepped up their propaganda.

The drawers of the imposing metal filing cabinet which stood at my elbow as I worked became increasingly full and were ever more frequently referred to.   I kept it locked, for several times ex-detainees, stung by my writings, came to try and " get " me or penetrated to my room, even in working hours, to try and raid the files.

Once I found one in our library, quietly going through our records.   I recognised him and turned him out, but a solicitor's letter which came to me a day or two later showed that he had been preparing notes for a libel case against me from our own material.   The letter was a try-on which we ignored.   I heard no more.

On another day a fascist made his way to my office but for a very different purpose.   A loose-jawed, pitiable creature, he had just come out of detention and offered to sell me information about his fellow-fascists who were still in jails and detention camps or to provide me with " background " on them as they were released.   He offered his services at what he called " the usual rates ".

He insisted that he was still a national socialist, still believed in British Union and in Mosley.   " But a man has to live and no one will employ me."

I told him I would pay him for any information I actually published, and his reports came in for a while.   Most went into my files, only a few were published.   He soon tired of being paid for so few items and, presumably, took his " services " elsewhere.

Each time a former fascist was released I published his record and then tried to keep an eye on him to see if anyone employed him.   As soon as he got a job I published his employer's name and address and the local Party would work to get a strike if he were not at once dismissed.

In addition to demanding the re-imprisonment of those whom the Government released I demanded that others, never inside the Government's net, should be jailed.   Among these was the Duke of Bedford, the landowner head of the British People's Party, who was, in fact, a Christian pacifist.

That Party's secretary, John Beckett, was in jail, so were other executive members. So, too, would the Duke be, I argued in the paper, were he not the Duke. Time after time I demanded his imprisonment. Questions were asked in Parliament. Meetings were held to demand his arrest. Trade unions, Labour Parties, Trades Councils began to pass resolutions naming the Duke.

Then, one day, I got a letter which seemed to me to be one of the oddest I had ever received—and the news editor of any national newspaper gets many in the course of his working week. It began:

" March 14, 1943

" DEAR SIR,

" I notice that you have been insistent lately in demanding my imprisonment and the suppression of political organisations of which you disapprove. There are certain questions I would like to ask you and points I would like to put to you, not in any unfriendly spirit, but in order that I may understand better the communist viewpoint. . . ."

There followed five hand-written pages, arguing that, in refusing men the right to say what they thought, I was different in no fundamental respect from Hitler and the Nazis.

The Duke ended with the advice " never to form a final adverse judgment of a man, no matter how black his apparent crimes or how trustworthy his accusers, until you have heard his defence."

The courteous tone of the letter astonished me but, apart from that, it seemed no more than a joke to be shown around the office.

My political world was one in which there was little courtesy shown, least of all to a political opponent whom we described as a sinister crank.

The letter seemed to reflect an extraordinary naïvety. Was I supposed to be shocked that I should be charged with using the methods of my opponents? That was the nature of the fight in the modern world. In the past, political opponents might possibly have been courteous to each other. They killed each other today, or, at the best, put them in jail.

In a collapsing capitalism methods of violence were a necessity.

We could not bring our new world to birth without a surgical operation, and by the very nature of capitalist crisis we expected the defenders of the old regime to attempt to maintain it by violence too.

To that extent we were both using the same methods and for that reason I was justified in demanding his imprisonment.

I decided that his courtesy was bluff, a political tactic such as we ourselves might use under similar circumstances. The fascists, having failed to silence me by threats, were now going to try kid-glove methods. I wrote a particularly bitter piece demanding his immediate imprisonment.

That was my answer.

A few days later a woman came to see me at my office. She told me that she was certain that I had got the Duke all wrong. He was, she said, a kindly man whom she had known for years. He was, she insisted, neither an anti-semite nor a fascist, had always been on the side of progress, and the attitude he was taking up with regard to the war arose from the fact that he was anti-war. There was no question of his supporting Hitler.

If I met him—and she was prepared to arrange a meeting—I would find that she was right and that I was wrong. With a journalist's nose for a story, I agreed that if she could fix things up I would meet him.

It was arranged and I was taken in her car from a sleepy Bedfordshire station one Sunday afternoon to meet him. It was a curious setting for a curious meeting.

The Duke's large mansion had been requisitioned by the military and there were armed guards to keep him—along with the rest of the public—out. In his extensive parkland roamed his world-famous herd of rare deer, but it had all been taken over by the Air Ministry. He was living in a lodge on his own estate, from the windows of which this anti-war Duke could see the fighter planes taking off all day long. As we drove up the long drive I could see in the woods on either side great piles of shells and ammunition stacked high for War Office use.

Around the parkland had been erected barbed wire and he had no more right than anyone else to go through it. He had succeeded to the dukedom (he was formerly the Marquess of

Tavistock) since it had all been taken over, and since then he had neither lived in the house nor set foot on the land which he had inherited.

All this he told me as we sat in the sunshine on the little lawn of the lodge which was his home. He opened the conversation with, " So you want me to be deprived of my liberty and caged in a cell, do you ? "

I replied that I did, that in time of war such things were necessary, that had the war taken a different course it would be I who would be in jail.

The entire conversation was most courteous and friendly. We argued for hours. I told him what I thought of fascists and anti-semites and said I thought that, whether he realised it or not, he was both or, alternatively, was being used by such people, which amounted to the same thing.

He, in return, talked pacifism and Christian tolerance, denying my charges but without convincing me that he was not equivo-cating. As he talked at length against the war I thought of the fight taking place at that moment on Soviet soil and my blood boiled. His world or mine, which is it to be? I asked myself.

We stopped awhile to go inside for a pleasant tea, then out again for several more hours of argument, after which he saw me into the car in which I had been fetched. As I left he said: " It has been a pleasure meeting you and hearing your point of view. I trust that you, too, understand me better now."

" I do," I said, " and I am more convinced than ever that you should be behind bars—and I shall say so."

The Duke waved me a friendly farewell.

On the following day I published my story. It began with the assertion that after four hours of argument with him I was more certain than ever that the Duke of Bedford should be in jail.

I went on to outline the views he had expressed to me. The result was a renewal of the demand by organisations all over the country for his internment.

There was a curious sequel to the incident some time later. A pacifist paper in which the Duke was interested quoted my article at some length and then went on to denounce me in forthright terms. That was the sort of fight that I as a communist understood.

But in the following issue of the paper the Duke repudiated the editor, saying that he had, in fact, been struck by my sincerity and regretting that I had been attacked the previous month. I told myself that this was, in fact, the cleverest tactic of all.

But the episode left me wondering whether, even though his politics were detestable, his Christian values might not represent something which, in the days when social systems were not cracking up, might have been worth-while.

Then came something else to keep my anti-fascist campaign going with renewed vigour. The Duke had told me how several alleged fascists whom he had known had, whilst in jail, become Catholics.

I had for a long time watched the Catholic Press for what we called " dirt ", which meant things we could attack. And I had become increasingly aware that, despite the prevailing " red haze ", sections of the Catholic Press were conspicuously cool towards the Soviet Union.

The *Catholic Herald* appeared to be taking the view that though the fight on the Eastern Front was an important one and its outcome was of great military consequence this provided no new argument for suddenly saying that the Soviet regime was good when all along you had said it was evil.

Such a line, of course, cut right across all we were trying to achieve by our propaganda. It made me more determined than ever to attack the Catholic Church whenever the opportunity arose.

From Party headquarters one day came some marked copies of a paper called the *Weekly Review*, accompanied by a note saying that I should at once expose it as a fascist platform.

Each of those whose articles had been marked, said the writer —a member of the Political Bureau—was a fascist, and he went on to give what purported to be their fascist records. The writer of the note described the paper as a Catholic one with a fascist policy.

This fitted in exactly with what I had expected. If some of

the fascists were becoming Catholics, then what more natural than that they should use the Catholic Press for their propaganda?

The *Weekly Review* was new to me—and I had thought that I knew all the most reactionary publications in the land. One glance showed that it was more outspoken in its suspicions of the future intentions of the Russian leaders than most I had read.

In one issue was an article on the corporate state, which failed to condemn it out of hand. In another was a not unsympathetic reference to Franco.

Here was something worth exposing. The fascists had done their job well—and more cleverly and subtly than I had expected.

I looked up the names of the writers who had been described as fascists in my card index but learned little more about most of them that way. There was a Jones; said to have been active with the British Union of Fascists in South Wales. The card index, not surprisingly, showed there had been several of that name active there.

There was H. D. C. Pepler, about whom the cards revealed nothing. Then there was R. D. Jebb. Here things appeared better, for an R. Jebb had been a Mosleyite prospective Parliamentary candidate in pre-war days. In addition there was Jenks, whom I had recorded as having been an agricultural writer who had contributed to B.U.F. publications, and A. K. Chesterton, who was described as co-leader with William Joyce of the National Socialist League, a body to which he had never belonged. About the printers, the Ditchling Press, I had no records.

I proceeded to check up on all those about whom there was any doubt. This was an important political job and it was going to be done well. When I had got it all in order I would not pull my punches. For years I had said that the Catholic Church was fascist. Here, at last, was the chance to prove it.

But next day came an angry phone call to the editor from Party headquarters. Why hadn't Douggie Hyde run the big fascist exposure story today? Here was a chance to tie up the Catholics with the fascists and he was letting grass grow under his feet.

" You must run it at once," said the editor, and, although I protested that it still needed checking, the decision was taken to go right ahead with a " red-hot " article. " We would welcome a court case," I was told, and the political value of a good case was clear enough.

On the morning after it appeared I received a number of phone calls from people who told me of other papers in which the same allegedly " fascist bunch " had succeeded in getting a foothold.

One man, a fellow-traveller, took the trouble to come round from Fleet Street to tell me more about Pepler, with whom he worked, and to congratulate me about my " splendid " exposure.

I told the editor, and the result was two more articles along similar lines.

Those three articles were among some of the most popular I had ever written in the *Daily Worker*. To blacken the Catholic Church and the fascists at once was the perfect communist exposure.

But I still went on checking and, despite the many congratulatory phone calls and letters and a few from superior people who expressed surprise that I had not got around to this particular hornets' nest long ago, I began secretly to wonder whether the facts supplied had all been in order.

Then came the day when I had one writ for libel after another served upon me, from all the writers with the exception of Jenks, and from the printers and publishers besides. We rubbed our hands in anticipation.

It was just what we wanted. Here was the chance to come before the public as *the* anti-fascist paper and *the* anti-fascist party. At the same time we would smear the Catholic Church as much as ever was possible.

The facts that I had the details of the fascist network at my finger-tips, was regarded as the foremost Left-wing writer on the question and in addition had had practical experience of defending myself and others in court all guaranteed, it was felt, that this would be a really big and successful case.

The aim of every communist in a capitalist country is to " do a Georgi Dimitroff ", in other words to dominate the court, turning from accused to accuser, using it as a platform for communist propaganda. This, I was told, must in its own way be another Reichstag Fire trial.

For that to be possible I must understand my enemy. I had no previous knowledge of the *Weekly Review*. Now I must acquire it. I sent a messenger to its office to buy as many bound volumes of past issues as possible and directed that a copy of the paper be brought to me on the morning of publication each week.

As I studied it, the paper's politics nauseated me. Its social policies seemed crankily, even self-consciously, reactionary.

But it seemed clear that what it stood for was not even by our standards full-blooded fascism. If I was to make out a case I should have to use to the full every tolerant reference to the corporate state, every failure to condemn Franco. I should have to play up its refusal to pay the appropriate tributes to the military genius of Stalin and the liberating rôle of the Red Army.

Most of all I should have to play up the names of those one-time fascists who had written for it. It should be possible, in the prevailing war atmosphere, to get the *Daily Worker's* first favourable decision in a capitalist court.

Libel actions are leisurely affairs and we calculated that, by the time the cases reached the High Court, the Second Front would have been opened, England would be under fire, British lads would be dying as Red Army men had died and the atmosphere would be more than ever hostile to anything that smelt of fascism or support for the Nazis. In the light of that, even the discovery that there had been a confusion of names on the part of the person who had supplied the original information did not daunt us.

R. D. Jebb, I found, was not the R. Jebb who had been a fascist candidate. The most careful research failed to reveal any personal or organisational connection on his part with the fascists at any time.

Jones, enquiries proved, had not been a pre-war fascist in South Wales. Other Joneses perhaps, but not this one, for he had no links, past or present, with the fascists.

Pepler was in an exactly similar position. No amount of

denunciation of him as a fascist could provide him with either a fascist past or present. The Ditchling Press's past was beyond reproach.

But, we reasoned, these men were reactionaries, it might be possible to make their policies appear fascist in the light of prevailing conditions and we could blacken them to a point where any judge could be forgiven for being prejudiced against them.

We got counsel's advice but were told we should settle their cases out of court and fight only what we hoped would be the "safe" one. We played for time, let the months drag on and left it to a solicitor whom we knew could well look after our interest.

Meanwhile I continued my studies of the *Weekly Review*. But although nine-tenths of its contents never failed to make me angry, there was always something in it I found interesting.

I first became aware of this when one day I found in it a quotation from William Morris. For such people to quote my Morris seemed blasphemy.

Then I found that the parts of the paper I had been deliberately missing because, being non-political, they had no bearing on my case, were very much in tune with Morris. It was almost humiliating to discover that these people were medievalists—and so was I.

For years almost my only relaxation had been reading Chaucer and Langland, visiting pre-Reformation churches, listening to plainsong and Gregorian chant or spending hours in the Victoria and Albert Museum studying the craftsmanship of the thirteenth and fourteenth centuries, revealed in gloriously illuminated books and, equally, in perfectly designed things for every-day use.

These were, it seemed, the *Weekly Review*'s interests too, and the articles and poems which reflected that interest were no less interesting because they appeared side by side, perhaps, with something which was political poison to me.

It was disquieting to discover that people occupying the exact opposite of my own ideological position could nonetheless have similar cultural interests and—who knew?—perhaps even similar dreams as well.

I resolved the problem by putting the medievalist attraction of the *Weekly Review* into one water-tight compartment of my mind and its politics into another—and continued to read the one part with enjoyment and the rest with fury, which was added to rather than lessened by the underlying paradox.

XVI

SECOND FRONT

HIGH spot of the anti-fascist campaign which I had started came when Sir Oswald Mosley, leader of the British Union of Fascists, was released from jail on grounds of ill-health.

From a secret Party member working in the Home Office we got news of his pending release. I immediately wrote a " forecast " to this effect, backing it up with a pre-war picture of Mosley in full S.S. uniform, calculated to arouse maximum indignation.

Our members in industry began at once to get resolutions passed in the factories. The first, as is usual on such an issue, came from a clothing factory in North London, followed by another from a cabinet works. Quite deliberately we used the Jewish fear of fascism and anti-semitism for our own political ends. It made the Stepney branch our strongest, with over 1,000 members. It was the Party's greatest asset in Jewish areas all over Britain.

Yet nowhere will one find a more cynical anti-semitism than in the Party itself. And the most anti-semitic communists of all are those of Jewish origin. Just as the Catholic-turned-communist tends to become the most anti-Catholic, so the man or woman from a religious Jewish home who turns communist will become anti-Jewish, identifying his religion with his race. In his anxiety to " emancipate " himself from earlier influences he will try to live down his Jewish origin and in so doing he will often react viciously against his old background and his former associates.

The Jewish communist who, in Party circles, says the most

outrageously anti-semitic things can do so without reproof. For coming from him it is seen merely as a proof of his successful " emancipation ".

Our reputation as the great opponents of anti-semitism paid handsome dividends during the next few weeks. Resolutions poured in, setting a snowball rolling which became the biggest thing in the paper's history.

Housewives took petitions from door to door demanding that Mosley should " remain behind bars ", they collected names in stores and fish queues. Men in the Forces set round-robin letters in motion to which the names of officers as well as men were appended. In the factories members of the management in many cases signed petitions or supported resolutions.

When Mosley was released nonetheless, I wrote one of the bitterest articles I had ever penned and again it rang the bell. Within a few days thousands of resolutions and petitions, allegedly backed by hundreds of thousands of people demanding his reinternment, were reported to us.

It confirmed us in our view that the anti-fascist campaign I had built up was one of our biggest political assets and was therefore to be continued at all costs.

Another one-time fascist leader who had been released was John Beckett, who was associated with the Duke of Bedford. In my post one day came an envelope addressed to me, inside which, however, was a letter written to Beckett, confirming the booking of a room in a hotel in Scotland for a small meeting of members of his Party.

A few days later I received a courteous note from Beckett in which he said that he was enclosing a letter which had come to him in an envelope bearing his name and address but the contents of which were clearly intended for me.

The security people at the post office, opening the correspondence of both communists and fascists alike, had, it seemed, had the two letters out at the same time and had put them back into the wrong envelopes.

Communists do not write courteous letters to fascists and so I did not return Beckett's letter to him. Instead, I had a crypto-communist at the appropriate date and time in the hotel in

Scotland and was, as a consequence, able to run an exclusive story of his Party's intentions.

As time went on my responsibilities on the paper grew. My news-editing had been a success and it was agreed that the paper's journalistic standards had been raised considerably. The quality of the news-editing was referred to in the professional Press and I had the satisfaction of knowing, and being told, that I was doing a good job for the Party.

When, each year, nominations for the Party's executive were called for, my name went forward from various Party branches, but, after consultation, it was decided that I should not go for election since my work on the paper eclipsed anything else in importance.

As news editor I was, of course, responsible for the reporting team and our local representatives and staff men throughout the country. In addition we had what the *Daily Worker* calls its Worker Correspondents—amateur journalists, working in factories, pits and offices or active in trade unions and other labour organisations, who keep the paper supplied with " inside " reports, some for use as stories, others for background.

In the Worker Correspondents' Department I had a filing clerk whose job it was to card-index, with half a dozen different cross-references, full details of everyone who sent a report to the paper and who might conceivably be of some future use.

Soon I had several hundred accredited Worker Correspondents sending in regular reports and receiving regular " leads " and directives from me, and thousands of contacts spread all over the country, to whom we could turn as the need arose.

I was put on the paper's business committee, which looked after management and administration, and was made responsible for the whole of the editorial and auxiliary departments—in all some forty people.

By the time I was brought on to the committee, an attempt was being made to effect economies. For some time after the raising of the ban it had been " easy come and easy go " with the money.

The knowledge that, after struggling for years, we had thousands of pounds in the bank went to the heads of some of the executives.

Shortly after the ban was lifted, for example, it was possible for
one man without any reference to anyone else to go out and spend
hundreds of pounds on a huge carpet for the editorial room (this
at a time when prices were at their highest because of war-time
shortages) which was worn out in a matter of months by the
constant coming and going of the staff. He bought at the same
time a set of new fluorescent lights, on delivery of which it was
discovered that they could not in any case be used because of
some peculiarity of our lighting system. It became a joke in the
office that if you wanted to spend sixpence you had to fill in half
a dozen forms but if you wanted to spend a thousand pounds you
need refer to no one. The days when we had gone around the
waste-paper baskets looking for paper clips and when we had
often gone home on Friday nights with no pay or only part-pay
seemed far away.

But a more sober mood prevailed by the time I went on to the
business committee, and plans were being made for acquiring
at a later date a bigger and more modern building for which
large sums of money would be required.

From time to time I reported to the Editorial Board, whose
proceedings I found interesting, even though every executive on
the paper knew them to be a farce.

The Editorial Board had neither administrative nor policy-
making powers. It could have ceased to exist at any moment
and not one ounce of difference would have been made to the
running of the paper. It was and is purely a " stuffed shirt "
body.

Professor J. B. S. Haldane, as the Board's chairman, would
preside, taking little part in the discussion and absent-mindedly
doodling in Greek as the Dean of Canterbury held forth at
length. Never on any occasion did I hear the Dean make a
distinctively Christian contribution to discussion. In the Board
room there was no evidence of any attempt on his part to
" Christianise " the paper's policy in any way whatsoever.

Neither Sean O'Casey, the playwright, nor Beatrix Lehmann,
the actress, both members of the Board, was present on any
occasion when I was reporting, nor was their presence ever noted
in any report from the editor to the Executive meeting.

Communist Party members were always in an overwhelming majority at the Board meetings and so there was never any possibility of things getting out of the Party's control. The existence of the Board, however, gave us the " evidence " to prove that the paper was " broad " in its administration and not just a narrow Party concern.

The People's Press Printing Society, a co-operative body created after the ban was lifted and which is nominally responsible for the printing and publication of the paper, is likewise so organised as to ensure the continuance of communist policies at all times.

Half-yearly members' meetings are held in London and the provinces at which all members of the society have the right to be present, but there is little likelihood of the policies adopted there ever being off the Party line and none at all that the paper itself will ever depart from official communist policies.

Communists are in the leading positions or have a decisive vote on each of the society's district committees and on the Board of Management. Yet the society organises around the paper several thousands of people who are not Party members and who provide another useful non-communist " front ".

At each district Half Yearly Meeting of the society a leading member of the *Daily Worker* staff makes a report which sets the tone of the discussion which follows. At the first I attended in that capacity everything had been carefully rigged in advance by the local Party office, where a " fraction " was held before the meeting proper began.

A committee had to be elected, along with a secretary and other officers. At the " fraction " meeting the secretary, a crypto-communist, was decided upon in advance, along with sufficient Party members for the committee to guarantee a clear majority. Those present then went along in twos and threes to the society's meeting, armed with the list of names, spreading themselves out among the audience when they got there and greeting each other as though they had not met before that day.

When it came to the elections, everything went according to plan, with one or two genuine non-communists being nominated from the body of the hall and elected on to the committee. It was, of course, the usual method used for capturing non-communist organisations applied to a body of the Party's own creation.

In fact the P.P.P.S. no more controls the paper's policy than does the Editorial Board. Control comes from the meeting of Executives which meets each week, which is one hundred per cent communist and of which three members are on the Party's Political Bureau. The direction and ultimate control of the Executive comes from R. Palme Dutt.

For communists who, like myself, had been long in the Party, the period of the Second Front campaign was one where the work of years looked like coming to fruition.

To stand on the plinth of Nelson's Column and look down on 50,000 faces, to see the hammer-and-sickle badge, openly and proudly worn by almost everyone present, to hear great masses of people singing the " Internationale " and " Sovietland ", was to be carried away with a terrific emotion.

For years I had dreamed of this. Through the years when the mass of the people had been bitterly hostile to us. Through the years when, to maintain one's morale, one had to tune in to Moscow Radio each night to hear the " Internationale " played in a land where it was not subversive. Through the years when people had frequently publicly demanded that I take the hammer-and-sickle badge from my coat. This was a foretaste of the Soviet Britain of tomorrow.

As one great Second Front demonstration followed another I would walk around the crowd, measure its size, judge its temper, listen to the conversation of the people on its fringes, climb on to the plinth and look out across the upturned faces and the proud banners and slogans.

The most unlikely people would be on the platform : Labour, Liberal and even Conservative M.P.s, journalists and writers whom we had attacked for years. One could see them react to the tremendous spirit of the demonstrations and be carried away by it.

At a great indoor meeting one Labour M.P., later a very loyal Junior Minister, brought the house down when he finished a speech with the words, " Forward to Soviet Britain ". How often in the past we had said just that to little bunches of hungry, doubting men.

But the campaign dragged on, and once again hostility to us began to come out into the open, expressing itself in sneers at the " amateur strategists ". We noted it and regarded it as a salutary reminder that that hostility would always be there so long as capitalism continued, and that communism would not come the easy way to Britain any more than to anywhere else.

I was working hard, if not harder than ever before. Proud to be at the heart of things, proud of the technical as well as the political job I was doing, I felt all the prouder when I was offered the news editor's job at a high salary on one of the " capitalist " dailies and could turn it down with the answer that I was doing something in which I really believed and that that was what mattered most to me.

I turned it down all the more emphatically, I suppose, because of a process which was beginning deep down somewhere in my own mind, in that other, water-tight compartment. I was coming to look forward to the arrival of my copy of the *Weekly Review* each Thursday morning. I still hated its politics. But I looked forward to H. D. C. Pepler's little Chaucerian rhymes, to the articles impregnated with love of the Middle Ages. I told myself that I needed relaxation and that this was it in its most perfect form—the exact opposite of the work on which I was engaged.

G. K. Chesterton and Hilaire Belloc had been the giants who had left their imprint on the paper, whose influence was present in all its columns. I had come now to know that the people behind it were the exact opposites of totalitarians. They were Distributists, and I began to find certain aspects of Distributism attractive. A tired man needing relaxation could be forgiven indulgence in a little nostalgia, I told myself.

The books of Chesterton and Belloc had not been among those I had read much in the past. Belloc I hardly knew, except through a single little Catholic Truth Society pamphlet on St. Thomas à Becket which years before I had taken from a literature rack in a Catholic church as I made room for some communist literature I was putting there.

I found it one night and read it for the first time. Its vigorous, polemical style appealed, for it had a certain similarity to that of some of our own Marxist writers.

The fact that it dealt with my beloved Middle Ages heightened its interest, but its religious side did not touch me at all. That was something which died, or should have died, with feudalism— all right in its day but not in ours.

I went through my library and rediscovered two books by Chesterton, *The Man Who Was Thursday*, which I had always loved, and his *Dickens*. I recalled reading and admiring his *Chaucer* years before. I had got it from a library on the day following his death and it had shed new light on the medieval poet whose works I knew so well.

Yet reading these books or the *Weekly Review*, late at night after a hectic day in the office, I had almost the same sense of guilt as that experienced by an adolescent indulging in a secret vice.

And when one day I bought a copy of *Avowals and Denials* in William Whiteley's store in Bayswater, I took it home with much the same sort of uneasy conscience I had had when in my very early teens I had smuggled home a pornographic—and very disappointing—book. The difference was that I did not tire of Chesterton. I wanted more.

As I read the *Weekly Review*, it came, in time, secretly to thrill me to think that Chesterton himself had once edited it. The trouble was that the more I read it, the more I found in it to interest me.

I hated big cities, longed for the sanity of rural life. The impersonal character of the suburb, its piddling values, nauseated me. The soil had a fascination for me that had never died. My years on the smallholding now had an almost mystical significance as I recalled them.

The smell of warm animal flesh and dung when one opened the goat-house doors in the morning. The joy of taking a stick and knocking the heads off nettles after rain and drinking in their intoxicating smell. The pleasure of simply taking a handful of soil and allowing it to run gently through one's fingers. The colossal satisfaction of spending hours quietly digging in solitude or kneeling weeding for hour after hour. The chance to think.

Yes, that was it. The chance to think for the sake of thinking. Not " applying " someone else's thought to some line of action. Just thinking one's own thoughts. I did not at the time consciously formulate my thoughts in that way. I never gave them the chance to crystallise from feelings into anything like a thought-out Marxist heresy.

I longed to think independently, and yet how far away it all seemed. It would mean an abandonment of the class struggle, a betrayal of all I had lived for. It was a luxury belonging to the past, to days when revolution was not on the order of the day, to the quiet periods which interleave those of revolutionary change.

But at home at night I could find it all there, implicit in so much that was written in that little Distributist paper. I was just indulging in a little more-or-less harmless vice, no more. There was no real betrayal, just a little nostalgia, a little conscious escapism, after a long period of overwork and whilst still living under considerable strain. And why the hell, I asked myself, shouldn't I try to escape for a few minutes a week? It did me no harm. Did me good, in fact. I worked all the harder for the Cause as a consequence. I grew resentful with myself for feeling guilty about it at all.

Then at last the Second Front was opened and for some time I was too busy to read anything at all except those things which related directly to my work, too involved in assisting the Party to want to be in any way disloyal to it, even in my subconscious thoughts.

I took only a quick surreptitious glance at the *Weekly Review* as it arrived each Thursday in the office. It was no longer part of my work to read it, since any public comment on the paper would be unwise in the light of the libel action still outstanding. I took it home at night but was usually too tired to read it.

The fly-bomb attack from the " rocket coast " of France meant organising my team to cover " incidents ", report the anti-aircraft and fighter resistance. I fought to get a reporter by one means or another to cover the Second Front itself but we were refused by the authorities. That last point was important for my own morale, and that of the Party members generally. One rarely has time for doubts about the Cause when having to defend oneself or the Party against attack, and that is the normal psychological atmosphere of the Communist Party.

The " little " blitz which had preceded the opening of the Second Front had necessitated getting Carol and Rowena out of London and I had taken a house in Wimbledon which, when the V-1s began to make their way to London, was damaged three times in quick succession.

There was no comfort and little rest. But there was plenty of enthusiasm, for the tide had been turned at Stalingrad and the Red Army was battling its way across Europe. " When the Red Army gets there it will never go," we said, remembering Latvia, Lithuania and Estonia and the way in which communism had come to them.

Jokingly we said that we hoped that the Red Army would get to the rocket coast of Northern France before the British and United States forces and so be able to liberate us as well. But we openly said that, now that the Western allies had waited so long, it would be better by far if the Red Army got to Berlin first and taught our people a lesson. The hopes of the Party's members were pinned on the East, not the West.

In fact, by the time of the landings on the French coast, leading members of the staff and of the Party were saying that it would be a bloody good thing if the British people were made to suffer a bit. They were winning the war on the cheap and at the cost of good Soviet lives. If thousands and millions of men had to be sacrificed to defeat fascism and make the Soviet Union secure, then let them at least be the lives of the people of the capitalist countries. There were too few Soviet citizens in the world already without sacrificing more.

The Red Army no longer needed saving; Russian soil was no longer in danger, and, left to themselves, the Russians could now finish it off, we believed. The only thing in favour of the Second Front by that time was the sharing of the sacrifices and the hope that the impact of British and Allied troops meeting those of the Red Army would make people still more Red.

The Party's line was to identify itself as completely as possible with the " masses ", reflecting their hopes, fears and sacrifices in our propaganda and in our Press.

It became the duty of our members in the Forces to set an example in courage and in leadership. For those in the factories it meant being " heroes of labour " who were models of efficiency on the job, who did everything possible to boost output and to find solutions for all production problems. For us on the *Daily Worker* it meant getting the stories of the achievements on the fighting and industrial fronts and telling them as skilfully as possible. And, since staff members also had the ordinary responsibilities of the Party member as well, it meant doing all we could individually to assist the struggle.

Our mood was very much that of those Party members on the Continent who were by now leading the Resistance. The short-term fight was important in itself and the long-term possibilities were enormous.

Typical of the spirit existing on the staff and in the Party at the time was something that happened when the fly-bombs began to fall on London. The *Daily Worker* staff was made up of both communists and non-communists. All the editorial staff, the business heads and a majority of the business personnel were Party members. But only a minority of those responsible for the technical production of the paper—the compositors, printers and others—were in the Party.

We had, therefore, a Party factory group in the building whose work followed more or less the normal lines of such groups, constantly working to spread communism among the non-Party members and also to exert a communist influence throughout the area in which the works was situated.

With this area at the receiving end of the fly-bomb attack the nearby hospital soon found itself in need of blood for the many civilian casualties which were being brought to it almost daily.

One day a circular letter was received at the *Daily Worker*, addressed to managers of establishments in the locality and asking for blood donors. On the business committee we decided to pass it to the Party group with the recommendation that they should appeal to the staff to volunteer.

The recommendation was adopted and backed by meetings of Party members in each of the departments, where they were told that they should set an example to the " non-Party elements " on the staff, and that the aim should be to make our workplace an example, too, to factories throughout the entire area. It would prove to people that communists not only talked but sacrificed as well. It would, moreover, be a chance of making contacts at the hospital, where we had wanted to have a Party group ever since we had moved into the area.

But soon a problem was created in the departments for which I was responsible as news editor and in which the staff was one hundred per cent communist. The Party members were going along to donate blood so frequently that some were fainting on the job and the general standard of work was being affected.

In the editorial stenographers' department, the girls who typed the urgent messages and reports as they were phoned by our reporters and correspondents were fainting at the most inconvenient moments and so threatening the production of the paper itself. A chief sub-editor passed out one afternoon just as the first edition was about to go to press. Reporters upon whom I depended were working at half-cock because of the quantities of blood they had given.

Finally I went to a specially convened Party group meeting and argued that the needs of the paper must come first, that their first responsibility was to the *Daily Worker*. I had a hard job to convince both the group's members and its leader. My job was made more difficult by the production, at a vital point in the argument, of a letter received from the hospital to the effect that the *Daily Worker* had set an example to the whole area and by a report that some of the hospital staff were on the way to becoming sympathetic to the Party arising from their admiration for what our people were doing. I won, but only after a fight. The keenness of the staff as Party members quite frequently led to such conflicts of interests between paper and Party.

Thus, for example, the Party group, at a slightly later date, decided that the editorial members should play a greater part in the activities of their union. It was not long before I regularly found myself, on the afternoon on which the Central London branch of the National Union of Journalists met, with hardly any staff. People who were supposed to be on reporting assignments were slipping into the branch meetings and neglecting their work. Again I had to fight it out with the group and to get a decision to the effect that the paper must come first.

In the factories our members, as at the time when Russia had first come into the war, were working for the settlement of disputes without strike action. Striking was denounced as all but treachery and our shop stewards were denounced by the Trotskyists as traitors to the working-class who had gone over to class collaboration.

The newer members and those of middle-class origin who had gone into the factories accepted the " line " with the greatest enthusiasm and carried it into effect with no misgivings. For the old stagers among the rank and file, it was more difficult to go into the campaigns of that period without the feeling that there were times when the Marxist dialectic could result in the queerest situations, where one had even to pay lip-service, it seemed, to patriotism, pay homage to those who died for their country and even to work harder in the factory, bringing increased profits for the bosses as a consequence. To be a Party member required a high degree of Marxist understanding—or so little as actually to be able to believe in the Party's pretensions—in a situation such as that.

There were troubled consciences among the old stagers, too, when the names of Communist Party members began to appear in the King's New Year's Honours Lists. For the first time in the Party's history I turned a reporter on to scouring the Lists, not for those " Judases " to the working-class movement whom we had annually denounced for taking honours from a capitalist regime, but for the names of our own members. We found several communist shop stewards and others, whom we publicised as heroes. But we only kept our self-respect by privately greeting the announcements with loud and cynical laughter.

Our military correspondent, Lt.-Col. Hans Kahle, fretted and fumed at British and U.S. strategy, comparing it despairingly with that of the victorious Red Army. The case of Hans was an interesting one. He was a German of " bourgeois " origin, a professional soldier of the Potsdam school. During the Spanish civil war he had gone to fight in the International Brigade, and there joined the Communist Party. When the Brigade was disbanded he was, of course, unable to return to Nazi Germany, so came to Britain, where, at the outbreak of war, he was detained.

By the time the *Daily Worker* ban was lifted he had been released, but was still a very suspect enemy alien. It was in the greatest secrecy therefore that he was brought on to the staff, but gradually, as the atmosphere became increasingly pro-communist, the need for secrecy diminished. Day after day, with considerable skill, he commented on the to-ings and fro-ings of the battles on the Eastern Front, and often we asked ourselves what the public would think if they knew that those comments and forecasts were coming from one of Prussia's professional officers.

It would be difficult to find a more courteous and likeable man than Hans. Tall, with short-cropped hair, he looked as though he had walked straight off a Potsdam barrack square. Until he smiled. Then his face was transformed into one of the most good-natured I have ever had the pleasure to see.

For years he had hoped to be allowed to fight against the Nazis. He volunteered for the Allied Forces but was rejected. Then, when the fighting reached German soil, he volunteered again, hoping to be able to assist in leading a German rising in the rear. Again he was refused.

Like most communists he still believed that there was a great anti-Nazi mass of ordinary German folk just waiting for the signal to rise. The Communist International and the Soviet leaders had believed the same when the Red Army first came into contact with the German forces. Bands had advanced playing the "Internationale", expecting that mass desertions would result. There were none. But in London Hans still sat waiting for the day when the anti-Nazi masses would rise. When they failed to do so he became bitterly depressed, having at last to accept the reports which the Party had for some time been receiving to the effect that practically no communist or anti-Nazi opposition existed within the Third Reich.

But his depression lifted again as the Red Army went hacking its way into his country and he impatiently awaited the day when he could join it. When the war was over he was allowed by the British authorities to return. He went straight to the Soviet zone and was given a tough assignment as a local police chief. Within a few months he had contracted an infectious disease. He died before the Soviet policies had hardened Germany off into two hostile zones. I learned of his death with sorrow, but perhaps it was as well. Sooner or later disillusionment would have come and with it the depression which had been his curse during his stay in Britain.

Also on our staff for some time was Ludwig Freund. Ludwig was a likeable Czech who came to Britain as a political refugee when Hitler went into Czechoslovakia. At the outbreak of war he was detained as an enemy alien and, because he was a communist whose Party like the rest was declaring the war to be an imperialist one, he was detained long after the majority of enemy aliens had been released. We called him, after the Coalition Government had been formed, one of " Mr. Morrison's prisoners " and campaigned for his release.

When Russia came into the war and the Czech communists in Britain, like the rest, gave it their wholehearted support, Ludwig was released and quickly got himself into Czech Government circles.

Anxious not to appear as an obvious alien he finished up by looking more English than the English, spending his days (and his nights, too, we said jokingly) in rough tweed suits and tweed caps.

The Czech liberal leaders were anxious to learn as much as possible of the workings of British democracy. As a part of this policy Ludwig was told that he could elect to work for a period on the British newspaper of his choice and that the appropriate financial arrangements would be made by the Czech Government, so that he should be taught as much as possible by whichever paper he chose. Ludwig, not unnaturally, chose the *Daily Worker*, who received the " premium " for his " apprenticeship " with joy, and under this official cloak he was able to become the liaison man between the British and Czech Communist Parties at the Czech Government's expense.

Working in my office he was at the hub of British communist activities and any time required for visits to our Party headquarters was, of course, gladly given him. He reasoned that communism, when it came to Czechoslovakia after the war, would draw on what he and the others had learned in Britain. It would take as much and no more than it wanted from communism as practised in Russia. " Our historic conditions are different," he would say, " and our communism will be different too."

In the company of other Party members he was kindly, considerate and excellent company in his quiet way. He achieved considerable standing with members of the Beneš Government and was able to put us in touch with them at any time. He was able also, of course, to keep us informed of most that was going on in Czech Government circles. Ludwig in co-operation with members of our Editorial Foreign Department would write articles to which non-communist members of his Government would willingly, at that time, put their names and which we in due course published.

The Czech communists were already certain that the post-war Czechoslovakia would be a communist one, and it looked as though the " liberals " in the Government thought so too and were playing for safety by keeping in with both East and West. Certainly they had already compromised themselves up to the hilt by the time they went back via Moscow to Czechoslovakia and—in a good many cases—to death or renewed political exile.

Ludwig went back, too, and in the strongly anti-German Czechoslovakia which he found quickly changed his Germanic name of Freund (he came from the Sudetenland) to a more Slav-sounding one. He was described as the Government's economic adviser and as such was responsible for the drawing up of the Communist Party's economic programmes introduced after the *putsch* of February 1948, and so was completely identified with all that followed. Yet Ludwig was likeable, intelligent and, I believe, fundamentally warmhearted and good. But he was also a Marxist.

London in those war days was full of members of almost all the nations of Europe. In each there were communists, all were planning for the post-war communist world and all were using

G

their Governments for that purpose. There were French, Belgian and Dutch communists; Czechs, Slovaks, Germans, Austrians, all using their various " centres " and emigré organisations to spread their influence, employing their ample leisure in perfecting their knowledge of Marxism and their plans for the seizure of power.

Co-ordinating their activities and pooling their experiences was a hush-hush body in London which came near to being a little Communist International in itself. Its administration was the responsibility of an old and trusted one-time Political Bureau member, Tommy Bell, who kept me informed of all that was going on in the various foreign parties. Had M.I.5 kept itself sufficiently aware of their activities too it is probable that the Fuchs case would never have occurred. The communist emigrés saw themselves as the rulers of tomorrow and were confident that they could deal with their respective Coalition governments when the day came.

All were also closely in touch with London Soviet circles, who saw their importance at a time when others thought that they counted for little.

XVII

THE TWO WATER-TIGHT COMPARTMENTS

DAY after day, in the months that followed the opening of the Second Front, the fly-bombs passed, or failed to pass, overhead. The chirpy Cockney heroism of the blitz days did not really return when the fly-bombs came. There was heroism still but it was more passive and stolid. But I sent my reporters out each time there was an incident within reach of the office and we made the most of every bit of heroism we could find in order to build up morale. Once a reporter I had sent out to an unidentified incident in the suburbs came on the phone to tell me that the incident included my own house, which was now minus its windows, doors and ceilings. I decided that there was no story in it and that he would be more usefully engaged in doing a few first-aid repairs to the house instead.

There were times when I found myself watching events curiously as though I were little more than a spectator. I was a trained Marxist and so spoke and thought as a Marxist without any conscious act of will. But there was not the same sustained and passionate belief in it all, the same colossal zeal for everything the Party said and did. It troubled me, I fretted inwardly and told myself I was tired and perhaps a little ill. I had lost a lot of weight and was visiting a hospital every week where they were trying to build me up. There were times, too, when the slaughter seemed a little senseless. I heard our bombers go out night after night and tried not to think of what was going to happen in Hamburg, Berlin or whichever was the target for the night.

I remembered the detailed reports which had reached us of what life had been like in Hamburg when all above-surface services had been destroyed. It made me sick and I began to doubt its necessity. Retribution had no pleasures for me.

Then, the fly-bombs having stopped, the rockets brought the suffering nearer home again. A rocket fell on the Farringdon Market one day as I was passing on my way to the office. My press card let me right on to the scene. It was a Thursday and numbers of Catholic working women from " Little Italy ", the nearby Italian colony, had been queueing for the next day's fish.

The projectile had fallen right in the middle of them, killing scores and maiming more. The blood and the mess, the bits of bodies mixed with the fish stalls and ruined market buildings numbed me.

I went back on my way home at night. Priests were standing near rescue teams who dug into rubble, shored up great weights, cut through girders with acetylene flames in order to release the men and women who had been buried alive.

Outside, beyond the barriers, silently stood groups of small dark men, Italian ice-cream and hot-chestnut men, knife-grinders, patiently waiting for news. It isn't their war, I thought to myself.

There were little children. And there was one old woman in particular whom I noticed standing there.

Next morning men were still digging, but not so frantically. And men were still waiting. But not so many of them now. The old woman was still there, standing on the same spot as before, her grey hair thick with dust, eyes black from want of sleep.

That night I went again. She was still there, but next morning as I arrived they were leading her protesting away. Nothing that was still alive remained behind the barriers. Nothing which could be pieced together into a human form was left to be brought out.

Another rocket, which brought down a shower of plaster on me as I worked, fell a few streets away, killing a large number of the leaders of the English Presbyterian Church who were meeting in conference. It killed, too, many men, women and children in the densely populated tenements of the area. Some days later a mass funeral was held for these local residents killed in the incident. All down the street outside the *Daily Worker* building that lunch-time stood hearses, in every one of which was a tiny, white, baby's coffin. Somewhat shaken, I went in to the editorial department and told a colleague about them. He looked up from his typewriter with a grin. " And I suppose on every one there is a card saying ' Our loss is heaven's gain ' in the approved British proletarian tradition," he said cynically. I wondered to myself whether I, too, had at one time been sufficiently hard-boiled and detached in my Marxism to be able to react as he had done. For me, this period of civilian suffering seemed at times almost as purposeless as had the first.

When the evacuation of Dunkirk swept the nation off its feet we had been cynical spectators. When others were swept along in a great heroic wave at the time of that first, big months-long blitz on London it was an imperialist war for us and so I had seen only the blood and the dust and the slaughter where others saw so much more.

Now we were saying: " Had they opened the Second Front earlier this would not have happened," and Party leaders scoffed together at the amount of time which elapsed before the Western Allies got to the " rocket coast " of North France.

But the Party's mood of cynicism passed as East and West rushed towards each other in Germany. We speculated on what would be the result when they met. Most of my colleagues thought that the British troops would be made still Redder than they were, that the last anti-Soviet prejudices on the part of the British public would melt before the impact made by the forces of the new Soviet world upon those who had come from the old, collapsing one. My own half-formed doubts and difficulties went back into their water-tight compartment in the mood of general enthusiasm and I thrilled at the thought that communism would sweep right across the Continent and that Britain would be much nearer the Revolution when the war ended than she had been when it began.

But the *Weekly Review* began to publish disturbing reports of the behaviour of Red Army men, and before long they were being confirmed by the letters which started to flood into our office from Forces men who were disappointed, disillusioned or outraged, depending upon the views they had previously held about Russia.

Raping, looting, black-marketeering—these were things we had expected of our own and the U.S. forces, products of a world in decay. But the Red Army was doing the same and worse. Our soldier-readers demanded explanations.

Party members in the Services appealed to us to explain the ignorance, the illiteracy and the complete lack of culture of the majority of the Soviet personnel. Our own over-bright propaganda of the past was coming home to roost, for we had published, too often, pictures of eighty-year-old peasants in the most backward Soviet area learning to read and write over the caption " Illiteracy is now ninety-eight per cent liquidated in Russia ".

The volume of letters and protests became such that we could no longer ignore them. We had a top-level discussion on the question and decided that the only thing for it was to explain the situation and to hope that not too much of our earlier propaganda would be remembered.

Most of the Red Army men came, we said, from the rural areas and from the least important industries. As in England, the skilled workers and the majority of the men in the industrial areas were in war industries and so had not been called up.

The people now misbehaving themselves in Europe were not in any way typical of the new type of Soviet citizen. Coming from backward areas, and after suffering so much, they were letting off steam and should be understood and sympathised with, particularly in the light of what they had suffered.

All of which was largely true. The trouble was that it was all so unlike what we had taught them to expect and what we had come to expect ourselves—for from top to bottom of the Party we had made the mistake of swallowing too much of our own propaganda. We had dealt out the sunshine stories for so long that we had fallen into the error of believing half of them ourselves.

In a good many cases our hopes that memories would not be too long were not justified and former supporters came back disgruntled, when not actually hostile. The reports, confirming what I was reading in the *Weekly Review*, depressed me, too. Once, I would simply have been concerned with putting over the " correct line "; now one half of me was concerned about the facts as well.

I was still interested in the success of the *Daily Worker* as an enterprise. But my missionary zeal had grown less because of my growing mental conflict. I reacted by taking an even greater pride in my craftsmanship as a journalist and in the efficiency of my department. I continued, of course, to take part in and to lead discussions among the staff and among the Party leaders and I found to my surprise that I was doing it better than before.

Marxist analysis was becoming a science to me without being an apostolic faith. I could use my Marxist methodology coldly for the larger part of the time, with the result that I was doing it more successfully than before. The process had been a gradual one and I had only slowly become aware of what was happening. No one else knew or even guessed.

The official announcement of the end of the war in Europe did not wildly excite any of us. Indeed, it seemed rather an anti-climax. With the Russians still claiming that there was much mopping-up to be done, the Party took the view that the British and Americans, having cashed in on the Red Army's victories, were now trying to claim a premature end of the war. And we could see that from our point of view there was still a lot for the Red Army to do.

But on the eve of V.E. Day I took a bus home, instead of going by my usual train, in order to get some idea of how the " masses " were taking it. To my amazement the mean little streets of South London were already a mass of flags and bunting, and preparations were manifestly going forward for a day of popular rejoicing. Money which had been collected over a period of years for precisely this moment was now being spent. It was an aspect of the war of which we in the Communist Party, living our own lives, fighting our own battles, pursuing our own distinctive course, had had no knowledge whatsoever.

I phoned the office a colourful story and prepared my reporters for the job of seeing that the excitement and rejoicing of the masses were adequately reflected in the columns of our paper. It was good communist practice to do so, of course, but to me it had a greater significance. The simple festivities which I had seen under preparation in those little back streets, and our ignorance of what the ordinary people had planned, seemed to me to cast doubt upon our claim to be " the vanguard of the masses ", their only real mouthpiece and champion. The simple joys and sorrows of the masses were, it seemed, something outside our ken after all.

My staff, in the months that followed, were impatiently hoping that Russia would quickly join in the war against Japan so that she might be in at least as strong a position there as she was in Germany.

The use of the atom bomb profoundly disturbed me even though I told myself that in balance, by bringing the war to an abrupt end, it had undoubtedly saved many lives. The existence of such a sinister and devastating weapon seemed to bode ill for the future and robbed the conclusion of years of war of any joy. For a few days, my colleagues hotly debated whether Russia had been wise to remain out of the war in the Far East until the last moment or whether the Soviet leaders had allowed themselves to be outwitted by the Americans. But that sort of discussion does not last for long in Party circles and soon the official line was made clear; the Americans had double-crossed the Russians by failing to reveal and share the secret of the atom bomb. Those who had for the moment queried the wisdom of the Soviet leaders now denounced the Americans' duplicity.

My own view was that the unconditional surrender policy in Germany and the " atomising " of Nagasaki and Hiroshima in Japan promised little more than Dead Sea fruit for the future.

During the months between V.E. and V.J. Day, the General Election had been held and the Labour Government returned. The Party had miscalculated the mood of the people to the extent of believing that a Labour victory was unlikely and that we must, therefore, be ready to support a Coalition. Had Labour not been returned the Russian leaders would most certainly have desired us to demand such a Coalition, for the war-time alliance was, allegedly, to last for a generation and Russia wanted a strong ally rather than a weak one.

Just as the Party under-estimated Labour's strength so it also over-estimated its own. Out of all the candidates we put into the field only two were returned to Parliament. The majority of the remainder failed miserably.

It had been part of my task to see that each of the candidates in turn got a boost in our columns, but the editor was himself standing for a London constituency and demanded for his own campaign what the other candidates regarded as a disproportionate amount of our available space. The result was a flood of protests and nasty letters from the others in the field.

On the night of the poll he expressed the view that, on the basis of the most careful and sober estimates, he had undoubtedly headed the poll. In fact he was ignominiously at the bottom.

That mood of almost unreasoning optimism was shared by all my reporters and created a multitude of problems and pitfalls against which I had constantly to guard. A girl reporter, sent to write up the campaign of two of our candidates in rural constituencies, wrote an enthusiastic piece about the way in which the " Red villages of Kent and Berkshire " were going to return communist M.P.s. Knowing the countryside, I doubted the existence of those " Red " villages and toned the story right down.

It was just as well. Out of tens of thousands of votes cast, our candidates got a few hundred each.

In Sparkbrook, Birmingham, R. Palme Dutt fought the Conservative, L. S. Amery, and a Labour man. Over and over again the Party declared that there were only two men in the fight, Dutt and Amery—and Dutt was going to win. When the results were declared Dutt had lost his deposit and the Labour man got in.

Parliamentary candidates usually publicly proclaim the certainty of their victory. The difference was that the Party really believed these things. For years we had derided all parliamentary institutions and at no time had we taken parliamentary democracy seriously. The result was that the vast majority of our members, including our leaders, had next to no experience of fighting serious election campaigns, and the Party had no electoral traditions on which to draw. My own experience as a " crypto " in the Independent Labour Party and the Labour Party had enabled me to estimate the possibilities in a more realistic manner.

On the morning that the election results began to come through we got a series of surprises. The first was the sweeping Labour gains, second was the communist defeats, third was the realisation that among the Labour men returned were a number of our own Party members who had slipped in almost unnoticed as it were.

My first realisation of this came when I answered the phone and the man at the other end announced himself as the new Labour member for his constituency. He followed it with a loud guffaw and rang off. I had known him as a Communist Party man for years. Then over the tape, among the new Labour M.P.s came others whose candidatures we had hardly taken seriously ourselves. By the time the list was complete we knew that we had at least eight or nine " cryptos " in the House of Commons in addition to our two publicly acknowledged M.P.s.

It was not long, however, before some of them were finding reasons for quietly dropping the Party, explaining that they felt they could do more good for the cause by doing so. Their political progress since then would suggest that there were other

reasons too.   Some of them may genuinely have come to feel that
the parliamentary way to socialism was the best or only way in
Britain, others became attracted by a political and parliamentary
career which they felt would not be helped by a secret association
with the Communist Party.   Others who were returned as Labour
men were subsequently among those " purged " by the Labour
Party itself and who, in the 1950 election, all lost their seats in
Parliament.

With the ending of the war things became a little less hectic.
The very nature of my work, of course, was such that life was
lived at top tempo.   With my phones ringing almost unceasingly
as I briefed my reporters or dictated letters, articles and reports,
I had little enough time for thought during working hours.
That is normal for any news editor on any daily paper.   But on
the *Daily Worker* we were chronically short of staff and so the
hustle was even greater.

Quite legitimately I told the Party that my state of health was
such that although I could manage my work I could do no more
lecturing or tutorial work.   The Party Chiefs agreed that writing
for the *Daily Worker* must take priority and so I began to get
just a little leisure for the first time for years.

Having got it I hardly knew what to do with it.   I no longer
wanted to read my Marxist classics, no longer wanted, for the
time being, at any rate, to read anything much at all of a serious
character.

I indulged in what I called " pure luxury " reading instead—
reading which did not connect up directly with any form of
action possible to me at the time, books about the countryside,
about farming, agriculture, gardening.   I dreamed of the day
when I could get away from it all on to the land.   One day, I told
myself, I would be able with a clear conscience to say: " I've
worked hard for the Party, I've done my best.   Now I'm going to
do what I want to do and live quietly in some lonely spot.   It's
necessary for my health and, in any case, I've trained others to
take over and do my job."

I read the farming press and wrote a certain amount on farming
questions myself.   I knew that the fire had gone from my communist faith, that it was no longer the driving force in my life

that it had been. But it was equally true that I consciously supported no opposing political theory even though I read of Distribution with growing interest. Some day to become a small-holder and agricultural writer seemed a desirable aim and an escape from my present position. It was not so much that I thought that communism was entirely wrong. It was rather that it was no longer a spur to action, and this had come about as a result of thinking along lines which were inherently contrary to those of Marxism, even though I could not contemplate accepting any other philosophy.

I still resented attacks on the Party and still continued to write bitterly against the fascists. If I had got past caring passionately about my future communist world and if I even secretly wondered in my heart of hearts whether I wanted it at all, I most certainly did not want a fascist one either, and so I wrote more vigorously than ever against the fascists. And, because subconsciously I resented the way in which Catholic thought had destroyed my peace of mind, I attacked Catholicism and the Church more viciously than I had ever done.

In time I came to look for those parts in the Party's policy which I could still support with conviction and to concentrate upon those. Here I found an increasingly wide range was open to me, which did something to restore my morale and which enabled me to retain belief in the usefulness of my job.

The Party was taking a " constructive " attitude to the post-war world. The war-time alliance with the U.S.S.R. was continuing, we argued, into the peace. We must help to make Russia's British ally strong. We must, therefore, do everything possible to assist post-war reconstruction, since the rebuilding of Britain's economy was a contribution to the rebuilding of the Soviet Union too.

For this reason we continued, after the return of the Labour Government, to assist production in every way possible. At the same time we retained the right to criticise unnecessary hardship and to speak out against social injustice. The tactic was not for the moment the direct fight for communism but for healing the wounds left by the war and for fair-play for the common people.

That was a policy that suited my mood perfectly and it was

upon those aspects of our policy that I concentrated the energies of my reporters and correspondents.

I sent my industrial correspondents out to look for examples of good production efforts in the pits, the shipyards and the factories. They looked, too, for anything which was holding up production—inefficiency, bottle-necks, out-of-date methods, failure to provide the workers with sufficient incentives—and we sought positive solutions in every case.

We decided to review each of the industries which the Labour Government was likely to nationalise, giving our readers a picture of the size of the job to be done.

Similarly I turned my agricultural correspondent on to finding positive solutions for raising production in agriculture, and myself wrote on the question from time to time.

In all this the Worker Correspondents were able to play an important rôle and I got considerable pleasure out of mobilising so many for purely constructive purposes.

A certain amount of criticism came from some of my fellow-editorial executives, who complained that I was concentrating exclusively on such things and neglecting others, but I stuck to my guns, said it was Party policy and carried on.

My general reporters I turned on to exposing social scandals, bad housing conditions, evictions, profiteering, anti-social practices. I urged the crime reporter not simply to concentrate on crime stories as such (for which there was all too much material) but to deal also with the social causes of the crime wave. But I lost the fight which developed around him.

In the Party there were two schools of thought about the advisability of the *Daily Worker* publishing crime stories, and they parted company on a fundamental issue. There were those (of whom I was one) who argued that if the paper was to attract non-communists it must give the readers what they expected to find in any other morning paper but that it should be given our own " slant ". There were others who argued that the *Daily Worker* should concede nothing to " bourgeois decadence " and should concern itself exclusively with those things which were directly related to the " class struggle ".

When I appointed a crime reporter the latter school of thought at once protested and, even though he made a good and largely successful effort to present crime as a social problem, still continued to protest. In theory the editorial executive was on my side. It had been more than once laid down, indeed, that there should be a murder on the front page of every issue—for preference a sex crime. Whilst I did not go as far as that, I held that in post-war Britain crime had become a social problem which we could not ignore and on which we should have something to say.

The paper's policy had in the past swayed to and fro between the two points of view. For a period it was held that we should increase circulation if we gave more lurid details than any other paper, and in our reports of the sex and sadistic crimes of that period nothing was left out. Then some of the anti-crime-story school of readers protested and we dropped our lurid-details policy. When I later appointed and carefully briefed my crime reporter I thought some sort of compromise had been found. But the protests still came in, and a letter from Douglas Garman, solemn-faced leader of the Party's Marxist education department, finally led to the sudden collapse of the editor's support for my policy and the dismissal of the crime reporter. But on my treatment of industrial, social and agricultural questions I came out on top.

XVIII

CONFLICT

ALL communist eyes were hopefully turned on Eastern Europe in the post-war world, for there the " new democracies " were being evolved. They had, of course, been established by a liberating Red Army and not by civil war from within, a situation which had not been foreseen by Marx, Engels or Lenin when discussing the means by which communism could be brought to a country.

So new theories had to be formulated, and in due course expounded, at the Party's study classes.

It was wrong to say that communism had come to the new democracies without the violence which had always been predicted, it was argued, but it had taken new forms. The war had been one against the blackest reaction the world had ever known and which had attracted to itself all the worst reactionaries in each of the countries occupied by the Nazis. So, in carrying through at the end of the war a thorough-going purge of all who could be dubbed collaborators, precisely those elements who would normally be destroyed in a period of proletarian revolution were being liquidated—quite legally, democratically, without civil war.

The big industrialists in what were now the new democracies had assisted the Nazis, the great landowners had done the same. Now, with the connivance and support of the Western governments, they were being destroyed as individuals by the firing squads of the new democracies, were largely being liquidated as a class and their property was being passed over to the people, exactly as in a civil war.

Where the Red Army was present in the background and the communists were in the ascendancy, the process could go forward speedily and thoroughly and no opposition need be expected from such liberals as Beneš and Masaryk, for example, who were wise enough or astute enough to appreciate the temper of the people.

In such countries as France and Italy, where the Party was strong but not in power, it was necessary for it to push for such a policy as vigorously as was possible under the circumstances in order to make the task easier later on.

In the early days after the war it was believed in Moscow, and so in the various Communist Parties, that nothing could stop France and Italy from in time falling into the hands of the Party, that the Party, strong in numbers and experienced now in the use of arms, was invincible there.

That belief, incidentally, affected the attitude of the French communist leaders, who had been given an especial responsibility for guiding the British Party and did so with the mixture of arrogance, intolerance and condescension one expects of people newly possessed of wealth or power.

We sent our correspondents one after the other to tour the Eastern European countries.

One who went to Rumania reported how the Party there had only some 300 members when the Red Army completed the country's liberation. But it was nonetheless now being made the dominant party, having to use every sort of former fascist, careerist and anyone else who was prepared to jump on the band-wagon, in order to rule. To me it all seemed rather remote from the exercise of the revolutionary will of the masses about which we had talked and written in the past.

Czechoslovakia was described as the great land of promise. There the Party had succeeded, under very favourable conditions, in recruiting millions of members. It had been liberated by the Red Army, the wave of gratitude and enthusiasm for the Soviet Union could be understood in the light of the " Red haze " which had resulted from the British people's appreciation for Soviet aid. In Czechoslovakia it resulted in the Party momentarily having the biggest membership, in relation to total population, of any Communist Party in the world.

It would, of course, require a large-sized purge later on to sift them all out, our correspondents warned, but for the moment it was of tremendous political importance that the Party should take on the character of a great mass movement. The liberal leaders were conveniently pliant and alive to the need for falling in with the wishes of the people, whose views were largely being made and moulded by the Party.

Off the record, we were given details of the mass expulsion of Saar Germans and of Hungarians from Czechoslovakia. It meant a great loss of personnel with undoubted suffering for some, we were told, and a serious loss of skill, for the Hungarians had been useful to Czechoslovakia in the past.

But the Czech leaders were adamant that, on the basis of past experience, all such minorities were possible trouble spots and there were going to be no festering sores in the body of the new people's republic. In any case those ejected were mainly going to countries who were also on the road to communism and they would become useful citizens in what was after all now a community of nations.

As our correspondent spoke I had a vision of trucks and hand-carts piled high with pitiful belongings, with weary mothers and children and puzzled resentful husbands tramping along behind. It was all so much like scenes on the road from Malaga for which we had blamed Franco, and the crowded, fantastic roads of France and Belgium when the Nazis were sweeping all before them.

It was hard enough that by agreement with Britain and America vast populations were being uprooted to make the new Poland. I had hoped that that might be the limit of such forced migrations and wondered whether this really had to be.

Czechoslovakia was quoted by communist speakers as being an example of what could be done where there was a determined mass Party in existence. Democracy could after all be used and converted so as to serve the purposes of communism. It was an indication that in the coming period the seizure of power by democratic means and without the direct use of violence might even be a possibility.

The Party's leaders streamed out from London to Prague and there found the red carpet laid down for them. They met the new bosses, mixed with those who were now among the most important in the land, or about to become so, stayed at the best spas. It was all very exciting for them and it gave them a sense of importance which they were denied under British conditions. Here was a chance of mixing with the great without fear of being accused of consorting with the class enemy. Rust, Pollitt and even our less-important correspondents told of being garlanded with flowers, taken around in great chauffeur-driven cars, fêted, wined and dined.

Our correspondent who went to Bulgaria and Yugoslavia told at private staff meetings how these two countries were proving that, under communist guidance, traditional enemies could become friends. What had been the cockpit of Europe was, in the new conditions, now becoming an integrated whole.

Both Tito and Dimitroff had told him that their aim was the virtual union of the two countries. Because of the bitter feelings of the recent past, little would publicly be said for the moment about a political union as such. Instead, they were so fashioning their economies that each would be economically dependent upon the other. Out of the reality of a virtual economic federation would come, as soon as propaganda and Marxist education had prepared the way, a political fusion.

Bulgaria would base her plans for industrial development upon a generous and adequate supply of power from Yugoslavia, who in turn would key her industries to those of Bulgaria. Balkan federation was not a thing to be talked about. It was something which was quietly being achieved.

Some day all the new democracies would be ready to take their place as federated republics in the ever-expanding Union of Soviet Socialist Republics. But the way would have to be prepared by economic integration first.

The correspondent who visited Hungary reported that there the Party had a special problem. It had the power all right but the population was largely Catholic and was resisting its activities. The suspicions of the peasantry had got to be broken and, since the majority were affected, it would have to be done by means of winning the support of decisive sections of the people whilst at the same time isolating the Catholic leaders.

He told us of the methods being used by the Party. Enquiries by Party members around the countryside had shown how the peasants were still so completely in the grip of Catholic superstition that, when asked what they wanted most, they had replied that above all else they would like to see their churches repaired.

The Party had risen to the occasion. If this was what the peasants wanted they should have it. Party members, all of them good atheists, volunteers from the cities, had been sent out each week-end to repair the churches in their spare time. When the job was completed Rakosi, the Party leader, would arrive and remind the peasants that the communists alone had bothered to do anything about their ruined churches.

Often, our correspondent told us, they would garland Rakosi with flowers, saying that they had been deceived by the priests who had told them that communists were hostile to the Church and would destroy it if they could. The story was greeted with laughter by the members of our editorial staff.

It was all rather on all-fours with what I had done myself, years before in North Wales, when I had pretended that communism and Christianity were compatible, in order to use nonconformist ministers and to deceive their flocks. But I was not at all sure, now, that I liked it. There were, actively at work, " two Douglas Hydes ", one whose spontaneous reactions were what they had been for so long, the other whose reactions were almost the exact opposite. Sometimes one seemed in the ascendancy, sometimes the other. Most often, still, it was the communist, for even though I was losing my health because of accumulating secret doubts and misgivings, I still could not think of myself as anything but a communist.

At any moment, after having quite serious doubts about some aspect of Soviet or Party policy, I might still react violently in defence of the Party, especially if I heard it attacked by anyone outside its ranks.

But I went on fretting inwardly and losing weight until, in the end, my doctor decided that, what with that and a seemingly incurable cough, it was time my lungs were checked up on. He feared that I was heading for tuberculosis.

I knew too much about tuberculosis hospitals and sanatoria to get any joy from the news, yet I found myself curiously apathetic about whether I lived or died.

The old zest for life, the desire to fight on to the revolution, the constantly maintained hope of opportunity-bearing crises being just round the corner, the deep longing to be alive when the pattern of the new Soviet Britain was being laid down, had disappeared.

I went to the chest clinic in a deadened, almost fatalistic mood. My interest in the outcome of the doctor's examination was mainly in my case as a case, rather than in what happened to me as an individual.

I had been given a time at which I should attend the clinic and was naïve enough to imagine that, being a big modern hospital, they had actually instituted an appointments system.

When I got to the waiting-room I was quickly disillusioned. Close on one hundred appeared to have been given the same time for their " appointments ". Seating provided was for not

more than thirty.   The remainder stood leaning against the walls
or, when there was no space left there, were just standing in the
middle of the room.

But not quite the middle.   That was occupied by two stretcher
cases brought from other hospitals, who were wheeled in on
trolleys, which then occupied the centre position.   One was a
plump elderly woman with closed eyes and blood-drained face,
to which stuck wisps of grey hair.   Sweat was the adhesive.   Here
was a chronic case of something else, but now tuberculosis was
intervening to shorten the weary way to an inevitable death.   The
other was an old man, with a persistent, revoltingly fruity cough.
They were later joined by other bed-ridden patients wheeled
through from the hospital's own wards.

Leaning against the trolley on which lay the old woman was a
woman in an advanced state of pregnancy who told me that she
had had tuberculosis years before, was cured but had just come
back for a routine check.

Her two-year-old child played around the trolley on which the
old man coughed and spluttered.   Other pregnant women stood
or sat in other parts of the room.

Opposite to me a little four-year-old girl with a tubercular leg
talked to another child who was said to be " wasting ".   And
amongst the chronically sick and the not-so-sick were distributed
people who, like myself, were merely " suspects ", presumably
in a condition where they were particularly likely to pick up
tuberculosis if they came into contact with it.

The suffering there appalled me as the problem of pain had
always done.   In my early communist years, confronted with
animal and human suffering I had often declared that, although
I could not believe there was a God of love, I would not find it
difficult to believe that the world was ruled by an all-powerful fiend.

Now, again, close proximity to sickness, as opposed to the man-
inflicted suffering I had seen in the war years, made me wonder
how anyone could believe in a beneficent God.

Three and a half hours after arrival I went through to be
weighed and measured (" 5 ft. 5 ins. and 7 stone 12 lbs.").   Then
to be X-rayed and cross-examined by the grossly over-worked
specialist.

Some weeks later the report came through: " This man, although organically sound, is heading for disaster unless he eases up. He appears to be living under great strain, possibly because of the nature of his work."

One result was that a decision was taken by the editorial executive committee that I should, at least, be given a deputy. From working a six-day week of twelve hours daily I was now, after several years of such hours joyfully and willingly undertaken in the first instance, dropped down to nine hours daily with a five-and-a-half-day week.

The doctor advised me to get more fresh air and so I took a small allotment garden, overgrown with great weeds and brambles.

With my work now finishing at soon after six, I was able regularly to put in a few hours each night gardening. As I cleared and cleaned the soil, built my compost heap and later dug and planted the garden from end to end, I was happier than I had been at any time since the end of the war.

The sun had set one night and no one else was left on the patch of gardens. I was working quietly on. As I went between the rows with my hoe I found myself repeating aloud the words of a hymn from my Methodist days:

" What though unmarked the happy workman toil
And break unthanked of man the stubborn clod,
It is enough, for sacred is the soil,
Dear are the hills of God."

It is enough. The healing of the soil. That was what I was looking for. Perhaps that could fill the gaps left in my life by increasing doubts. Give me the chance one day to just potter about on the soil, I told myself, and I shall find peace and satisfaction. No need for thanks from anyone. To work on the soil is its own reward.

On wet nights I read books about humus and organic soil culture and joined what is derisively called by the superior and the ignorant the " muck and mysticism " school. My great, steaming compost heap became my greatest pride.

What happened at the *Daily Worker* during those summer and

autumn months of 1946 became almost secondary to my few hours on the garden at night. I continued to keep a reputation for efficiency on my job, I sent my reporters out on the assignments that appealed to me most.

Our correspondents came and went in the " new democracies" and I heard their reports with increasing cynicism.

I had always had the reputation among the staff for a bitter cynical humour. Now that humour appeared more outrageous than ever. I wisecracked about everything which my colleagues held to be most sacred—the Soviet leaders, our own most revered British Party members, the Party line. And I more than half meant what I said. In those cracks the two water-tight compartments came together.

Then, under pressure from the local communists I agreed to act as tutor at a series of classes on communist leadership. I had, the year before, been the one selected by the Party to instruct its tutors in precisely that course. All over London they were teaching the Party members the things which I had taught them. Among them was a well-known dance-band leader whom I had trained and who had since run classes for members of almost all the best-known West End bands, making Marxists in each as a consequence.

Surely, despite the fact that I was now supposed to take my leisure quietly, I could at least do the same for them, said the local Party branch.

I told myself that this might bring me back to my old un-questioning faith, restore the old fire, the passing of which I regretted and wanted to resist. I took the classes but found that I was making my points without conviction, arguing a case which, deep down, I did not really feel.

I reacted by defying my doctor's orders and taking on some public speaking, defending my communism aggressively, attack-ing the enemies of communism with extravagance. But still the old fire would not come and I went back to my books on the land, to my beloved Chaucer and Langland, to studying the Middle Ages, reading of their art and architecture, listening to their music, angry at my defeat.

Winter brought with it greater opportunities for reading than

I had had for years, but my Marxist text-books remained on their shelves, except when required for appropriate quotations for use in my work.

I had been doing a certain amount of free-lance writing, as did most of the paper's executives, in order to supplement my *Daily Worker* salary. Now I took on more.

I had time for thought, to review the road I had travelled. I was surprised at how far I had gone, how much of my old faith I had lost. I saw that my feelings about the land, which I had had during the summer months, much as they meant to me and would always mean to me, did not alone represent a philosophy of life. They would not fill the gap left by the withering away of my communism—for when I was completely frank with myself I now knew that that was what was happening.

For years I had had something to live for, something to believe in. But where did I go from here? The *Weekly Review* had begun a process which had destroyed a good deal, but something like a vacuum was being left as my old beliefs shrank and shrank. I was becoming increasingly aware of the appeal of an almost completely opposite philosophy, but it hardly seemed possible that it could ever be mine.

I still read the Catholic Press for " dirt ", but could find little. Instead there appeared to be a good deal of sound common sense mixed with what seemed crude and extravagant anti-communism.

XIX

TWO IN HARNESS

In addition to reading the *Weekly Review* with sympathetic interest now, I was similarly reading the *Catholic Herald*, whose attitude to terror-bombing and unconditional surrender at the end of the war had struck a sympathetic note. I took copies home at night, and left them about, half hoping that Carol might also be reading them. I dared not discuss with her what was happening to my communist faith. She had made big sacrifices for the movement and I had no reason to doubt that she still felt the same towards it. She had sacrificed a comfortable life for the Party, giving her time and energy to it and working with me on the *Daily Worker*. When I felt my communism slipping I desperately hoped that we might not drift too far apart, for it would be a poor home where the one went on giving her all to the communism in which the other had all but ceased to believe. Our second child was coming and she had given up her work on the paper and had for the time being dropped out of Party activity.

One day, reading the *Weekly Review*, a thought struck me which was so obvious as to be almost laughably so. Yet it was so opposed to all that I had held for so long that it cast doubts upon almost all my thinking to date.

For twenty years I had been troubled by the evidence of the unequal distribution of wealth and the social injustices which appeared to flow from it. I had reasoned: " The unequal distribution of property gives rise to great social injustice. Therefore private property is wrong and should be abolished." Millions have reasoned along similar lines. It has influenced an entire generation.

Now, suddenly, the slipshod character of such pre-fabricated thought struck me between the eyes. The maldistribution of property did not *necessarily* prove that private property was wrong in itself. If it proved anything at all it was surely that its distribution was wrong and that a means must therefore be found to spread it more evenly over the population as a whole. The formulation should have been: " The unequal distribution of property gives rise to great social injustice. Therefore property should be more equitably distributed."

It had hitherto seemed axiomatic that those who revolted against inequality should turn to Marxism for a solution and that those who stood for the perpetuation of inequalities and injustices should oppose communism as a consequence. That there could possibly be a solution which was not a Marxist one had hardly occurred to me.

If one of the main starting points of my years in Marxism had depended upon such phoney thought, then what right had I to accept, more or less as gospel-truth, the superstructure—all the imposing philosophy, the political programmes, the strategy and tactics, the way of life—built upon that foundation? I was opening my whole mind receptively at last to anti-Marxist ideas.

I got hold of everything of Chesterton's and Belloc's on which I could lay my hands, tried to find out more about their Distributism and the philosophy behind it.

Then, after buying a cheap edition of Chesterton's *Orthodoxy*, I went on from that to books by other Catholic authors.

I re-read the history of the Middle Ages I had thought I knew so well and of the Reformation period, and found each book appealing more strongly than the last. A new light was thrown on the end of the Middle Ages, the ages with a Faith.

I had believed that Catholic culture had been outgrown at the time when the new economic system of capitalism had broken the fetters of feudalism, that it could all be explained in terms of economics.

But had men outgrown it? There appeared to be a convincing case for saying that it was not outgrown but that there had been an attempted murder which had not quite succeeded. My old love of the Middle Ages, their art and literature, for pre-Reformation architecture and for plain-chant bubbled up anew as I sought to recapture the spirit of the days whose passing I so much regretted.

As we came to mid-winter I tried to recreate the spirit of Christmas, the feast I had lived for for years. Even in the days of my most complete acceptance of communism I had clung to Christmas, arguing that it was a grand old pagan feast, anyway. I had written about its pagan antecedents and survivals for the Press fifteen or sixteen years before.

I tipped carol-singers with abandonment in order to ensure return visits to my door, sang carols—and the older the better—from morning till night. It was all very nostalgic and somewhat synthetic.

I was trying to capture what lay behind them, what had given them meaning and significance. But I realised sadly that the

Babe was not a living person for me. He was just a nice idea which some lucky devils, even in these days of greater knowledge, could still believe in. I envied them as I envied my little girl Rowena, who was still guileless enough to believe in gnomes and fairies, although she had never heard of God.

The inner knowledge that I had lost most of my communism, had grasped at Catholicism and found my hands empty, was shattering. There was so much I could accept and yet so much more that eluded me. The art, the culture, the way of life, what I knew of the philosophy, attracted me. But their Divine foundation was something against which my mind was closed.

Again my health played tricks with me. I was run down and sleeping badly. Then I developed what my doctor thought to be some sort of heart trouble, and after much examining and various tests he told me that my symptoms were those of *angina pectoris* and ordered me to stop work at once.

Down from the shelf at home came the big medical book which informed me that the disease (a) was incurable, (b) resulted in ever more frequent attacks, each more painful than the last, which continued until the patient succumbed to one of them. So, maybe, the candle was going to be snuffed out. Ring down the curtain, the farce is done.

I went back to my garden, quietly avoiding any sort of strain, as befitted one who was thought to be an incurable heart-sufferer. The future was obscure, with no real certainty that even after a long rest I should be able to take up my old work.

A month went by during which I tried to adjust my mind to the new situation and then I went to a hospital for diseases of the heart for examination.

If possible the heart hospital was even more fantastically depressing than the chest clinic had been.

It was a dark and ancient building, approached through a draughty stone corridor in which the out-patients waited for the doors to open. The waiting-room was small and square but as high as the building itself. The only light came from a fanlight high up in the roof. Row upon row of men and women, with the blue complexion of the chronic heart-sufferer, sat on wooden benches looking hopelessly at the wall before them.

On it was painted a legend in dark lettering picked out by the cold, late-winter light which filtered down through the dusty air in a slanting ray. It read: " I shall pass through this world but once. . . ." It must, I felt, have been put there by some monstrous practical joker.

With gloomy faces and numbed minds we sat hour after hour looking at it, wondering whether it was intended to cheer or to depress us.

Then, stripped and with just pyjama coats over us, we stood shivering in corridors, occasionally passing from one group of students to another, to be prodded and questioned, photographed, X-rayed and cardiographed. For many there it was normal routine, just part of life.

I came away knowing that I had *not* got *angina pectoris*, that my heart was at least without disease and that, once again, " this man is suffering from strain ". After my month in the legion of the incurables I returned to my old position on the *Daily Worker*. I had not slept for several months and so was put on to drugs in order to keep going. Otherwise life on the paper went on much as before.

I read Ronald Knox's *The Belief of Catholics* and found myself in intellectual agreement with it. But it did not make me believe in God. That belief had been dead too long. Nothing stirred, nothing clicked.

The B.B.C. news had just finished one night. It had been much the same as the news of any other night for a long time past, with a dismal recital of the evidences of the disunity of the United Nations.

Then, as I was about to switch it off, Carol, who had been listening too, said angrily: " I'm sick of old Molotov saying No, No, No, the whole of the time. And I'm utterly fed up with Russia's behaviour since the end of the war."

It was as though a reputed saint, living in a Christian home, had followed up a broadcast of the Mass with a string of outrageous blasphemies.

And such is human nature in general, and the twisted skein of my own position at that time in particular, that I turned on her, shocked and outraged.

" That's a bloody fine way for the wife of a leading member of the Communist Party to talk," I exploded furiously.

" I don't care," was her defiant rejoinder, " I meant every word of it and I'll repeat it all if you like."

She followed it up with a wholesale condemnation of all that had been taking place in Eastern Europe since the end of the war and a prediction that before we knew where we were we should find that Russia had succeeded in giving us a third world war.

Then came a broadside on the British Communist Party leaders and a defiant declaration that she was fed up with the whole lot of them.

By this time I was getting over the initial shock and my heart was leaping. " You talk like the *Universe*," I scolded half-heartedly. " What the dickens do you think you're doing? Are you becoming a Catholic or something?"

My heart leaped still more when she said wistfully:

" I wish I were."

" And I wish to God I could do the same," I answered.

Then, for the first time for months, we came clean with each other. I told her just how far I had travelled.

How I had come to realise that the culture of the Middle Ages had not died with feudalism but was alive today, a living Catholic culture. How I for one had had enough of hatred and class war; that I believed that that went for millions like us. Men were ready today for a message of love and peace. (In all the years we had been together I had not used the word love to her except in its sexual connotation, and the word came strangely to my lips.)

How communism was proving wrong in practice and the old Catholic teachings were being shown to be one hundred per cent right. How the world might or might not be subject to Marx's law but that that did not account for the world.

How man, too, might have evolved along historical materialist lines, but it did not explain man.

How my reading of Chesterton, Belloc and the *Weekly Review* had convinced me that they were right on fundamentals and we had been wrong.

How St. Thomas Aquinas's five proofs of God seemed to me

unanswerable, but how, also, I was obliged to admit that whilst they carried with them intellectual conviction they had not made God come alive for me. That I could accept His existence intellectually but that was all.

Then Carol talked. She told me how she had for some time had a secret wish that Rowena should not grow up in a communist home.

Rowena was a good-looking child and a mother's instinct was telling her that hers were the sort of looks that might last.

Supposing she grew up a " good-looker " and with nothing but Engels' ideas on the home and family to guide her, mixing from the start with the Party's leaders. With the Party's morals being what they were, what would happen to her? She would spend her time going from one to the next.

Carol had read the Catholic papers which I had been leaving about the house and from them she had got a picture of what a home and family might be like—a picture the exact opposite of that which we had known as communists.

As she talked I saw that vision too. I looked back over the years. I had accepted communist morals and had practised them. Many of my colleagues had been able to love as irresponsibly and as indiscriminatingly as barnyard fowls. For me that had never been possible. My experiments in that direction went only to show that happiness and fullness of life did not lie that way, but that their exact opposites did.

We both agreed that all our experience showed that the Marxists were wrong, whether we judged them in the light of our own lives or of the broken homes of the comrades we knew.

But the Catholic Church stood, foursquare, like a rock, utterly uncompromising on this question. How right it was.

And Carol admitted too that, though the Catholic " case " appealed and convinced, she, like me, was unable really to believe in God.

We decided half-jokingly yet very wistfully that we had better call ourselves Catholics who didn't believe in God. And there we stuck for many months, learning more of Catholic thought from books eagerly devoured and from its application in the Catholic papers, but still unable to get that belief.

XX

LONG LIVE THE INTERNATIONAL

MEMBERS of the *Daily Worker* editorial staff were given the opportunity of cheap holidays in Czechoslovakia the following summer and many of them took it. Our editor, William Rust, went to Yugoslavia, then on to Czechoslovakia.

In Belgrade, Tito warned him that Gottwald was out of favour; that whilst the rest of the " new democracies " were imposing what amounted to the classical dictatorship of the proletariat on their peoples as a necessary pre-condition of communism, the Czechoslovak Party was arguing that under the peculiar conditions obtaining there it would be possible to go forward to communism by using the democratic forms of organisation— which was precisely what we had been telling our people too.

This, said Tito, was regarded by the other communist leaders as rank heresy and was causing difficulties for them. It made it a bit hard if they were deriding bourgeois democracy and telling their people it must be destroyed whilst at the same time another set of communist leaders were saying the opposite and putting it successfully into practice. A showdown, said Tito, was expected soon.

So, thus warned, Rust did not stay long in Czechoslovakia. It was of the Yugoslav advances towards Sovietisation that he talked to the staff and to the executive meeting when he returned to Britain.

Tito was the special hero of a whole generation, as it were, of communists; those who had come into the Party during the war. The first Soviet-made war film we had seen after Russia was brought into the war was a glorification of the Tito-led Yugoslav guerillas.

Tito had for years been an almost legendary figure, his picture taking its place side by side with that of Stalin in many communist homes.

Of the two, Tito appealed most to the communist youth in particular. Stalin had become the kindly-looking (or kindly-

pictured) statesman and strategist.   Tito was handsome (or made
to appear so), dashing, colourful.

My own second secretary had decorated her corner of the
room in which she worked with a little art gallery of her own:
Stalin, Tito, Paul Robeson and by way of contrast Frankie
Sinatra.   She was a good little girl, product of a broken home,
living with Catholic relatives and fighting hard to keep her communism despite their hostility to her views.   She had an essential
decency which not even the Communist Party could destroy; she
was full of idealism, and her pin-up corner reflected a colossal
hero-worship which took on an almost religious character.   And
Tito was her great hero.

Yugoslavia's communist leaders, Rust reported, were going
ahead more quickly, but more cleverly, than any of the others in
Eastern Europe.   They were proceeding with what was, in reality,
the Sovietisation of their land even though the mass of their own
people did not realise what was happening.

" There is only one underground Party now and that is the
Communist Party," was the inner-Party joke there, for the Party
deliberately concealed its face from the public.

The man who had driven him all over Yugoslavia had only
revealed after four or five days—and only then under pressure—
that he was actually a Party member.

" The Yugoslav Party talks least about itself and does most,"
was Rust's summing up.   " I felt nearer to the Soviet Union
there than at any time since I was in Russia."

I wistfully recalled to myself the words of the Communist
Manifesto: " The communists disdain to conceal their aims. . . ."

There seemed to be nothing heroic left in post-war communism.
It was revolution by stealth.   Again I thanked my lucky stars
I was not the Foreign Editor, having to sell Soviet foreign policy
and the new democracies to our readers.

I could, at least, still feel that my own department's work was
useful and even honest, so far as I could make it so.

Our assistant editor (now editor-in-chief), J. R. Campbell, was
busy working on solutions for Britain's post-war economic
problems and doing it with all the skill and patience with which
he is so well endowed.

Johnnie is a friendly, peaceable, understanding little man who nonetheless has been in the forefront of many a riot, has fought in many street battles and has made speeches which have led to many more. He has a capacity for grappling with difficult economic problems which is the envy of all who see him at work. He can attend a Government Press conference at which statistics are reeled off for an hour at a time, then walk straight out of the conference room to the nearest telephone and dictate his story, with all the facts and figures interpreted and simplified for the reader—and still never slip up.

He can take a huge official publication and digest it in as long as it takes the average journalist to read the preamble. It was almost uncanny to see him take a thick Government statistical digest, run quickly through its pages standing at his desk and then sit down and start writing his story interpreting it.

As leader of the Communist Party's economic sub-committee he had a grand chance of using his gifts. The Party has created a number of such sub-committees, on Colonial questions, on social services, on industry, on youth, on women's problems and on scientific questions. Their personnel is, in many ways, the most interesting of any. Their purpose is to use, under the guidance of a Political Bureau member who occupies the position of chairman, the specialist knowledge of " under-cover " members who hold more-than-usually useful jobs but who are not necessarily political leaders. For in the Party's ranks are university professors, Government research scientists, civil servants in confidential jobs, sometimes in Ministries, and a host of others who cannot be " open " members of the Party and who would be wasted on ordinary Party work. Such people are drawn into the work of the various sub-committees.

Johnnie Campbell at that time had the advantage of having many such people on whose experience he could draw. At any meeting of the economic sub-committee one at least of the universities would be represented by a professor of economics along with people from a Government department or two and a leading financial paper. Together they worked on an economic plan for post-war Britain, putting into it a vast amount of time and thought.

The social services committee, headed by William Rust, was approaching its work in an equally constructive frame of mind, backed by the experience and inside knowledge of someone serving on a " hush-hush " Government committee on housing research, a London professor, leading medical men serving on official commissions, and a civil servant in a Ministerial department concerned with housing.

After years in the Party it seemed perfectly normal to me that, in tackling the job, we should use every channel of knowledge, information and experience open to us, " milking " official and confidential documents as a matter of course. Those had been the sources of many an exclusive story we had run, they provided the background essential to a knowledge of what was happening in the enemy camp and for being able to analyse the situation with a view to laying down lines of action. The ethics of the thing just did not enter into it.

It was taken for granted that any Party member coming into possession of information useful to the cause of communism or the Soviet Union (which meant the same thing) would pass it on. It would be treachery not to do so.

Thus a doctor in a position to know or discover the course of talks between the British Medical Association and the Ministry of Health on the projected National Health Service would, as a matter of course, disclose what he knew to a discreet *Daily Worker* reporter, whom I would select for the job, and also to the appropriate Party sub-committee.

A specialist serving on a Government committee on housing materials would keep us informed, as part of his Party duty, of any decisions made and any proposed changes or, especially, modifications of the Government's housing plans.

A civil servant working in a Government department in which internal memoranda circulated freely would keep an eye open for anything which affected Party policy or the interests of the U.S.S.R. Even a junior typist could pick up useful material in this way, and it was often such people who would take the greatest risks. A Board of Trade contact could keep us informed of Government intentions when trade talks with Eastern European countries were pending or in progress. The *Daily Worker* would then, if it was considered expedient, publish an "informed" story full of intelligent anticipation and aimed at putting pressure on the Government, but not revealing enough to show what were its sources.

The full information would, however, be passed on to the appropriate Embassy, so that when the negotiators next met all the cards would be in their hands.

During this period a new "contact" was found, with precisely such connections. The internal memoranda which she passed on to us—and which in due course found their way to the Czecho-slovak Embassy—were often far from calculated to improve relations between the two countries.

The Party knew that the British Government viewed all the Eastern European countries with suspicion and it believed that, unless pressure was exerted upon it, trade with our "new democracies" would be kept at a minimum. The internal memoranda confirmed this view. I recall one such, in particular, which said that the Czechs were behaving rather like poor relations who have suddenly found themselves with something to sell and immediately ask fantastically high prices as a consequence. But if its frank phrasing made the Czechs feel like an individual who reads someone else's correspondence and finds in it uncomplimentary references to himself, they also learned a good deal from the facts and figures relating to British intentions.

The girl who passed on those particular documents was a simple, idealistic, very nervous, highly indiscreet young woman, new to the Party and terribly in earnest. We had the utmost difficulty at first in preventing her from using her office phone to pass on the more exciting tit-bits which came her way. Yet we knew that she was actually scared about what she was doing and her indiscretions were the result of a great naïvety and an even greater enthusiasm.

But a nasty flavour was left in my mouth when, on the basis of one of her documents, there was an editorial decision that a story should be run on Yugoslav trade which must, inevitably, reveal her identity. When I and the reporter who had been her contact protested that it would get her into trouble we were met with the answer: "So what? She's a bloody little fool anyway."

H

In industry we were beginning to take the line that " the legitimate demands of the workers for higher wages " should have our
support, but not (except in purely luxury trades) to the point of
strike action.   Even this marked a considerable development on
our latter war-time policy of opposing all strikes and preventing
all disputes at whatever cost.

The Party " fractions " at the various trade union conferences
were organised with particular care, as this was a situation from
which, it seemed likely, we could not fail to benefit.   We would
support the official, Labour Government line, back constructive
policies and, at the same time, give sympathetic support to the
growing demands for higher wages.

The Party takes its work in the trade unions seriously, organises
it with considerable skill and reaps the benefit in terms of positions
and influence as a consequence.

The headquarters' Industrial Department begins planning its
work for the year's trade union conferences on January 1 and
does not let up until the last " fraction " has been steered through
the last conference.

Each conference is approached with the same care.   Months
before a conference is due to take place leading communists in
the union are called together, resolutions are framed and
branches selected from which they shall be sent for inclusion in
the agenda.   Branches from which communists can be sent as
delegates are also noted and in due course the Party members
there are informed that they must work to get one of their
members adopted.   Headquarters constantly checks on the
implementation of the decisions taken at the " fraction ".

When the delegates have all been officially elected from the
branches and districts, and the preliminary agenda has been
published, a full " fraction " is called at which will be present, in
addition to the communists who are to go to conferences as
delegates, leading members of the Party's Industrial Department
and, in most cases, a *Daily Worker* industrial correspondent or
some other member of the paper's industrial team (who is not,
of course, a member of the union concerned).

Together they will go through the agenda, decide on those
resolutions which shall be supported, those which must be

opposed; which people are to be supported in election of officers and what, if any, emergency resolutions should be moved. They will choose their spokesmen for the various issues on which the Party wants to make its voice heard.

In due course, they will meet again on the eve of the conference to check last-minute arrangements and then go into action as an organised team, knowing just what they want and how they are going to get it. Such tactics work unless the non-communists are organised to resist them or are more than usually alert and vigilant, so that even a very few communists may achieve a very great deal and a large minority can sweep the conference.

The Party's influence in the trade unions was still in the ascendancy and our " fractions " that year often got almost everything they aimed at. And, by and large, I felt the policies they stood for were constructive and useful. I knew, of course, that, as always, those policies were keyed to the conquest of power for communism, but I was by then concerning myself solely with short-term aims and not thinking too much about the ultimate goal. After all, the Party might not succeed in achieving Soviet power but so long as present policies continued it was doing good rather than harm.

I told myself these things, but not with entire conviction, for the situation was an impossible one. I could not continue indefinitely to feel enthusiasm for our home policies and at the same time be appalled at the persecution of non-communist leaders in those lands where the Party ruled.

I was profoundly disturbed by the execution of the Party's opponents in Eastern Europe and by the melancholy procession of those who were driven from their homelands. I was concerned about what would be the fate of Stanislaw Mikolajczyk, the Polish Peasant Party leader who had flown out to Poland from London for the elections which had been staged by the Polish communists earlier in the year and who, my colleagues gloatingly prophesied, would never be allowed to return alive. Their cynicism, which had been my own for so many years, began to revolt me. The trouble was that I was beginning to think in terms of individual human beings and their fate and not just of the impersonal masses and the political policies which I had believed to be for their ultimate good.

I had done so when, in September 1946, Archbishop Stepinac was arrested by Tito's Government and put on trial. I knew, as every communist knew, that he was not, in fact, being tried for being a war criminal, an associate of subversive movements, but for the views he held. He was on trial for being a Catholic. His deportment in court, his refusal to discuss the things with which he was charged and his courageous statement of the things for which he, too, knew he was being tried impressed me tremendously.

" The Catholics have their Dimitroffs, too," I thought. But although the personal courage of Dimitroff before Göring had been held up by the Party as worthy of admiration in itself, the courage of Mgr. Stepinac met only with sneers from my colleagues. And Dimitroff, once the giant, had shrunk visibly and ignominiously to pygmy proportions when he found himself with Petkov in his power.

Everyone in the office took it for granted that Archbishop Stepinac would be shot or hanged; it was simply a question of which would it be. My reporters and fellow-executives viewed with relish, as I would have done not long before, the execution of a prince of the Church. When he was given a sentence of sixteen years' forced labour there was acute disappointment, which, however, was quickly soothed by political explanations to the effect that it was not yet time for an all-out attack upon the Church. That show-down would come later. In Party classes and at branch meetings the coming struggle with the Church was discussed and looked forward to with pleasure.

Members of the Political Bureau who had been to Czechoslovakia had been told that it was believed that the fight against the Church could be carried through without too much difficulty in the Czech lands, so strong had the Party become there. But the Slovak Catholics, they were told, were much more completely in the grip of the priests and bishops, and " special measures " would be required. At a *Daily Worker* executive meeting we were told that those special measures would probably have to take the form of armed action at some point. Sooner or later the Catholic peasants could be provoked into violence, some incident would be presented as the intended forerunner of armed insurrection and tough counter-measures would then provide the chance for conducting the thorough-going purge which was required. A bit of terror would soon settle them.

Again, I should most certainly have approved and justified such schemes before I began to read and think along Christian lines. Now I was filled with an uneasiness which at times amounted to revulsion as I heard it all explained. It was not communism but I that had changed, but I now found the application of our theories and tactics clashing with all I felt to be right.

But that was just it. I was beginning to say that some things were right and some were wrong. I was judging communist behaviour on the basis of ethics and not expediency—a thoroughly un-Marxist thing to do.

It was still not always a fully conscious process, but I became increasingly aware of what was happening and found myself viewing it from outside myself as it were, an interested and often astonished spectator of my own mental and spiritual processes.

Thus, for example, in a break between editions, one of my reporters, son of a well-known author, who had worked on the Yugoslav Youth Railway, was describing some of the things he had seen.

He told how at communist meetings the local populace would be brought together to hear a speech from Tito, or from one of the other communist leaders. At pre-arranged points during the speech Party members in the crowd would start to chant " Tito, Tito," or maybe " Tito, Stalin, Tito, Stalin," and the crowd would take it up, repeating the names over and over again. It was a technique used by Mussolini and Hitler and was now being turned to good account in the cause of communism.

He went on to describe how, when he had turned up at one such meeting, the word had gone round that an English comrade was present and they had quickly switched to " Tito, Stalin, Harry Polleet, Tito, Stalin, Harry Polleet," which they had kept up for an astonishing length of time. My reporters laughed uproariously at the story. Suddenly I realised that I was making myself conspicuous by not laughing at all; instead I was feeling utterly disgusted.

It was not sufficient now to tell myself that the end justified the means. Once a Marxist begins to differentiate between right and wrong, just and unjust, good and bad, to think in terms of spiritual values, the worst has happened so far as his Marxism is concerned.

The British Party had been given no indication whatsoever that the Communist Information Bureau was to be formed. On the *Daily Worker* we first learned the news when it came over the agency tape machines, accepting it with reserve until it was confirmed by the Soviet Monitor, then passing on the information to Party headquarters.

The Parties invited to the initial meeting had been those of Russia, France, Italy, Poland, Yugoslavia, Bulgaria, Czechoslovakia, Hungary, Rumania. They were those which were already ruling Parties or those which Moscow thought would soon be so. The British Party came into neither category.

We decided that, until we learned otherwise, we must treat it in our columns as though it were simply an Information Bureau. But everyone was asking: " Is it the Communist International re-formed ? " Most answered their own question with a very definite yes. They were told by the Political Bureau that they were guilty of wishful thinking—but the P.B. was thinking the same whilst it anxiously awaited more light on the subject. At the editorial executive which followed the announcement, Bill Rust opened with his usual political review of the situation. He declared that little useful purpose would be served by discussing the new development until more information was available. The others, however, brought it into the discussion. The Foreign Editor thought that it was undoubtedly the forerunner of a new International. He complained at the lack of service from *Tass* and Soviet Monitor. Others supported his estimation of the rôle of the new organisation but J. R. Campbell declared that it might after all be what it was described as and no more. There were now common problems for most of the Communist Parties concerned, arising from American Aid to Europe, and it was natural that they should set up such an information bureau. The others listened with sceptical smiles on their faces and the argument became acrimonious. R. Palme Dutt quickly brought it to an end by declaring that we were all equally in the dark until more information was received so we might as well save our breath.

When no inside news came a Party member was sent to Belgrade to find out what it was all about and, approximately at the same time, the French Party vouchsafed the British Party a certain amount of information. It was all very " hush-hush ", and the British leaders were at first told only as much as was considered good for them. But an indication of what it was going to mean in practice soon came my way.

For years my industrial reporters had been writing stories aimed at raising production and ending impediments to all-out industrial effort. One of them had made a study of railway problems. Reports were being received of increased output in the Yorkshire coal-field and it occurred to me that the value of this would be largely lost if a bottle-neck, which we had previously exposed, still existed at the important Doncaster rail centre.

I discussed it with my specialist and he agreed that, unless things had improved, the coal would pile up at the pit-heads and, in time, would slow output right down again. We decided that no matter whether the bottle-neck had been cleared or whether it still existed, there would be a story either way. If the former, it would be a story of achievement—a morale-building story— if the latter, it would mean yet another exposure. I informed the editor that I had sent the reporter to Doncaster and he agreed that it was a good and necessary assignment.

In due course the story was phoned to me. The bottle-neck had been cleared by a combination of managerial efficiency and workers' effort.

" There's no scandal in it," said the reporter, " just straight good work by all concerned." With the editor's approval it was made the leading story on the main home news page. It came in for a word of special commendation from the editorial chair when the first edition was examined at the conference which preceded commencement of work on the second edition.

But half an hour later, when work on the edition was just about to start in earnest, the editor called me to his office. We should, he told me, have to lose the story. When I asked why, he replied that it was " pure sunshine " and went on to explain that a new approach to such stories was now needed. Increased production " under present conditions ", he said, meant, not a higher standard of life for the British people, but higher profits for the American capitalists, and, moreover, it simply assisted them with their plans for the defeat of communism in Europe.

It was all in flat contradiction to the prevailing Party line, not only as officially and publicly proclaimed, but also as understood by the Party rank and file and even by the Executives.

The story which half an hour earlier had come in for special praise was thrown out. The new line had arrived from Belgrade. At the next editorial executive meeting we were given a confidential report to the effect that, although the Cominform line was not yet known in full detail, it was now clearly understood in main outline. It would mean the gradual reversal of the Party's previous line in industry, but the executive committee had not yet been made aware of this and no public statement would be made until they had met, by which time more information should be available and we would then know just how far to go. Meanwhile all " sunshine stories " would be dropped and the solution of production problems would no longer be our concern.

There was, as yet, no instruction to the effect that we would go over to impeding production. For the moment we were " neutral ", awaiting further orders. But I saw then the possible significance of a remark made by a Political Bureau member not long before, and began to prepare my mind for the worst.

When American Aid was first offered to Europe the Czechoslovak Government had alone among the " new democracies " come forward to accept it at the Paris Conference. Then came a quick step back into line again after an angry protest from the U.S.S.R. At an editorial meeting we had discussed the incident and agreed that there would be difficulties ahead for the Party leaders who had refused the proffered aid, especially if that aid led to a quicker rate of recovery in the West than in the East of Europe. Then the Political Bureau member had made his remark, which was followed by the sort of silence which follows an obvious indiscretion.

It would not be possible, he said, quickly to raise the standard of life of the people in the new democracies, since theirs were mainly peasant economies. But there was another way of raising their *relative* standards and that would be by reducing that of the countries of the West. " And that shouldn't take the Party long," he added.

It is rarely that the Party's real aims are put clearly into words in that way. Even at top levels they normally talk in the language of the Party's public propaganda, whilst the real and concealed meaning is understood by all present who share the same knowledge of Marxist-Stalinist theory, jargon and methods of thought.

In the light of the new developments, my colleague's words seemed sinister in the extreme. Our home policy alone had held me for some time. Now that too, it appeared, was about to go.

XXI

THE CUL-DE-SAC

EVERY shock, every disappointment, every occasion on which I found myself troubled by what the Party was doing at home and abroad made me turn the more eagerly to my Catholic reading and set me thinking the more furiously about it. Here were constant values, an appeal to reason which stood up to scrutiny, an ethic which was attractive and obviously right, a view of life which was clearly satisfying for those who could accept it in its entirety and who knew from their personal, spiritual experience that it was true. But I was still not one of these.

For Carol and I had remained stuck as " Catholics who did not believe in God ". With all our hearts we now yearned for that belief but it would not come. We read " the Catholic case ", as we called it, and intellectually we accepted what we read, for it stood up to examination, even in our new, questioning frame of mind. But we knew it was not enough simply to accept intellectually the truth of Catholicism. We must feel it, know it from the experience of our own inner lives.

We had found it difficult to accept the existence of God intellectually. We had quite sincerely believed that we knew all the answers without Him. Dialectical materialism had explained, to our satisfaction, the whole universe for us; like Nietzsche it had proclaimed that " God is dead " and we had believed it and felt it to be true.

For us He had been dead for years. We had appeared to get on all right without Him. We had been aware of the existence of no inner life, no spiritual needs. Our communism had been our whole life. When doubts had come about the policies of the Party, about its methods, even about the desirability of its goal, they did not necessarily and immediately undermine our dialectical materialism nor prove that it must, therefore, be wrong in all its main assumptions.

Even the exciting realisation that the culture of the Middle Ages which I had loved for so long was still alive, that it was a Catholic culture which had not died with the Reformation, did not prove the existence of God, although it helped. Belief in God might be but the product of a certain stage of man's historical development, surviving into a later period along with the rest of the " ideological superstructure " that went with it. That superstructure of the Middle Ages might be attractive, it might include a great outpouring of human genius in terms of magnificent churches and cathedrals, glorious music, works of art which took one's breath away, literature which gripped as nothing else could—and still not prove that God was alive or even necessary as an explanation for it all, even though faith in God had been its inspiration.

But that phase had passed. We had come to accept the intellectual case for God, to see that without it not only Catholicism but the universe itself made nonsense. We had discovered with some surprise that the great thinkers and philosophers of the Church had made out a better case for God's existence than Marx and Engels had done for His non-existence.

Yet we realised that that was not enough. Belief meant being able to *feel* the existence of the spiritual, to *know* God and not just to know *about* Him. Christians even said they loved Him, they talked to Him and listened to Him. That was still outside our experience and, in moments of depression, we feared that it would remain so.

Yet all paths seemed to lead to Rome. I was asked to review Avro Manhattan's book, *The Catholic Church against the Twentieth Century*, along with a pamphlet by the Rev. Stanley Evans. The first was a large book which set out to prove, by means of telling the story of Vatican policies since World War I, that the Catholic Church was fascist.

The other had much the same intention, attempting to show that the Church was against all " progress ". Once, I should have had grand fun with them, using them to smear Catholics and fascists at one and the same time. I tried to do the same now, failed and hated myself for even attempting it. It was a last desperate attempt to salvage the way of life I had loved. It failed completely.

Instead I found myself saying: The Catholic Church against the twentieth century? So what? So am I, if the twentieth century means the crazy world I see about me which has endured two world wars and goodness knows how many revolutions already, and with the war-clouds gathering so soon after the last war.

Against the twentieth century? Against the century of the atom bomb? Against a world right off the rails? Against those beliefs which lead to people persecuting men like Archbishop Stepinac and preparing a Red Terror against the Slovak peasants? Against the crazy post-war conditions right here in Britain? Why not? So am I.

Instead of gaining ammunition against the Church from Manhattan's book, I learned, despite the tendentious writing, something of the Church's social teaching. It was written to make anti-Catholics. It helped to make me " pro " instead.

The Anglican Stanley Evans I knew already and I knew his type of parson-cum-communist-sympathiser well enough. The Party uses such people, but it rarely respects them. I had used such types myself. I read his pamphlet with distaste. He wanted to show that the Church was opposed to " progress " everywhere.

And again, so what? It all depended on what you meant by progress.

Was Nagasaki progress? When the story, one of a vast number which make such things normal to newspaper life, came over the tape machine about a boy of eighteen sent to jail by a London court for theft and described as living on the immoral earnings of his twenty-year-old divorcée wife, was that progress? Or was the trap for Mikolajczyk, laid by the Warsaw Government (and from which he had now escaped), progress? Were the preparations now going forward in Hungary for the persecution of the Church and suppression of the religion of the vast majority of the people there progress? Was it progress for our generation more and more to move away from the idea of the worth of the individual to that of the impersonal masses?

And in any case was it really so certain as we had imagined it to be that the world must inevitably " progress ", that the past was necessarily less good and civilised than the present and still less so than the future? Must the new always, automatically, be superior to the old?

Somewhere I had seen a reactionary described as one who, finding himself on the edge of a precipice, sees the danger and steps back in time. On the basis of that definition I was a reactionary. And again, so what?

Perhaps, in one of life's grand Chestertonian paradoxes, the " progressives " were really the reactionaries—in the light of their own definition of the term—and those who saw the danger and stepped back might yet be the progressives, possessing a new solution which was really the oldest of all. The line of thought those two anti-Catholic publications set in motion helped me along on my road to Rome.

The way in which the whole of medieval life was steeped in Catholic thought, even in its lightest and most ribald moments, was brought vividly home to me as I listened to the broadcast version of *The Canterbury Tales*. I had thought I could at least claim to know my Chaucer. Now I saw that a whole world, implicit in every line, had escaped me as a communist.

I had still not been in a Catholic church, but listening to Fernando Germani's organ broadcasts from Westminster

Cathedral took me right inside. Then I saw advertised in my local Town Hall a Brains Trust, organised by the Wimbledon branch of the Sword of the Spirit. I had never been to anything Catholic, had never known any Catholics personally, never seen Catholics together in the mass. I wanted to go and, almost shamefacedly, told Carol so. We decided that I should attend, keep well in the background, lest I should be seen, and tell her what I felt about it in due course. We wanted to know if we could " stomach " Catholics as persons.

I went late so that I had an excuse for remaining at the back. I crept in as though I were taking part in a conspiracy, my emotions strangely mixed as I slipped into a back seat in the half-light. Here was an assembly of the people who stood at the opposite pole to that at which I had stood for the past twenty years.

On the platform were two Jesuits (stories from my non-conformist childhood and my days in communism cast heavy shadows on them); Richard Stokes, Catholic Labour M.P., whom I had often denounced as a friend of the fascists; Commander Bower, former Catholic Conservative M.P., whom I had similarly denounced with even greater venom; Dr. Letitia Fairfield, about whose " reactionary " views I had heard a great deal from an enthusiastic communist whom we both knew, and Robert Speaight, the actor, viewed in communist stage circles as a reactionary and obscurantist. Instinctively one half of me reacted away from them. Yet simultaneously the other half said : " These are Catholics, they belong to the tradition you love. They hold the views you now admire. Their philosophy is the one you have all but embraced. Their way of life is the one for which you have yearned so long."

Before long I was warming to them. The political questions asked and the answers given seemed naïve, the cracks which brought the biggest laughs seemed oddly unsophisticated; it was a straighter, simpler, cleaner world than mine. I liked it. " I *can* stomach Catholics after all," I told myself.

I had feared it would not be so, for I had retained all the quite unreasoning prejudices of my early nonconformist days: I thought that all priests, nuns and monks were immoral, that

Jesuits were sinister and crooked. And I still had my communist prejudices, too. In the Party we had held that the Catholic population in Britain represented the most backward, illiterate, politically moribund section of the people, sunk in superstition and hopelessly priest-ridden.

I saw priests in the audience, and when the meeting adjourned for sandwiches noted the friendly, free-and-easy relationship which existed between clergy and laity. The stories I had believed for so long seemed a good deal less reliable now. But, I told myself, anxious not to rush into hasty and possibly incorrect judgments, " Even if all nuns, monks and priests are in fact immoral hypocrites, if the Catholics *are* the most backward and uncultured of the British people, it does not make *Catholicism* wrong. Catholicism could be right and good even though the whole of the Catholics were bad. It is irrational to judge the Church by Catholics; it must be judged on the basis of its teachings."

I wanted to know how one became a Catholic, in case I should ever succeed in getting over that last hurdle, belief in God. So when the meeting was over I waited for the Question Master, Fr. Francis Devas, a kindly and, it seemed to me from his appearance and behaviour on the platform, an understanding Jesuit.

In the few minutes that it took to walk to the station from the hall I told him who and what I was, keeping my eyes about me as I did so lest I should be seen by one of the local communists. I told him of my past twenty years as a militant atheist, of the practice of my Marxism and the misery I had left behind me, of the tangled skein which was my life: " Could such a man become a Catholic?" I asked. He replied that the Church existed for sinners. It sounded oddly old-fashioned. I had not used the word " sin " since my local-preaching days. Sin finds no place in the communist's vocabulary.

I said that my communist past must dog my future whatever it might be; that you cannot play with dirt without soiling your hands, nor would the consequences of twenty years in communism end because I renounced it. It almost seemed as though I was arguing against myself, my own devil's advocate.

With a twinkle in his eye he told me that if one could not be a good Catholic one could at least be a bad one; that even the bad Catholic had a great deal that the communist had not got. The Church was not full of saints, he said. If I could not be a good Catholic at least I might be a bad one and it would still be better than communism.

I realised then, and still more clearly today, that the man who had seemed so unworldly on the platform was displaying a shrewd (Jesuitical if you like, in the best sense of the word) understanding of human types. I might grasp at the hope of being even a " bad " Catholic, but he knew that I was not the person to be content with being a bad anything at all.

He told me that before one became a Catholic a course of instruction was required and that I might get in touch with him at Farm Street at any time.

I all but ran home to bring the news that we might become Catholics if ever we should be ready for it. We talked half the night, covering the same ground over and over again, always getting back to the same point: we would be Catholics if only it were not for that first premise, belief in God.

And there we stuck, making no perceptible progress, reading, discussing, yearning, but never arriving. We became hopelessly depressed, decided that it was all nostalgia. Some lucky devils might be able to have that faith but it was not for us. It had all been a nice idea, but it could be nothing more. The wasted, misspent years were reaping their reward.

Then one night as we ate our supper I said that I thought we should face up to reality: either we should abandon the whole business or we should be prepared to take an act of faith. Even as I said it I remembered the derisive definition of faith I had so often quoted in the past: Faith is that thing which enables us to believe that which we know to be totally untrue. As had so often been the case in recent years I felt as though I were cut in two, two Douglas Hydes or two consciences urging conflicting lines of thought and action.

One half of me supported my suggestion as being the obvious one, the other derided it, drew back instinctively as from something degrading.

I heard my voice saying: " It is five to ten and we still don't believe in God as a living reality. In five minutes' time, at ten o'clock, let's start. Let's act and think as though there really were one."

At ten o'clock we started. Nothing happened. And weeks later nothing had happened. We hadn't expected visions, or manna from heaven. We still did not feel we believed in the supernatural, so how could we expect miracles? But at least, I thought resentfully, there might have been some psychological consequences from that act of faith. There were none.

At the office things were going from bad to worse. The new Cominform line was clearly going to work out as I had feared, although both the Party Executive and the rank and file had still to be informed of it. Slowly, through the columns of the paper we were adjusting their minds to the pending official reversal of policy. There seemed nothing left, anywhere.

Leaving the office in a mood of the deepest despair one evening, I decided on a sudden impulse that at all costs I must go to a Catholic church. I remembered the Italian church in nearby Clerkenwell Road and hurried there. As I went up the steps a man locked the doors.

I tried to remember any other I had seen, and thought I recalled one in the Exmouth Market, not far away. I dashed through the side streets until I reached it. Then I looked up at it through the darkness. It seemed fortress-like and forbidding. I funked it and hurried away.

I had not slept for months without drugs and that night I didn't sleep with them either.

Next morning I went on my usual train to Holborn Viaduct station and took the road I had taken for years to the office. Passing Ely Place, I observed a notice I had seen hundreds of times before: " St. Etheldreda's Catholic Church ". I looked down the short cul-de-sac at what I had always thought was the most monstrous piece of church architecture of all time. I had seen plenty of ugly Catholic churches, but this, I felt, must be the world's worst. I decided I would go to it nonetheless. If I could stand that I could stand anything.

The ugly building which had revolted me so often proved not

to be a church at all. There was no way into it. It was simply the back wall of a warehouse which formed the cul-de-sac's end.

Then I saw a little church, lying back out of line with the Queen Anne buildings which flanked it. I had passed by without it even occurring to me that *this* could be the Catholic church, for it was quite obviously pre-Reformation. Its exterior, bombed and blasted as it was, quite clearly indicated that it belonged to the period I loved best.

I went in, down through its quiet half-lit cloisters and straight into a Gothic gem, right there on the fringe of the old City of London whose paucity of pre-Reformation churches I had so often deplored.

I was at home at once, taken back to the magnificent church in the Mendip village which was my home, back to the West country, where every hamlet boasts a church fit to be a cathedral. But this was different. There were Holy Water in the stoups, saints in the niches. These were not museum pieces, as had been those in the Gothic churches I had haunted in the past; these were serving their functional purpose. This place was alive.

Black roofing-felt was nailed where stained glass had been before the bomb fell, making it half dark inside, and it was, thank heavens, empty. I took a seat at the back. One or two people came and went. And I just sat.

I got to the office very late that day, and my staff were already waiting for their assignments. I sent them out as quickly as possible so that I should have the place to myself. I had gone into my first Catholic church, found it to be a Gothic gem— and I had just sat. I had not prayed. I had done nothing.

I left the office early and told myself I would just go in for a moment before I caught my train. I stayed an hour, sitting in darkness, lit only by the tiny spluttering altar flame.

I was back there next morning, careful to slip in only when I was sure that the coast was clear. It was reminiscent of the early war days when I was always tailed by a detective.

The more I saw of St. Etheldreda's the more I loved it. But still I could not pray. It was ridiculous and degrading to get down on your knees (better die on our feet than live for ever on

242 I BELIEVED

our knees, had said the Spanish woman communist leader, La Passionaria). It was a sign of submission, of cringing, crawling humility. Fantastically superstitious, having got on your knees, to talk to someone who wasn't there, did not even exist. But I went back again day after day, night after night. On the Friday morning I bought a copy of each of the Catholic papers in the porch and stuffed them into my case. As I walked into the *Daily Worker* I almost chuckled as I asked myself what would be said if the case flew open, depositing them all on the office floor.

Suddenly I realised just how tight had been the strait-jacket. Others could read pretty well what they liked. If it was known I had bought those papers to read sympathetically I should be sacked as quickly as possible. As quickly, that was, as it would take to frame something against me, for they would not be such fools as officially to dismiss me for reading Catholic papers. I knew what I should have done not long before had one of my staff been crazy enough to do such a thing. He would have been told he was going, for whatever reason we had thought would most damage his future career.

But after weeks of sitting I was back again where I had begun. I loved Etheldreda's, I loved its architecture, its atmosphere, its peace. But that was not what I had gone there for.

As I was leaving the church one Sunday evening I heard footsteps following me through the already dark cloisters, stopping when I stopped, quickening their pace when I quickened mine. I had been followed too often not to be familiar with what was happening. But I saw no one. Much later, I learned that a thief had been regularly visiting the church, rifling the money-boxes, stealing the candles, and a lay brother living with the little community in the adjoining presbytery had been told to keep an eye open for the culprit. He had seen the stranger who came at such odd hours and who observed none of the Catholic practices, appeared never to worship, simply to sit and sit and sit. He had decided that I must be the one responsible and was trying to catch me red-handed. In fact, he caught the real culprit shortly after, right in the act of taking away the altar candles.

My train left the station in that brief period of the evening when impatient night paints every object black against a daylight sky still loth to make its departure. I was weary and unwell, as empty as I had ever been; I had lost a faith and found a vacuum. I had my roots nowhere. Nothing remained.

I looked out at London's buildings outlined black against the magnificent fading blue of the sky. And sharp and clear against that sky was a cross, high above the city, fixed to the topmost point of a high tower. I watched it, as we hurried past, then turned back towards the city to follow it until it went from view. Then I saw another. That, too, was on a building; and as that went from sight another and another appeared.

Through my mind, in rhythm with the wheels, ran a verse from Chesterton's " Ballad of the White Horse " I had re-read not long before:

> " Therefore I bring these rhymes to you,
>   Who brought the cross to me,
> Since on you flaming without flaw
> I saw the sign that Guthrum saw
> When he let break the ships of awe,
>   And laid peace on the sea."

Could there be so many Catholic churches? I asked myself, as cross followed cross. Why had I not seen them before? Through Herne Hill, Tulse Hill, smug, suburban Streatham, the crosses came and went. And still the wheels hammered out Chesterton's lines:

> " Out of the mouth of the Mother of God
>   Like a little word come I;
> For I go gathering Christian men
> From sunken paving and ford and fen,
> To die in a battle, God knows when,
>   By God, but I know why.
> And this is the word of Mary,
>   The word of the world's desire;
> No more of comfort shall ye get,
> Save that the sky grows darker yet
>   And the sea rises higher."

As I travelled up the line next morning I looked from side to side for the crosses. There were none there, not even on those buildings that I could recognise from the previous night; but there were lightning-conductors on high grey towers and television aerials on suburban homes which, for one night at least, had inscribed the cross of God magnificently on the night sky of London.

That morning something happened. I was sitting in the gloom of St. Etheldreda's in the backmost seat as usual, when a late-teen-age girl came in, drably dressed and blessed with no good looks. I took her to be a little Irish servant girl. But as she passed me I saw the expression on her face. She, too, was worried. Like me, she clearly had something big on her mind. She went purposefully down the aisle to the front, then round to the left, to a kneeling stool on which she knelt before Our Lady, after having lit a candle and put some coins in a box.

Through such light as managed to creep through the blacked-out windows and by the flame of the candle, I could see her busy with a string of beads, her hands moving, her head nodding every now and then. This was Catholic practice, of which I knew nothing. This was the world of the Ages with a Faith. This was the world I had been groping for. Was it superstition? Was it the world of mumbo-jumbo? Two opposing answers came simultaneously to my question.

As she passed me again on her way out I looked at her face. Whatever had been troubling her had gone. Just like that. And I had been carrying my load around with me for months and years.

When I was sure no one was about I went, almost hang-dog fashion, down the aisle as she had done. Down to the front, round to the left, put some coins in the box, lit a candle, knelt on the stool—and tried to pray to Our Lady. Might as well be hanged for a sheep as a lamb, the two voices told me together. If you're going to be superstitious and pray to someone who isn't there you might just as well go one step further in your superstition and pray to an image and have done with it.

How did one pray to Our Lady? I did not know. Did you pray *to* her or *through* her, using her as an intermediary? Did you gaze at the figure to see the reality behind it or was it to that figure alone that you addressed your words? Again I did not know.

I tried to remember some prayer to her from medieval literature or something from the poems of Chesterton or Belloc. My mind was empty. The candle spluttered and flickered, growing shorter and shorter, but no words came.

At last I heard myself mumbling something which seemed appropriate enough when it began but which petered out, becoming miserably inappropriate. But it did not matter. I knew my search was at an end. I had not talked to nothing.

Outside the church I tried to remember the words I had said and almost laughed as I recalled them. They were those of a dance tune of the nineteen-twenties, a gramophone record of which I had bought in my adolescence:

> " O sweet and lovely lady be good,
>   O lady be good to me."

XXII

MAKING THE BREAK

ABOUT a week later I had encouraging evidence that my attempts to carry some of the new-old values I had now accepted into the *Daily Worker* office itself were not entirely wasted.

I had just briefed a reporter for an assignment when I found myself alone in the room with a colleague. He was a friendly, helpful man who never used a short word where a long one could be employed.

With his thumbs in the armholes of his waistcoat and looking very much concerned he said: " You know, old man, I've noticed with growing perturbation recently, when you have been briefing the reporters, an increasing tendency on your part to make references to the need for truth and honesty and fair reporting."

He gave me a puzzled anxious look: " What the hell's coming over you? " he asked.

I had hardly been aware that, without consciously planning to do so, I was introducing something new and alien into that office, but the realisation that even there I was able to achieve something filled me with pleasure. I also realised that at any moment I might equally unconsciously let something slip which would end the chance of achieving anything substantial before I left, as quite obviously I would sooner or later have to do.

I used my reputation for cynical humour to protect myself and found that not only could I thus defend myself, I could say what I felt quite openly and it was simply regarded as further evidence of the news editor's outrageous sense of humour. It provided a safety valve and at the same time gave me a certain grim amusement.

I normally had my lunch brought to me from the canteen by a messenger-boy each day, eating it in my office with plates around me on my desk so that I should be near at hand if any of my reporters phoned from the provinces. I told the boy one day that he must always bring me fish on Fridays. (I did not know that a war-time dispensation from " abstinence " was still in force.) When someone asked me why, I replied, " All good Catholics eat fish on Friday." The staff regarded it as just a curious, twisted joke, and still more so when I soundly rated the boy one Friday for daring to bring me meat. Inwardly I felt a Catholic now and wanted to practise something externally, too, even there on the communist daily paper's premises.

I went, night and morning each day, to St. Etheldreda's. One Sunday I went to Benediction at my local Catholic church and, the following week, to Mass, slipping in furtively, sitting at the back and slowly coming to understand what was happening at the altar. I had read sufficient Catholic books to know its broad significance, but had still to comprehend the meaning of each move leading up to the Sacrifice. I went straight from Mass to organise the production of the next day's issue of the *Daily Worker*.

A week before Christmas, we told Rowena, now five and a half years old, the Nativity story. Although in the past we had blasphemed freely we had not done so in front of her, lest other

parents should prevent their children from playing with her if
she, too, blasphemed.   And so she heard the words God, Christ,
Jesus, used for the first time and absorbed all that we had to tell
her.   Christmas became Christmas.

On the political front a public Cominform statement had at
last been issued which made it clear that my colleague's prophecy
that it might be our task deliberately to depress the standard
of life of the West in order to assist the East was an accurate
forecast.

The new line, laid down clearly enough in that statement, was
at last solemnly discussed by the Party executive and, of course,
adopted without dissent.   Most of the leaders and the rank and
file were, in any case, only too glad to get back to the class war
again after years of what had seemed to many of them curiously
un-Marxist co-operation and deplorably positive policies.

Henceforth those who aided production aided " dollar imperialism ";   those who impeded it aided the cause of communism.   In short, as always, our home policy was to be but an
extension of Soviet foreign policy—this time the war against the
West.   Once I should have been proud to strike like this at
" capitalist Britain " if it meant aiding the Workers' Fatherland.
Now I was appalled at the thought that, all over Europe this side
of the Iron Curtain, my Party comrades would be working
consciously and deliberately to produce economic crisis, unemployment, social misery, malnutrition.

Shortly before, a confidential document had come, I knew, to
the office, said to have been copied from an internal Treasury
statement outlining what would be Britain's position if she
refused the proffered U.S. Aid.   It had suggested that among
other things the Government would have to be prepared for
three million unemployed.   I had asked a Political Bureau
member if he thought that figure a correct one, and if so, could
we justify opposing American Aid.   His reply had been in the
affirmative on both counts.   " We would be a bloody sight nearer
communism if we had three million unemployed right now," was
the answer I got.

The way in which the " line " would be applied on the *Daily
Worker* and in the Party was outlined by J. R. Campbell at the

first staff meeting of the new year. We were going to support grievances and disputes wherever the Party was strong enough to be able to do so with a reasonable hope of success. We would work up to widespread strikes, but that, after our period of collaboration, would take time. Meanwhile, for 1948 we would set ourselves realistic targets.

In the docks and engineering industry, where we were strong and where there was " plenty of inflammable material lying about ", we would work for national stoppages. If we could do the same on the railways we would do so. All our forces in London's dockland would concentrate their activities on the riverside workers. Our campaigns would be carefully planned.

He went on in this vein for an hour, then finished with the words, " Whatever else 1948 may be, comrades, it will not be lacking in excitement."

Hardly any questions followed, just a common, excited acceptance. Johnnie packed up his papers and went down to his room humming happily to himself. Remembering all the work that he and his Economic Committee had put into their great plan to save Britain, and that would now have to be entirely re-cast, I told myself that he *must* like the new line a lot.

When I had first seriously contemplated the idea of becoming a Catholic, anti-Catholic campaigns were being conducted in many Eastern European countries. It was the Catholics who were being persecuted and martyred, and I had felt that this put me beyond the charge, from my comrades and from my own conscience, of going over from the persecuted to the persecutors, from the struggling cause to the winning side.

Now, however, since the Cominform statement, a new anti-communist campaign had been started in labour circles. Purges were being demanded, and I felt that if the situation should develop in Britain as it had done in the U.S. I might seem after all to be leaving the hunted to join the pack, which would further add to the misunderstandings which must inevitably follow my departure. It seemed urgently necessary to link up with the Church to which my allegiance now belonged.

Reading the Catholic Press I had learned of a new Papal

Encyclical, *Mediator Dei*, which dealt, among other things, with the demand in some quarters for an increased use of the vernacular by the Church. Looking back to the days when all Europe enjoyed a common faith and so possessed a common language, Latin, for its religious and cultural life, I strongly favoured the use of its ancient language by the Church.

I wrote a letter to the *Catholic Herald* and left the *Daily Worker* early one evening to deliver it at their Fleet Street office, hoping that I might meet some member of the staff there. I saw only the cleaner; the rest had gone.

But on Friday, January 9, the letter led its correspondence page. It had been headed: " From Communism to Catholicism ", and read:

" Sir,—May I, as one who is not yet even an accepted convert, but merely feeling his way towards Catholicism from communism, say how useful and timely I feel the new Encyclical, *Mediator Dei*, to be at this precise moment.

" The divisions of our post-war world are all too apparent; the lack of any sort of political stability in the world situation weighs heavily on men's hearts and minds. The generation which came to manhood between the wars—my generation—pagan though it was, grew up in the belief that some sort of universal harmony and lasting peace was possible, that men need not remain divided. We looked to the new organisations to achieve this for us—some to the League of Nations, some to world communism. But the League has been dead, murdered, for eight years. No one has the same hopes of the United Nations or, if they ever had, bitter reality has long since brought disillusionment. The Communist International, far from uniting the human race, is splitting it both horizontally and vertically. Its values, which once seemed so fundamental, so stable and immutable, we find in this hour of communism victorious may be changed overnight to meet a new situation.

" At 11.30 p.m. on Christmas Eve I was twiddling the knob of my radio. Unable to get out to Midnight Mass I wanted at least to bring it to my fireside. And as I switched from one European station to the next I tuned in to one Midnight Mass after the other. Belgium, France, Germany, Eire, yes, even behind the Iron Curtain, Prague. It seemed as though the whole of what was once Christendom was celebrating what is potentially the most unifying event in man's history. And the important thing was it was the *same* Mass. I am a newcomer to the Mass but I was able to recognise its continuity as I went from station to station, for it was in one common language. This aspect of Catholicism is but a single one, and, maybe, not the most important. But I have a strong feeling that it is precisely the Catholicism of the Catholic Church which may prove the greatest attraction, and will meet the greatest need, for my disillusioned generation." It was signed: " A NEWCOMER ".

I wondered what the Party would say if they knew the identity of the anonymous correspondent.

But I believed I had a useful job still to do with my own staff which was by no means completed and so I was anxious not to reveal my position prematurely.

Carol had got over the last hurdle, the " problem of the first premise ", more easily than I had done and had slid quietly, almost imperceptibly into belief at a time when I was still battling for light. Now she began to urge insistently that we should, without delay, have our two children baptised. I agreed, knowing that this must be the decisive step. Once the children were baptised we should have to create for them a Christian home.

At half-past eight on the evening of January 16, 1948, I phoned the local Jesuit college. " I want to have my two children baptised," I said.

" Half-past three on Sunday," said the voice at the other end of the line, obviously coming from someone who believed in being brief and to the point.

" Won't some godparents be needed ? " I questioned.

" Bring them along, too, at half-past three on Sunday," said the Voice.

I began to get desperate. " But we just don't know a Catholic in the world," I said.

The Voice now began to show a lively interest. " Aren't you Catholics yourselves either ? " it asked.

" No," I answered, " and we want to have a chat with someone about that, too."

That telephone conversation meant the end of twenty years of communism.

The Voice at the other end of the line went on to tell me that the priest responsible for my area was away but he would ask him to get in touch with us on his return. We had to wait impatiently until the end of the month before a mutually convenient date could be found.

Then Rowena and our six-months-old baby boy, Jocelyn, were baptised in the little sacristy behind the small local church and our instruction began under Fr. Joseph Corr, S.J. Hardly any discussion preceded that instruction. We wanted to learn about the Catholic faith, and that was enough for Fr. Corr, a saintly, scholarly old Jesuit from Northern Ireland, who quietly got on with the job without asking any questions. It was weeks before I told him who I was.

At the same time I told him how I was trying to influence my staff, in so far as I was able, and we agreed that it was a job worth attempting. It had taken me five years to travel the road from the Kremlin to the Vatican, but there was always the hope that I might accomplish something with someone before I left. But if the strain of working on the *Daily Worker* became too great, or if I felt that events made it impossible for me to continue, I should leave at once.

That attempt to influence my colleagues was only undertaken after considerable thought. I knew that I should appear to any communist who really knew what I was doing as a saboteur. Yet, quite obviously, if I believed that my Catholicism was right and communism wrong I was under a moral obligation to try to combat the evil and promote the good. Many Catholics would, I felt sure, give a great deal to have the chance to try and spread some truth or to defeat error in such a place. Once I had gone, my chance would be gone too.

Quietly I prised the Marxist armour of the individuals on my staff and, if I found a weak point, tried to extend it. I met with some success. After some weeks of patient work I had brought one reporter to the point where he agreed that he no longer believed in either the current or long-term policies of the Party, that logically he should leave it. He agreed that if and when I left the paper he would consider following me. But I got him no further. Religion was a language he simply did not understand, and I decided that where only weeks had been required to destroy his old faith it would take infinitely longer to give him a new one. Whether I could stick it out remained to be seen. There were others who were responding too, but more slowly.

Meanwhile I endeavoured to establish new standards in the paper itself. The new type of briefing given to my reporters and noted by my puzzled colleague continued. The new Cominform policy was getting the least possible application in the news pages, and for this I was constantly under pressure from other Executives. To counter this I aimed at the highest possible standards of efficiency and journalism.

It was a difficult position, spending my time between two worlds. I went to Mass on Sunday, then on to the *Daily Worker*. During the week I still called night and morning at St. Etheldreda's; often in the evening I went straight from my train to the local presbytery for my instruction. For the first time, possibly, in its history, many a silent prayer went up from the *Daily Worker* building.

At Executive meetings I kept out of policy discussion, but vigorously defended the work of my own department. I began to see our routine meetings in a new light. Present at one of our meetings were the editors of a number of German communist journals who had come with a Press party to London. They told us of the Party's work in post-war Germany. One described how, after the arrival of the Russians, the handful of Party members in the Soviet zone had been told they must get out a daily paper at once. If they had not the forces for the purpose among their own members they must use others.

The Party was so weak, he said, that they had not enough people to spare to fill even the executive positions on the paper. At the end of the first week the communists on the paper got together to review the week's work. When they checked over the personnel of the staff they found that the majority of those employed in a journalistic capacity had actually been Nazis until only a few weeks before.

At another Executive meeting someone from our foreign news

department said that in his view we should campaign against the
" concealed reparations " taken from Germany by Britain. It
was a good propaganda line, he argued, and calculated to damage
the Government. Johnnie Campbell argued that there was no
foundation for such a campaign. A few objects of scientific
interest might have been brought back to Britain, he said, a
certain number of rare and specialist books, but, for the rest,
what we were spending on Germany was vastly in excess of what
we were getting out of her and was, in any case, on the record.
The Government had published its own statistics, and there was
no reason to suppose that it had faked them, if only because it
could so easily be found out.

But when the editor, William Rust, summed up, he brushed
aside Johnnie's arguments. " The Soviet Press and radio ", he
said, " are campaigning on this and think it is worth doing. If
it is good enough for them it is good enough for us." It was
decided to take up the campaign and Johnnie, along with the
rest, concurred in this.

When the same colleague on another occasion suggested that
an explanatory article on the situation in Palestine would be
useful and would be particularly appreciated by our Jewish
readers, Rust clamped down on the idea.

" We don't know yet what Russia is going to do on the question
and it would be wiser to wait until we do before committing
ourselves," he said.

The Italian elections, shortly to be held, were discussed. A
confidential report given to the Political Bureau by a visiting
Italian communist was passed on to us. It was to the effect that
the Party thought its chances of winning the elections stood about
even. But the Party leaders were not worried about the results
because, even if they lost at the polls, they could, with the new
Cominform line being what it was, make life impossible for any
Government, and in the resulting crisis, come to power backed
by armed workers.

I listened to those routine proceedings almost in wonder, not
because they were in any way new in content but that I should
have travelled so far as to think that what had been the stuff of my
daily life for years should now seem so immoral and degrading.

Just how far I had travelled was brought right home to me one lunch-time by a handful of pictures sent over to me by the art department as I ate my lunch. They comprised a series, taken in Greece a week or so earlier, which had been smuggled out to us.

One showed a number of keen, alert young intellectuals and intelligent-looking young workers standing spaced out at even intervals across a mountain side in the early morning light. They wore handcuffs, and each was chained to his or her neighbour on either side. The caption gave their names, ages and occupations. Young school teachers, students, factory workers, farm hands who had joined the guerillas and had now fallen into the hands of their enemies.

The next picture showed them still standing on the mountain side, but someone had struck up the words of the "Internationale" and they were singing it together, heads proudly, defiantly thrown back, waiting for the shots from their executioners.

The last in the series showed the line of crumpled young bodies lying among the rough mountain grass just as they had fallen. I read and re-read the captions " aged 22 ", " aged 24 ", " aged 23 ". . . .

I leaned against the filing cabinet feeling sick, my lunch uneaten. " Grand, idealistic, intelligent types," I found myself saying, " who have thrown away their lives for something which is unworthy of them. They thought they were dying for a new, cleaner and better Greece. In fact they died for a Soviet foreign policy which cares nothing for Greece or for them."

Then I became aware of the nature of what had been my spontaneous reaction. I realised perhaps more fully than I had ever done before just how far it is from the Kremlin to the Vatican. Once those pictures would have made me work harder than ever for my communism. " You can hound us, persecute us, kill us," I would have said, " but history is on our side. We shall win. We shall build our new world and these young comrades of ours will be avenged. And God help you then." Not very long ago, they would have given my dying communism a new lease of life, a new injection of anger and hatred to revive it. Now I felt only a great sadness.

Betty Wallace, from our foreign news department, came into

the room. "What have you got there?" she asked. I passed the pictures to her without a word. "*They* ought to stir our readers and make them *very* angry," she said. At our Executive meeting it was decided to clear the front page in order to give them maximum display.

My resolve to try to undo some of what I had done in the past by staying at the *Daily Worker* as long as was morally and physically possible had been taken with a convert's zeal to make converts, but was proving even harder than I had expected.

The *Daily Worker* Party group started a new drive for " raising the theoretical level of the comrades ", so that they should be equipped to carry the new Party line into effect. The method employed at such classes is for the tutor to make a brief statement lasting only a few minutes; the whole of the remainder of the proceedings is then conducted by means of questions put directly to individuals by the tutor. A lot of preliminary " necessary reading " is required on the part of all who attend and any theoretical weaknesses or tendencies towards deviation are quickly revealed.

I had no desire to attend such classes (although I had to see that all my staff did so), for I knew that I should either have to lie or give my position away under such public cross-examination.

Five identical courses were run at different times during the day so that no one should have an excuse for being absent, despite the many shifts and duty turns operating on a daily paper. Every Party member from the editor down to the youngest messenger-boy was expected to attend.

I was told the time of the series considered to be most convenient for me, found reasons for not attending, was given another and found other reasons. By this means I missed the entire first series. Then another began and I had to prepare to repeat the process. It was not easy, for pressure from the group leader was considerable. Although occupying a relatively subordinate position in the editorial department, he had considerable power by virtue of the position he held in the group. I had reason to be aware of the latter point for I had been group leader myself during the difficult period following the raising of the ban on the paper.

A note was sent to all Party members, announcing the second series, and was, as usual, an instruction rather than a request.

"This is to inform you", it said, "that you are requested to attend Series 2 in the Educational Course for all comrades. . . ."

On the day I received that order from the "Party boss" I read something of a different sort. The *Weekly Review* had come to an end and in its place was now a little monthly review, *The Register*. In it I read a brief article entitled "Fellowship of the Heart" by H. D. C. Pepler, one of the writers whom I had libelled years before, and in it he told the readers that he now had *angina pectoris* and would be unable to play the part in the future of the paper which he had hoped to. I remembered how I had felt when I had been told a year before that I, too, had *angina*. I understood exactly why in his little piece he sounded so depressed. I remembered too what I owed to Pepler and the others on the *Weekly Review*. Perhaps if I told him where their influence had led me it would cheer him.

I wrote telling him the story, making him my first Catholic contact, apart from Fr. Corr, who was instructing me. By return I got a reply, sent from a Sussex nursing-home, which began:

"Your news provides me with an Eastertide in the middle of Lent, and I thank you very much for so magnificent a welcome into the Fellowship of the Heart."

He asked me to go and see him. I was hungry to meet Catholics and determined to see him as soon as a visit could be arranged.

The February *putsch* in Czechoslovakia, in which armed communists by threat of civil war took over what remained of the democratic state and converted it into a Soviet-style dictatorship, was the last straw. In its classes all over Britain the Party had held up Czechoslovakia as an example of how it might be done in Britain, how a Communist Party, functioning within a Western democracy, could gradually take over the organs of State, changing the very character of the capitalist State in the process until, with the consent of the mass of the people, it arrived at the same goal as that towards which the other communist countries were working.

Czechoslovakia had been held as proof of the way in which communism adapted itself to the different conditions found in a land with the traditions and culture of Western Europe. It had given hope to those who wanted to see a distinctively British communism evolved which did not slavishly follow the Russian model, whose background was so different.

The significance of Tito's warning that Gottwald was " under a cloud " because he was out of step with the rest was now clear. The Czech communist leaders whom I had known in Britain in the war days, and who had spent their time making plans for their own Czech-type communist State, had now climbed down. The Moscow-trained Gottwald had done what he was told. Henceforth they must be complete Russian stooges.

At an editorial meeting, the " copy-taster " reported that a message had just been received over the tape machine to the effect that the body of Jan Masaryk, the Czech liberal leader, had been found on the pavement under an open upstairs window. Czech Government sources had stated that it was known that he had been suffering from sleeplessness and it was clearly a case of suicide.

As the message was read out there was silence, except for a low whistle from the chief sub-editor.

" That's a trifle difficult, boys and girls," he said; " they don't worry too much about poor devils like us who have to explain these things to the customers." But it was all nicely explained to the customers, nonetheless, and soon the staff were cynically asking : " Did he fall or was he pushed? "

For myself I was finding the atmosphere there too suffocating to endure. I felt I must be able to talk to someone belonging to my new Catholic world. I phoned the *Catholic Herald*, thinking that I would have most in common with fellow-journalists, and, one night in a little Italian café just off Fleet Street, met the Editor, Michael de la Bedoyère, and two members of his staff. They were the first " live " Catholic laymen I had talked to, although already my children were baptised and I was under instruction.

A few days later, coming out from Benediction in our little local church, with the children, Carol walked straight into the local Communist Party treasurer and her husband. It was the sort of situation we had known might arise but had tried to avoid.

I

" My God, what on earth are you doing in a Catholic church, of all places? " one of them asked. Carol explained it away by saying that only in a Catholic church could one hear good plain-chant and that they should know our musical tastes sufficiently well to be aware of how keen we were on all early music.

The man, himself a music-lover, appeared convinced. His wife seemed to find it more difficult to understand. " No matter how much I loved music you wouldn't find *me* going into a bloody church," she affirmed. " Least of all a *Catholic* church."

When I got back from the office that night Carol insisted that we must come out into the open as soon as possible. " We can't let a situation continue where we have even to half-lie about our religion," she said.

By now, I knew that I could hope for no converts to Catholicism inside the *Daily Worker* office for a very long time, even though I had won some of my staff away from communism. I believed, too, that if I went now I might make an effective protest against the infamous things which were happening in Czechoslovakia. I agreed with her, and we decided that it should be the following week-end.

The editor was missing when I went to resign on the Friday night and so I decided it must be on the Sunday.

All the week I had been debating in my mind how I could go without causing more harsh feelings than were necessary. Debating, too, whether there was any hope at all of influencing Rust when I explained to him the reasons for my going.

I calculated, rightly or wrongly, that if I talked Catholicism to him it would simply be a language he did not understand. I think, today, that, given the same situation, I would at least attempt it. Instead, I decided to discuss with him my political position and hoped that thereby I might perhaps make even him have his first doubts. I now knew well enough that for a Marxist to have any doubts at all is to ensure the ultimate death of his Marxism.

The difficulty was, I felt, that almost certainly there would be an angry scene and that any sort of appeal to reason might thus be rendered difficult. At the same time I found myself, against my better judgment, almost hoping for a scene, since I knew that if I, too, grew heated it would be much easier to speak my mind and to see it through.

When it came to actually making the break I found it to be the hardest thing I had ever done. For years we had looked forward to having a great modern building in which to produce the new and, we hoped, improved *Daily Worker*. The money (nearly one-third of a million pounds) had at last been raised after years of sacrifices, of pleading, of special efforts. Work on the new building had begun. Long before, I had planned my own office and the whole editorial department just as I wanted it. I would never work in that new building, never use that carefully planned office.

I found a new affection for my own team of reporters. I had been fond of most of them, as individuals, for years. I looked at my colleagues, during the week I was preparing to go, with new eyes.

Most, beyond doubt, had come to communism because of the good that was in them. They had come with idealism, with anger at bad social conditions; fundamentally they had, in most cases, come because no one had ever shown them anything better. What had happened to them afterwards, as they were turned into the new Marxist men, the steel-hardened cadres which the Party makes and moulds, was another matter. I wished I could stay and make them see what I now saw, could share with them the truths which I had found.

There were some, it was true, who had come because they loved power, they " had an eye on the main chance ", I knew that the higher you went in the Party's organisation the more you would find of this type. I could leave them without regret. But that did not apply to Sam, Len, Rose, Ben and a good many of the other members of my team who had worked, hoped and sacrificed with me for so long.

The knowledge that I should almost certainly be misunderstood by them had helped to hold me back for a long time. I knew that when I went they would say: " Just another Judas Iscariot. We didn't think *he* would go "—and then set their teeth, close the ranks and work all the harder for the thing which was their life, as it had been mine. *They* had not changed, it was *I*, and I saw no reason for wishing to hurt them. In any case the Party members were my only friends. I had been too busy— and too cut off from the non-communist world for many years— to make others.

On the Friday night I took those who had been nearest to me out to the " editorial hostelry ", as we called it, to have a drink together. I had told them that I was going on the Sunday, told them I had fundamental differences with the Party, and pledged them to secrecy. They were puzzled and saddened and took steps, I later discovered, to see that they were not on the Sunday duty rota.

XXIII

OUT OF THE STRAIT-JACKET

I SENT my reporters out on assignments early that Sunday, just keeping one around the office in case of emergency. With great care I checked all my files, my diary of events, all those things necessary to continuity in my work, to ensure that everything was in order. After years of holding a reputation for more than usual efficiency I did not want to leave it in a state where it was difficult for my successor to take over the reins. I was almost obsessed with this idea, even leaving a skeleton schedule of assignments ready for the following day.

It is difficult to explain my motives for taking such care. Partly, I suppose, it was professional pride, partly a great desire not to hurt my old friends in any way I could avoid, partly because I was realising just how proud I had been when first I took over the news editor's chair, how I had loved the work and lived for the Cause.

I wondered whether I could see it through. I remembered hearing of couples who had planned to part, because life together had become hell, and who on the last night relented and made it a first night instead. I felt almost as though I were in the same position and likely similarly to relent.

I left the office and took a walk around a neighbouring block, discovering just how much I loved even that sordid area. Out into Swinton Street in which our building was situated, and in which there had been two murders in the past twelve months. One had been the wife of Paddy, the cheerful Irish cobbler at the bottom of the road, a Communist Party supporter who, living in unbelievable squalor above his little street-corner workshop, nonetheless mended our shoes for nothing when he knew we came from " the good old *Daily Worker* " and then told us to give the money to the paper's fighting fund. He had murdered his wife with his shoemaker's knife, then slit his own throat, leaving behind a toddler whom he had idolised to be sent to a home by the police.

The second had been a stabbing affair after the pubs turned out one Saturday night. We had followed the trail of blood which led zig-zag down the road past our offices.

At a huge bomb-site, cleared by a stick of high explosives late in the war, I watched a great rat rummaging among the rubbish in the ruins. A small female cat leaped on it and ran with it into the doorway of a nearby tenement building. She put it down to play with it and it dashed under the door into the dwellings beyond. Frustrated, the cat came out to look for more, and I continued my walk around the block, debating whether it was really necessary to go to Rust and argue with him. Why not simply write my reasons and leave them when I went?

I prayed as I had never prayed before, then went back to see it through.

It seemed nothing was to be made easy for me. Bill Rust did not create a scene, he did not get into one of his ungovernable rages, was not even sarcastic. I quietly told him how I disagreed with current policy, giving him my reasons. At first he seemed speechless, sitting looking white and shaken. Then he asked me questions, incredulously. He suggested that my differences could be cleared up if we had a longer talk, but I replied that they were fundamental, and went on to explain that I equally disagreed with the Party's long-term aim, that I was no longer a communist.

I had expected him either to be furiously angry or ice-cold. Instead he came as near to showing genuine warmth as he was able, nearer than I had ever before seen him. " I reproach myself," he said. " You've been obviously ill for a long time; you must be ill or you could not throw up your communism like this. I should have taken steps about it long ago."

It may have been that he knew it would all have to be explained to the Political Bureau in due course, that he would come under fire for allowing such a heresy to develop and such a heretic to remain so long. It may have been something more worthy. I do not claim to know, but I prefer to think it was the latter.

He suggested that I should go away, that the Party would fix up something for me, and mentioned making an arrangement with the French Party for a long stay in France. I replied that it would be pointless and at last made him see that this was so. We agreed that I could no longer remain on the paper and I quietly left, telling him I would summarise what I had said in writing on the following day.

I locked my desk and filing cabinets, still filled with the dossiers of fascists compiled over the years, handed the keys to the night reporter and left the building for the last time.

Suddenly, as I went out into the street, my depression left me for a moment. " I'm free. I'm out of the strait-jacket," I said to myself. " Now I start life all over again as a Catholic."

Early next day I wrote Bill Rust the letter I had promised. It read :

" 15th March, 1948

" DEAR BILL,

" You suggested yesterday that a further discussion about my views might be useful, but quite frankly I do not think it would serve any useful purpose.

" I am today resigning from the Party following my resignation from the *Daily Worker* yesterday. For some time now I have been increasingly disturbed by the Party's policy, both home and foreign.

" My first serious doubts came in connection with Russia's activities in Eastern Europe. The more I heard about what was happening behind the ' Iron Curtain ' the less I liked it. The reports to our Executive and staff meetings made by leading comrades returning from those countries, whilst inspiring other members of the staff, served only to increase my conviction that I could not honestly support such activities and brought increasing disillusionment as to Russia's intentions and as to the desirability of communism.

" When I first found myself in disagreement with the Party's foreign policy, our home policy was one I could still support and for that reason I carried on in my job as news editor, since my main responsibility was to see that the home news was adequately covered. Our campaigns for increased production, I felt, were useful and were meeting with success. I was proud of the part I played in them.

" But the coming of the new line on production and opposition to the Marshall Plan meant that I lost my last point of agreement with the paper's policy. I do not think that anything could justify that change of policy in the light of the misery which the success of the new line would bring.

" For me it meant that I now neither believed in the paper's home or foreign campaigns.

" Czechoslovakia seems to me to be the last straw. Events there in the last few weeks prove conclusively that any country which ' goes communist ' must conform to a single mould regardless of its orientation and traditions.

" I don't think there is any point in discussing these questions at length. I know all the ' correct ' answers—but for me they just don't ring true. Since I now neither believe in the Party's current policy nor its ultimate aims it was obvious that I should resign at once.

" For me the position was an impossible one and I know the paper well enough to be aware that there is no room on the staff —least of all in executive positions—for people who are not one hundred per cent convinced of the correctness of the Party line. And you would certainly *not* want someone who has resigned from the Party about the place for a minute more than is necessary.

" I want you to know that my decision has been taken in no light-hearted manner. I need only remind you that I have spent my whole adult life in the movement, and the last eight and a quarter years in the service of the paper.

" I appreciated very much what you had to say yesterday about the way I had worked and the efficiency with which I had performed my duties.

" I have taken steps to see that everything connected with my work is in order and right up to date."

To Harry Pollitt, the Party's General Secretary, I wrote:

" 15th March, 1948

" DEAR HARRY,

" I last night resigned from my position as news editor of the *Daily Worker* and now wish also to resign from the Party.

" I have explained my reasons fairly fully to Bill Rust, who will no doubt communicate them to you.

" Briefly they are as follows: I have been increasingly disturbed by Soviet foreign policy and by events in Eastern Europe. I am appalled by what has happened during the last few weeks in Czechoslovakia. I believe the Party's new policy on production is a profound mistake and that our campaign against the Marshall Plan, if successful, could bring nothing but misery to the people of Britain.

" Under the circumstances, I have no option but to resign from the Party at once. I joined my first Party organisation in 1928 and have spent the whole of my adult life in the movement. It is, therefore, only after very serious thought that I have arrived at the above conclusions, and only the belief that the Party is absolutely wrong has prompted me to make my decision."

On the same day Rust wrote to me, and our letters crossed.

His letter reflected the same mood as that in which I had left him. In it he repeated his " shock and amazement " with the views that I had expressed. " Over a long period of years ", he wrote, " I have regarded you as a talented, faithful and hard-working comrade who has done a job in spite of poor health."

He wrote of how " poorly " I had looked as we had talked together and " what a strain must have been imposed on you during recent months both because of the heaviness of the work and the political doubts that were growing in your mind ".

As I found myself " so uncertain with regard to the main

political aspects of our fight ", it was, he said, of course, better that I should leave. But he could not believe that the point I had made represented a fundamental change in my outlook, which would result in my separation from the Party to which I had devoted all the years of my active political life. " Writing as a comrade who has a deep personal regard for you," he said, " I would like to repeat my offer to arrange a thorough personal discussion on all of these questions so that we can get to know exactly where we stand."

He offered to come to my home to talk things over and then went on to say that he was enclosing a month's salary and asked me to let him know what I proposed to do in the future.

From Pollitt I received a similar request to have a conversation " before you give final effect to what is in your mind ".

I deducted a week's pay, for the time I had worked, and returned the remainder of the money Rust had sent. Along with it I enclosed a reply to his letter in which I said that whilst I appreciated his offer of further discussions, I thought that no useful purpose would be served by them since I was already on the way to becoming a Catholic.

I had so far withheld that information, believing that it would result in such blind prejudice that no one on the staff whom I might hope to influence would approach the question with any understanding at all. By talking exclusively in the political language they understood, I had hoped that it might achieve something at least and that the editorial staff might be told my reasons.

Just how right I was about the blind prejudice was demonstrated as soon as it became known that I was hoping to become a Catholic.

The *Catholic Herald* had asked if they might report my resignation and the fact that I was being instructed in the Catholic faith. I had agreed, had been interviewed, and the story was to appear on the Friday morning, which meant it would be circulating around the Press on the Thursday afternoon.

To save phone calls and requests for interviews which I guessed might come when the *Catholic Herald* was read in the other newspaper offices, I sent a copy of the interview to the main papers and news agencies on the day before, knowing, as a news editor, what a lot of bother can sometimes thus be saved for all concerned. I then went to meet some of the *Catholic Herald* staff in their Fleet Street office, thinking that at last I could relax.

By the time I got there, however, Carol was on the telephone imploring me to return as quickly as possible. The phone had been ringing almost unceasingly, journalists and photographers were in and around the house, others were coming shortly. I turned round and went straight back.

The tables had been turned on the news editor with a vengeance for I had to hold a Press conference then and there. The journalist who for years had shot his questions at others now had a taste of his own medicine. Most of those who had come, I sensed, had expected a stunt. I had the satisfaction of knowing that almost all, if not all, went away convinced, at least, of my sincerity. They were a friendly crowd doing a job, who had come for slick stories, but left with a sympathetic interest in the views and action of a fellow-journalist.

No sooner had they gone than the telephone rang. A woman's voice said: " I've just heard the six o'clock news on the wireless. Tell me it isn't true, Douggie. You can't be leaving the Party. You can't *possibly* think of becoming a Catholic." It was a Jewish girl in Bethnal Green, a Party member who had followed my writings for years, acted on my every suggestion, tireless in the war she carried on against the fascists and in which she had often shown considerable courage.

She sounded as though she were on the verge of tears. " I never thought that *you* of all people would let us down," she said as she rang off.

She was the first of many who found it impossible to understand how, after years in the Party, I could come to see that Marxism was wrong, and in particular to see that Catholicism could possibly be right. Each was a friendship lost.

All that evening the pressmen came, first from the British papers, later from the foreign ones too. I was talking to an American after one o'clock next morning and taking the first of a new flood of phone calls and callers five or six hours later.

For the next few days life was hectic, with broadcasts, newspaper articles, endless interviews. On the Sunday, Palm Sunday, British Movietone News came and filmed us in our home.

It's a nine-days wonder, I told myself; it can't go on like this. I've registered my protest at what has been done in Czechoslovakia and elsewhere behind the Iron Curtain; I've given my reasons for becoming a Catholic, which may help someone else as I have been helped. Soon I shall be able quietly to start living my new life as a Catholic.

But in the first ten days I received over 900 letters, which came from every part of Britain, from the United States, the Continent and, later, India, Australia and elsewhere. It was clear that I had set in motion something bigger by far than anything I had expected.

Among the letters were, of course, many from puzzled and indignant Protestants, quite a surprising number of whom took the view that of the two it was better to be a militant-atheist communist than a Papist.

But there were others which made me feel very humble when I considered the charity which they exercised in welcoming me to Christianity, regardless of which camp I had joined.

There were ones which thrilled me, too, such as that from the man who had been a communist, had been troubled by the Party's policy and now wrote to say that he had been considering doing what I had done. Now he could follow my example. The last time he was in a Catholic church, he wrote, was when he stabled his mule in one, as an International Brigader, during the Spanish civil war.

The reporters who had interviewed me proved to be as fair as I had hoped they would be. Only one wrote the sort of story which is made to fit into a pre-conceived pattern regardless of the facts.

We were at that time living in a house which was unnecessarily large, and very inconvenient, but which we had taken during the bombing when any sort of roof over one's head was better than none. But the reporter had come with a fixed idea of what our conditions would be like. His story next morning talked of our " little four-roomed dwelling " and described a state of affairs which, though heart-rending, bore little relation to the facts. Such is the perversity of life, however, that it was this story which got syndicated to many lands and finally provided the basis for the editorial introduction to something I wrote for a symposium published in the United States and which has since had a wide sale in this country too.

The *Daily Worker*, on the day following the broadcast of my resignation, had plainly found it difficult to know what to do about me and so dismissed me in a short acid little item. The news that I was becoming a Catholic had changed everything. The editor's kindly consideration of two or three days earlier had at once disappeared, as I had guessed it would, and in due course there appeared an editorial item to the effect that it was now known that I had been " a Vatican agent since last October ". The paper indicated that this would be the last reference they would make to such a creature. But soon they were bringing Sean O'Casey to the rescue to write a feature article against me. But, having worked there myself, I knew how Sean is often brought in to spin fine-sounding phrases when the Party leaders have no solid facts to support a campaign.

But I regretted deeply the break with old comrades and their hatred for me, even though I had known it would surely come.

Only the ignorant or the naïve would expect to find no comradeship or consideration among men working together in an evil cause. In some ways we had been thrown together all the more closely because of the very nature of that cause. But all that was now gone. The communists have no comradeship for those who leave them, least of all for the first of their better-known figures in Britain to go straight from the Party to the Catholic Church.

Nonetheless I heard a few weeks later of what had taken place in the *Daily Worker* office after I left.

When my resignation became known there was, it seems, a tense, witch-hunting atmosphere in the building. The situation was explained to the reporters collectively and then each was interviewed in turn to discover how far they had been influenced by me, whether they had had any suspicions as to my political " soundness " and, if so, why they had not passed on the information to the people at the top.

The Party has had a considerable international experience of gaining information in this way, and just how effective its methods have become even under British conditions is illustrated by the fact that the number under suspicion was narrowed down to a short list of three and that those three were in fact the right ones.

Each of the three suspects was then told to prepare a written " statement "—non-communists would call it a " confession "—which was to take the form of a Marxist analysis of how and why my " deviation " had occurred and an outline of how they had come to allow themselves to be influenced by me. On the basis of a solemn undertaking that they would take special steps to strengthen their own Marxist theoretical understanding and work loyally for the Cause in future they would be allowed to continue in the Party and on the staff of the paper.

One, who was under the strongest suspicion, had in fact intended to resign at the same time as myself, but at the last moment had drawn back for domestic reasons which I fully understood.

In the atmosphere which had been created in the office that morning, however, he began to feel genuinely penitent; I had been painted as such a criminal that, with a dozen or more years of communism behind him, he began to regret having permitted himself to be influenced by me. By the time he wrote his " statement " he was ready for a complete recantation. He attributed my deviation, in the best Marxist style, to my " petty-bourgeois origin ", attributed his own backsliding to his failure to rehabilitate himself after some years in the Army, undertook to attend his Marxist classes with renewed regularity and interest, and to work harder than ever for the Party and the paper. From years of journalistic habit he put a carbon in his typewriter and in due course put the duplicate copy of his " statement " into his desk.

For a few weeks, still under the influence of all that had been said about me and those whom I had influenced, he tried to re-adjust himself and to re-kindle the sickly flame of his communism.

But, in a quiet moment, one Friday evening, rummaging in his desk drawers he came across the copy and, since no one was about at the time, proceeded to re-read it. When he saw again what he had written about me, and remembered our former friendship and our many quiet talks together, he was nauseated by what he had done. " I should have resigned rather than degrade and humiliate myself like this," he told himself. The full realisation of the falseness of his position during the past weeks came to him. With the " statement " in his hand he made straight for the editor's office with the intention of resigning on the spot.

He found that the editor had already gone up-country to speak at a meeting on the following day.

" I'll resign as soon as he comes in on Sunday," he told himself. Feeling unsettled by the anticlimax to his impulsive move he went to the " editorial hostelry " nearby and started morosely to drink alone in a corner. Soon he was joined by a girl who had only in the last few weeks come to work on the paper, doing an obscure clerical job in one of the business departments.

He had seen her before, mixing with various members of the editorial department, chumming up with one and another and made rather conspicuous by a pronounced foreign accent.

He bought her a drink, then she stood drinks for both. Over her gins she appeared to expand; she criticised some of the Party's leaders and the leading figures on the paper in particular. He responded by criticising more vigorously and saying some of the things that were in his mind. By the time they had spent several hours together and had had a good many drinks he had told her how he would already have resigned that night had the editor been there.

He made a point of being first to arrive at the office on the Sunday, so that he might catch the editor as soon as he arrived. When he heard Rust's step in the corridor he braced himself for a scene, then hurried down to his office.

But as he went through the door Bill Rust asked him: " Have you come to resign? " With the wind knocked out of his sails he lamely answered that he had.

Rust produced a sealed envelope and pushed it into his hand. " You are too late," he said. " Here's your notice. You are sacked."

A heated scene followed during the course of which he said all the things he had longed to say for months. Rust, for his part, told him what he considered to be his principal weaknesses in colourful, Cockney language. As he was leaving, the editor had one last fling at him.

" There's another thing the matter with you, which I had forgotten to mention."

" What's that? "

" You talk too bloody much. You should have kept your mouth shut on Friday night."

Later, when he looked at the dismissal notice, he saw that the political reasons for which he had been sacked were not, of course, mentioned. Instead it was so worded as to be a professional liability rather than an asset when he began, as he would have to do at once, to look for another job.

Weeks later, still out of work, he got in touch and told me his story. He was convinced that he had been led into a trap by a fellow Party member who had, in fact, been an *agent provocateur*, put there for just that purpose. He believed, too, that he had been double-crossed by the editor. He had had weeks of unemployment and he no longer believed in the Communist Party's current policy, its long-term aims or its leaders. Yet he was, he admitted, still active in the Party.

I asked him why. " It's been my life for so long I can't bring myself to make the break," he said. " It seems easy enough when I remember the way I've been treated or when I think of some of the leaders. But then when I think of some of the rank and file who are the salt of the earth and who have believed in me for so long, I just can't bring myself to do something which will seem to them like a kick in the teeth."

It was not until months later, after the Tito incident had provided the last straw for him, and after months without work, that he at last brought himself to make the break.

That is the hold which communism has on many people who joined its ranks as starry-eyed idealists or who were attracted by what seemed its great work for social justice and who have been drawn into its life to a point where they find it almost impossible to escape.

The Party is so organised as to make communism the whole life of its members. They lose all their old friends. All their present comrades and associates are in the Party; it takes the

whole of their waking time, at work, in their leisure, wherever
they go. It controls their whole thought life. They spend their
days thinking of how best to " apply the Party line " to their own
milieu.

They genuinely believe that the Party gives them ample scope
for thought, but are unable to see that it is never original thought,
never anything more than applying to their own little world
what has already been laid down in the greatest possible detail
by the political bosses. To break from that vicious circle is not
easy, as was shown when an old friend and Party member got in
touch with me a few days after my resignation.

" You've worked hard to keep me a good Party member in
the past. Now come and explain what you have done," she
said.

I accepted her invitation, and discovered that she had bigger
doubts than she was prepared at first to admit. After hours of
discussion there was nothing left of her communism and she
agreed that she now found herself, too, in disagreement with
both the Party's immediate policy and its long-term aims.

" There is, then, no logical reason why you should remain a
Party member," I told her.

She was cultured, intelligent and had a forceful dynamic
personality. She had gone from university to journalism, got
drawn into the Party and had worked hard for it, putting some
even of the proletarians in its ranks to shame with her untiring
efforts for the cause. Now there was nothing left.

" Logically you should resign," I repeated.

Her answer startled me. " I will do it if you think I ought.
But don't hold me responsible for what happens next, because
I may do what poor old Jan Masaryk has just done. You see,
I'm terrified of the vacuum that would be left in my life if I
went."

Under the circumstances I could only advise her to follow her
conscience and tried instead to fill that vacuum. She thought
I had become a Catholic only as an " escape " until I told her that
the order of events did not support that view, that the Catholic
influence came first and that my communism went later, and then
only after years of resistance.

Each time she tried to think in terms of religion—and she had, it seemed, tried since hearing of what I had done—she recalled a professing Christian she had known as a child and whose memory filled her with loathing—and then boggled at the thought.

Yet it is precisely the existence of that vacuum which gives communism its chance. Communism, I believe, has had its origins in precisely that spiritual vacuum which exists all over what once was Christendom.

One has to be potentially good or intelligent even to be aware that it is not enough simply to drift along without sense of purpose or direction, with neither faith nor ideal. That is why communism so often claims the best—those who feel the miss. It is why it has spread in our day and no other. It is not the presence of poverty which is new. The new factor in the situation is the presence of millions of modern pagans. Communism is the child of unbelief. Bad social conditions are only the things on which it feeds.

And that is why communism has been able to take what is essentially a religious instinct and to use it for evil ends, take good qualities and use them for evil too.

It is why, confronted with the choice of remaining attached to a cause in which she did not believe or facing a vacuum, she chose the former and, to my knowledge, was still working for it months later.

There have been just a few who have been prepared to come all the way with me but I know the length of the journey involved and do not now expect it to be a quick process. There have been more who have simply been influenced sufficiently far, at least, as to lose their communism.

There has been more to do than I had ever imagined likely, not the least important job being to attempt to spread a better understanding of communism and particularly of *communists*, for it seems to me that those who have seen communists only as political adventurers or power-crazy morons tend to help the very cause they wish to destroy.

Life is so much more complex, and so are men's motives. I would say that the majority who come to communism do so because, in the first instance, they are subconsciously looking for a cause which will fill the void left by unbelief, or, as in my own case, an insecurely held belief which is failing to satisfy them intellectually and spiritually.

I do not want to suggest that all the best men are inside the Communist Party and all the worst are outside. But I most certainly believe that there is magnificent material in the Party's ranks, that communist atheists often put to shame by their energy and devotion those who possess a faith which has the only real and lasting answers to our problems.

I know from experience that many good people annually go into the Party. But after accepting an evil creed how can their lives fail to become evil too? The " steel-hardened cadre " is an artificial product, he is something made and moulded by Marxism, often from some of the best materials, into something which is perhaps the most deadly thing on earth today. For the " steel-hardened cadre " there are no spiritual values, no moral or ethical considerations. No human compassion influences his Marxist judgment, neither love nor pity nor patriotism has any room in his make-up, nor has truth nor honour, except within his immediate circle of comrades. Conscience has become something which prompts him to lie, to deceive, to betray. Communism has become an end in itself and that end will always justify the means.

It would be tragic enough if there were increasing thousands of already bad men going year by year through this process. In a way it becomes even worse when it is realised that the majority are essentially good and come with good intentions.

When I look back on the people who were for so many years my comrades and friends I know that among them were some who were super-careerists, some who were bad, who came to communism because they were bad and were attracted by the bad that was in it. I know, too, that the majority would make magnificent Christians if once they were given a better cause in which to believe. And I am certain that millions more could be prevented from ever joining the communists' ranks if they were made more aware of something superior, something able to make even greater demands upon them, claiming the whole man and using him for noble instead of ignoble ends.

XXIV

THE GOD THAT DID NOT FAIL

I HAD been promised nothing "save that the sky grows darker yet and the sea rises higher". The gaining of a new faith and the resultant losing of the old one which had for twenty years been my very life had left me for the moment physically exhausted. I wanted more than anything to have a period of peace and quiet; fully to enjoy my new-found freedom to think; live my life as a Catholic, breaking completely with my past—which had obviously been impossible so long as I was trying to carry on in the *Daily Worker* office.

I wanted to forget the communism from which I had at last escaped. I was tired enough even to identify peace in my own mind with inactivity and to want to do nothing more than to write—since that was my job—and, most of all, to be left to sit back and think out my own position. My acceptance of Catholicism had so far been a completely personal thing. Now I wanted, too, to be able to apply it to the world I knew.

My future was uncertain. I believed that as a journalist I could hold my own professionally. But I was anxious to have the maximum possible independence. The communist engineer who becomes a Catholic may continue his work as such very much as before. For me, a journalist, it was different. I was determined not to tie myself to any paper or organisation which would involve constant compromise. Later, when I was more sure of myself, I might perhaps feel free to take work anywhere. Meanwhile I wanted to be able to work out my own ideas, solve my own problems. I knew that my foundations were this time right and firmly established. But the form of the superstructure was still unclear.

I had never liked public speaking and lecturing. Always when I had done it, it had been only out of a sense of duty. Now I would do no more.

Painfully, reluctantly, I had arrived at the firm belief that communism was wrong. Now I wanted to concentrate on positive solutions. But soon I began to feel that this desire to disappear into an ivory tower was a form of selfishness. Most certainly it was a form of spiritual luxury I could not justify. For the fight was on. In Eastern Europe, communism, aggressive and triumphant, was sweeping ahead. It was doing battle against the ideas, the organisation, the culture, the faith I had accepted. Whatever others might think, I knew from my years in communism that it was war to the death. If communism came out on top, then the soil of Eastern Europe would be dyed red with the blood of martyrs—the people who were prepared to die for my new faith. Worse still, if Marxist-Leninist theories and tactics went according to plan, the bloodless victory over the mind might be more fatal in its consequences than anything they could do to the bodies of the Cardinals and Bishops whom they would martyr.

I understood the danger. I knew the difference between the communists' professions and their true aims. I understood their technique. My ability to think as a Marxist had not departed with my resignation from the Party. Marxism was not for me just a theory to be learned from books. It was a methodology. Dare I abandon the struggle just because I wanted to forget my past? Was it not, in fact, that I was permitting myself to be influenced by the thought that I did not want to appear to my old comrades as having turned from friend to foe?

It was so easy to think that the way that suited best my present condition and my spontaneous desires was the right one for me to take. But, I decided, it was phoney. If I thought that Christian culture was worth fighting for, then I should be in that fight. If the Faith was today, as so often before, assailed by the pagan, then I must be in the crusade. So could my past be turned to some good purpose.

The work I had done for communism had not stopped just because I had left it. It still went on. I could not pick up a copy of the *Daily Worker*—still cannot—without seeing the name of someone I brought into the Party, still working for the Cause. Every issue contained stories by old friends whom I had trained. And, nationally, the Party had replied to my defection in typical Marxist fashion by carrying the fire right into the enemy camp. It was making direct appeals, by means of special pamphlets and in all its public propaganda, to Catholic working men to join the Communist Party, quoting the Acts of the Apostles, St. Ambrose and St. Thomas More to prove why they should become members of the most militantly atheistic movement of all time. This was the Party's reply. If I sat back, the result of my coming to the Church might well be a net loss to it. I took a vow to try and make more converts to the Faith in the next ten years than I had made for communism in the past twenty. I decided that the ivory tower was not for me. Once again I must get out and fight.

If I knew from my own experience that communism was wrong, I as a writer must say so. That did not mean that I should suddenly start writing and talking as though all my old comrades and colleagues whom I had been proud to call my friends were now a bunch of crooks and morons. At all costs I must hold fast to what I felt to be the facts, those which I knew from my own experience to be true, the belief that the most evil thing in communism is that it claims some of the best and moulds their minds and twists their consciences so that they can be used for the worst.

So, when a " safe and comfortable " job was offered me I turned it down almost rudely. But one idea which almost obsessed me was that, come what may, I was not for sale. I knew that most of my old associates would not be able to understand what I had done except in such terms, but at least I would keep my own self-respect by refusing any over-generous offers which might come in the early days from those who might want to use me for purely political purposes.

I took on free-lance work, writing for papers all over the world but keeping my independence. I had undertaken to write a series of articles for the *Catholic Herald*, giving my journey from communism towards Catholicism in brief outline, and some news stories as well. The series created wide interest and, more important, clearly helped quite a lot of people, as the resulting correspondence showed. The articles appeared as a pamphlet which quickly became a best-seller and had soon been translated into a dozen or more languages. Some of my writings were distributed among Greek communist guerillas, others were used in Red China. A pamphlet written for the Catholic Truth Society was translated into Indonesian for use among the communists there. The ivory tower was soon very far away.

When the series for the *Catholic Herald* was completed, others were needed. Soon I was a regular contributor, and, later, became a member of the staff, spending part of each week in its Fleet Street office and the remainder working on my own. On the *Catholic Herald* I did not have to compromise. I wrote what I believed and no attempt was made to direct or influence me. The editor prided himself that his paper was one of the last strongholds of free speech in Britain and the contrast with the *Daily Worker* was as great as it could be. With my communist background, I almost expected directives to come from the Cardinal as once they had come from Party headquarters. None came. Soon I was enjoying to the full the freedom that comes from the self-imposed discipline of the mind, which springs from a belief in that absolute truth which so many of our generation have rejected or forgotten.

At the end of the Easter term we took Rowena from the little private school run by Left-wing atheists which she was attending to send her straight to one run by the Ursuline nuns. She took to the new atmosphere as a fish takes to water. The new life presented no problem for her, at least.

From all parts of Britain came requests that I should lecture, from political bodies and, of course, from the myriad Catholic societies. At first I stuck to my original intention of lecturing no more. Then I decided that I must not, could not, at such a moment, abandon the fight to the communists. In a few years' time it might even be too late. In my lifetime the issue would most probably be resolved one way or the other. Christianity or communism.

Out of a host of invitations I chose one from Dowlais, in a South Wales mining valley, for my first lecture. The Welsh valleys, with their record of strikes and unemployed demonstrations, had for years had a magic ring for me about their very names. I would start with a reputedly " Red " area. If I could get through a meeting there, I could stand up to anything. The meeting was packed and widely reported. The result was a new shoal of requests to lecture. I booked up every minute of my leisure that I could possibly spare, mainly with the Catholic societies.

I made no attempt to pick and choose, just took them as they came. Those who invited me were more likely to know the value of a meeting than did I, the newest of recruits. I went, no matter whether it was to a meeting of six nuns in a little convent or to talk to five thousand in the largest hall in town. In two years, I lectured at hundreds of meetings in my spare time, travelled thousands of miles. The job, I felt, was, first and foremost, to get Christians moving, not just because they were anti-communist, but because they had been made to see that their actions, the fight for their principles, were what would decide the course of history for centuries ahead.

In those two years I probably talked to at least half a million people. I found that other-worldly nuns invariably ask the most down-to-earth questions; that the most searching ones come from senior school girls and boys; that professional politicians usually have the least original queries. I slept in trains, in monasteries, presbyteries and hotels—and wrote wherever I went. I had no time to gauge the relative value of large meetings as opposed to small or of lecturing as opposed to writing. I simply took on everything I had time for.

I came to the Church with most of my old prejudices still very much alive.

I had thought as a communist that British Catholics were among the least politically alert and were the most illiterate section of the public. We had accepted that as a matter of course. Until I had evidence to the contrary I saw no reason for rejecting that notion even though I was now in process of accepting their Faith. But after meeting them in their thousands I came, not unnaturally, to realise that they were in fact, when encountered in the mass and seen or addressed from platforms, much the same as any other audience. Because they were human—and the Church is very human—they had all the faults, all the vices of other human beings. But as I met them individually I came to see that there was a difference: that whilst they had their share of vices they had virtues which were not to be found in the same developed form among comparable numbers of modern pagans. The desire, the intention to do good and to be good has its effect. Kindness and charity are there in greater quantities because consciously developed—and there are too little of both in our modern, streamlined, hard-headed society.

I had even believed that all monks, nuns and priests were immoral. Those ideas had been planted early in my childhood when I belonged to a militantly anti-Catholic organisation.

And again, until I had evidence to the contrary, I saw no reason suddenly to change those opinions. To dismiss the truth of Christianity because of the existence of " bad Christians " would be as irrational as to argue that communism is good because it attracts people with good intentions. Catholicism was right and that was all that mattered to me. I found, of course, that there were priests with the ordinary human failings and laymen who were uncultured or apathetic. But what was more important was the presence of vast stores of unsuspected goodness in presbyteries and convents and among the ordinary layfolk too.

For years I had been watching and commenting on world events, meeting and passing judgment, as a journalist, on public figures and people in every walk of life. Now my world was turned upside down, so much so that, needing some rough and ready guiding lines when continuing to write on men and affairs, under the usual rushed newspaper conditions, I found that if I took the exactly opposite approach to that which I would have taken in the past, I was likely to be somewhere near the correct application of the Christian principles I had accepted. Everyone, everything, had to be given a new assessment.

As a communist I had had a vested interest in disorder, in economic crisis, social injustice and chaos, military defeat. My hopes had been pinned on world unrest and national instability. The aggressiveness of the leaders of the East, the growing problems of the West would have raised my hope of an early victory for communism. Marxism had always provided easy answers for difficult situations. The world had not consisted of millions of imperfect men striving for something better but of two warring classes out of whose conflict would come our new order. The problems and solutions had been simpler, more clear-cut—and utterly phoney.

As a Christian I now believed that our current problems were the outcome of the failure or inability of nations to live up to the ideals they once had held and of men to live up to the Faith which some still retained and others had scornfully rejected.

In the old communist days I had judged men in the light of Marxist teaching. On which side of the barricades would they be if a revolutionary situation developed tomorrow? Where did they stand in relation to the Soviet Union and current Communist Party campaigns? This was the only test of character we recognised, the only questions we asked of them. So, in judging people, as in assessing the world situation, everything had a starkness, an unrealistic simplicity; everything and every-one was either black or white, there were no greys. The whole of the working-class, with the exception of those who had actively gone over to the enemy, were potentially white. The entire " ruling class ", with the exception of the few who joined the ranks of the workers, were black. All Catholic politicians were reactionary. All Catholic trade union leaders were corrupt.

Even as for the first time I met a Catholic M.P., as a friend, I found myself still under the influence of oft-repeated lies and the old blind prejudices. I was almost surprised, despite the distance I had travelled, to discover that he, like the majority of my new associates, was trying to lead the Christian life.

To stand waiting for someone in the Central Lobby of the House of Commons and see one old comrade after another among the fellow-travellers and the " crypto " M.P.s come towards me, remember what I had done and swing away with a look reserved for one who was regarded as a Judas Iscariot was a salutary reminder, unpleasant as it was, of what I should have thought of them had the boot been on the other foot—and a test of my Christian charity, too.

It was useful, and grimly amusing, to meet a Catholic trade union leader whom I had attacked for years and whom I still subconsciously suspected and to find that he, too, had suspected me right up to the moment we met. The shame I felt was necessary, too, when quite simply and naturally he offered to help me at any time in any way he could.

The day we became Catholics I felt that I was now linked with the sanest thing in the world to-day. Not just the sanity of men, but the vaster sanity of God, without Whom in this age of atomic madness there is no sanity or meaning in life at all. The God whom once men had proclaimed as dead is needed more than ever today to save the world from destroying itself.

The sanest things on earth are those for which the allegedly reactionary, unscientific, obscurantist Church stands and for which she is doing battle. The Church will always appear reactionary to those who see " progress " as an end in itself and who believe that everything which is new must by virtue of its newness be superior to that which is old. To react against a progression towards disaster is a sign of sanity and one which will appeal increasingly to a generation confronted with the possibility of scientific " progress " leading it to total extinction. To those who say that at all costs we must progress, the Church asks : Towards what?

Similarly, on social and political questions the Church has refused to be carried away by the prevailing belief that so long as we are changing conditions we must inevitably be improving them. It has been taken for granted by those attracted to communism that the man who can see and denounce the evils of a social system is thereby qualified also to lay down the lines of a better one and, in due course, to administer it. Experience shows that there is little to warrant this assumption. For one evil thing to attack another is normal enough. It does not make either the attacker or that which is attacked less evil because one is attacked by the other.

The communist may be able to put his finger on what is bad in our society, but only the Christian is fitted to expound the good. One of the greatest errors of our time was put into words by the Webbs, who grandly disposed of the Soviet rejection of religion with the statement that there the worship of God has been replaced by the service of man. It has been that sort of facile thinking which has opened the way to the destruction of the culture of the West.

The communists have headed the self-conscious " progressives " for a generation now—and the regimes they have established have proved to be the most " reactionary " (in their own interpretation of the term) on earth today.

But modern trends are tending to prove that in her social teachings the Church has been truly progressive—that the policies she has recommended make for true human betterment. That is why people are taking the social encyclicals, *Rerum Novarum* and *Quadragesimo Anno*, more and more seriously. The only thing against them ever was that they were ahead of their time.

When Leo XIII condemned the class war, whilst at the same time asserting the worker's right to a living wage, he was denounced as a reactionary by the Left and as a trouble-maker by the Right. But the saner elements of the Left and Right are today advancing his ideas as their own—and as the last word in " progress ". Pius XI was condemned as a fascist for the suggestions he made for the reform of our social system—and the most " progressive " firms and politicians are now just getting round to putting them into practice.

Whilst careful not to get things out of focus, the Christian, seeing men as creatures made in the image of God, must, if he is consistent, be actively against social injustice and anything which degrades or hurts his fellow-men. That is why, too, some of the most significant social movements I have seen, in Holland, in France and in Ireland, too, are the results of that inspiration.

The Christian Church has proved more scientific than the scientists who have believed that they could isolate one section of human knowledge, their own, from all others, and in particular from that represented by Christianity and its teachings. They have reasoned that nothing should be accepted unless it can be weighed in scales and measured with rulers. Men were more scientific in those days when the scientist began his studies with a course of theology to enable him to keep things in perspective. The Christian is more scientific, too, when he declares that the most important things cannot be tested in this way; that the supernatural may, after all, be more important by far than the natural.

That, of course, is a language which many today simply do not understand. That is why they can go to Ireland, for example, and see, as once I should have seen, only the urban and rural slums (both, let it be said in justice to those at present responsible, a heritage from earlier days).

The significant thing about the lands in which the ancient Faith still lives is that there the supernatural is as real in the lives of the people as are the things of the natural world. The frontiers between the two are so blurred as hardly to exist, and that is why those people who have retained the Faith have retained also the art of living, where our more paganised countries have lost it. The explanation lies in the fact that life is only half lived when it operates exclusively on the natural plane.

Marx, in his famous Eleventh Thesis, declared: " The philosophers have only *interpreted* the world in various ways; the point, however, is to *change* it." With its combination of intellectual arrogance and emotional appeal it was calculated to attract both the new, pagan intelligentsia and proletarians looking for an ideal. " Change the World " has become a slogan which has inspired rank-and-file communists in every land—as though change were an end in itself. They have hardly stopped to ask whether it was for better or for worse.

Marx realised, as do the communist leaders today, that his new world required new men. Equipped with the knowledge of modern psychology and propaganda technique, they have set about the parallel tasks of moulding minds, even as they sought to change the structure of society to their own pattern. But the very nature of that pattern cannot but be false, for their starting point, that this is a purely material world, is a falsehood. And, moreover, it is a dangerous falsehood at that, for their goal, since they recognise nothing higher than themselves, can be anything they care to make it. Mind-moulding in the hands of Marxist materialists becomes the most deadly thing the world has known. World-changing dare not be left in their hands.

The communist becomes increasingly unattractive as he perfects himself as a Marxist. The new Marxist man, the " steel-hardened cadre ", is terrifying in his potentiality for evil. The more the new Marxist society is brought into being the less it is liked, so that in time the communist regime must depend entirely for its survival upon false propaganda, the eulogising of leaders made utterly unattractive by their Marxism, and upon terror, open and concealed.

Exactly the opposite is true of Christianity. The more it is practised the more it attracts. It has been when Christians have failed to practise their Faith and to carry its truths into the society around them that men have been repelled.

The Christian has believed that a changed and better world could come only from changed and better men. But the changes he would make are based, not upon his own whims or selfish interest, but upon supernaturally revealed truths and the vast body of Christian doctrine which has been developed from them. It is precisely the belief of the Christian in the supernatural which makes his Faith so sane and his goal so desirable. It guarantees that the changes he achieves in men and in society will be for the better and not for the worse.

Six men who, like me, were once communists or fellow-travellers and who left the Movement disillusioned, called their story " The God That Failed ". They lost a faith, even though it was a bad one, and, in most cases, found only a vacuum. That has been the tragedy of many of the best of our day. Communism took their best years, claimed their whole mind and soul as of right, then left them with nothing but their disillusionment and an unbounded cynicism.

I was more fortunate. I lost my communism because I had been shown something better. I did not find it easy to get to know my new God. And the love of God did not even then come automatically. Just as one has first to get to know a man or woman, and love comes later on the basis of common interests shared and intimacies exchanged, so, slowly, I came to know that love. But one thing is certain: my God has not failed.

THE END

ished, so that in time the communist regime and depend entirely
for its survival upon false pretenses, its conspiracy of leaders
... entirely undertaken by their blackmail and ... on terror
... open and concealed.

Exactly the opposite is true of Christianity. The more it is
practised the purer it attains. ... it has been what Tolstoy have
... tried to practise that I am able to carry on a life in the life ...
society around them that men have been repelled.

The Christian has believed that a changed and better world
could come only from changed and better men ... but the student
... he would make for ... upon his own whims, or even
interest, but upon rationally received truths and the ... vast
body of human doctrine which has been developed from them.
... it is precisely the belief of the Christian in the supernatural which
makes his Faith so sure and his goal so desirable. ... it transpires
that the change he achieves in men and in society will be for the
better and not for the worse.

Six men who, like me, were once communists, no fellow
travellers, and who left the Movement disillusioned, called this
story "The God That Failed". ... They, too, found, as I found,
... was a bad one, and in none it was found only a personal. ... That
... has been the tragedy of many of the best of our day, of so many
who mock their year, ... chained their whole mind and soul ...
of right, then left them with nothing but meaningless and
an unbounded egoism.

... I was more fortunate, I was no communist because I had
been shown something better. ... I did not find in Marx to go to
know my new God. ... And the love of God did not even then
come immediately. ... first no one had ... taught me to know a real
man ... woman, and love comes later on the basis of communion, of
shared and ... common exchanges. So, slowly, I came to know and
love. ... But one thing is certain: my God has not failed.